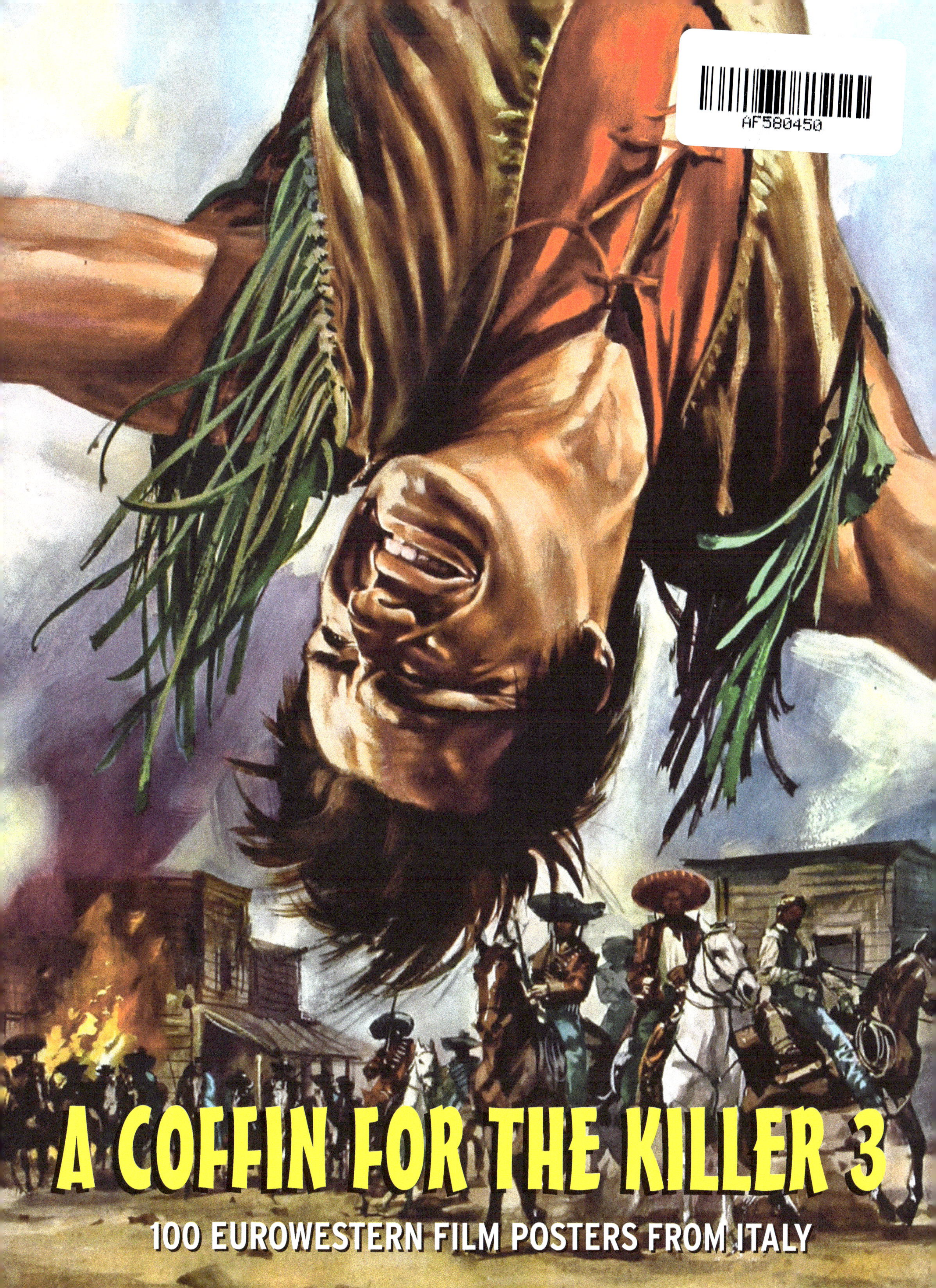

A COFFIN FOR THE KILLER 3
100 EUROWESTERN FILM POSTERS FROM ITALY

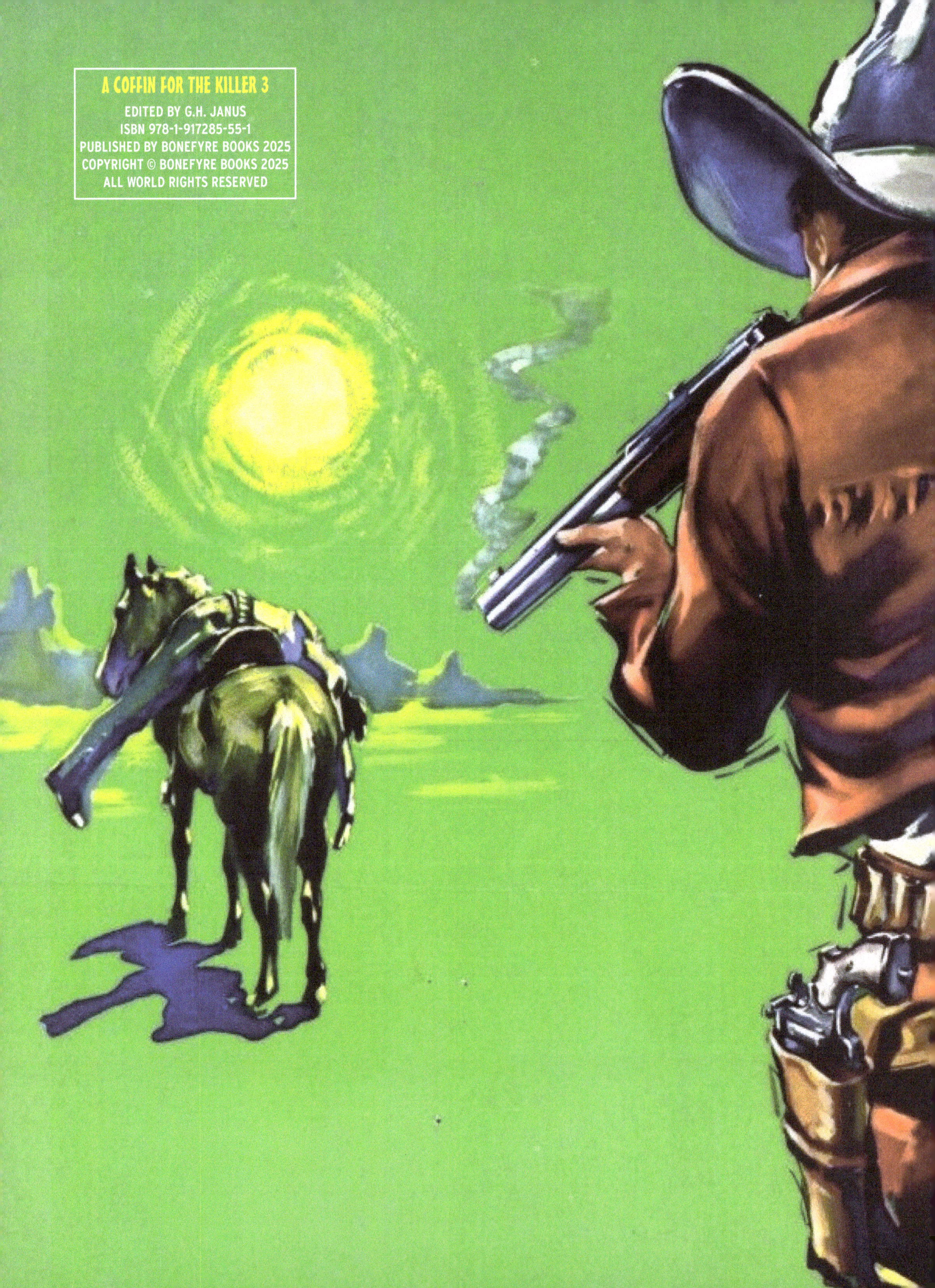
A COFFIN FOR THE KILLER 3
EDITED BY G.H. JANUS
ISBN 978-1-917285-55-1
PUBLISHED BY BONEFYRE BOOKS 2025
COPYRIGHT © BONEFYRE BOOKS 2025
ALL WORLD RIGHTS RESERVED

POSTERS

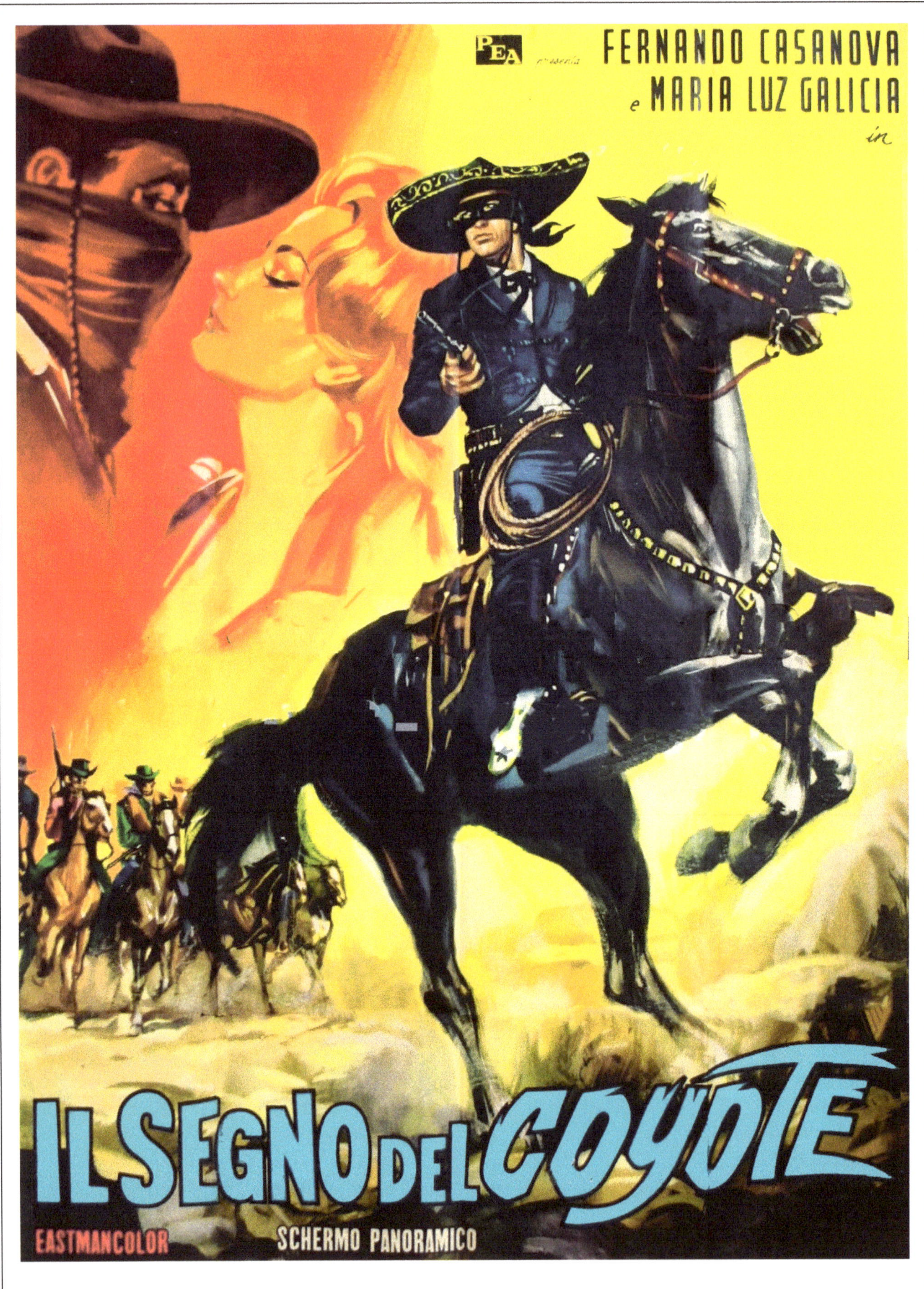

IL SEGNO DEL COYOTE

("The Mark Of The Coyote"). Artist: Renato Casaro. Original Title: **Il Segno Del Coyote** (1963, Italy/Spain).

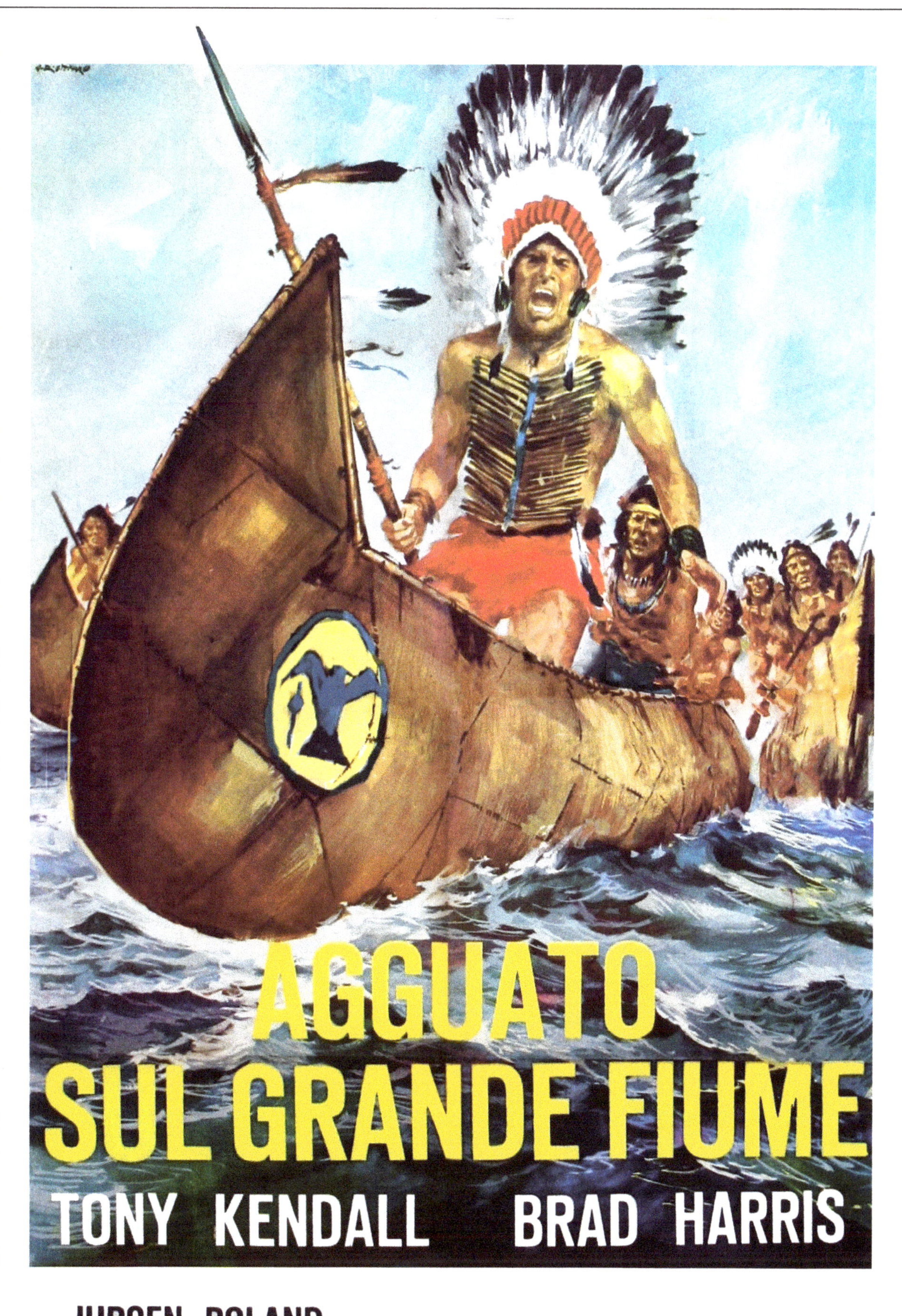

AGGUATO SUL GRANDE FIUME

("Ambush On The Great River"). Artist: G. Di Stefano. Original Title: **Die Flußpiraten Vom Mississippi** (1963, Germany/Italy/France).

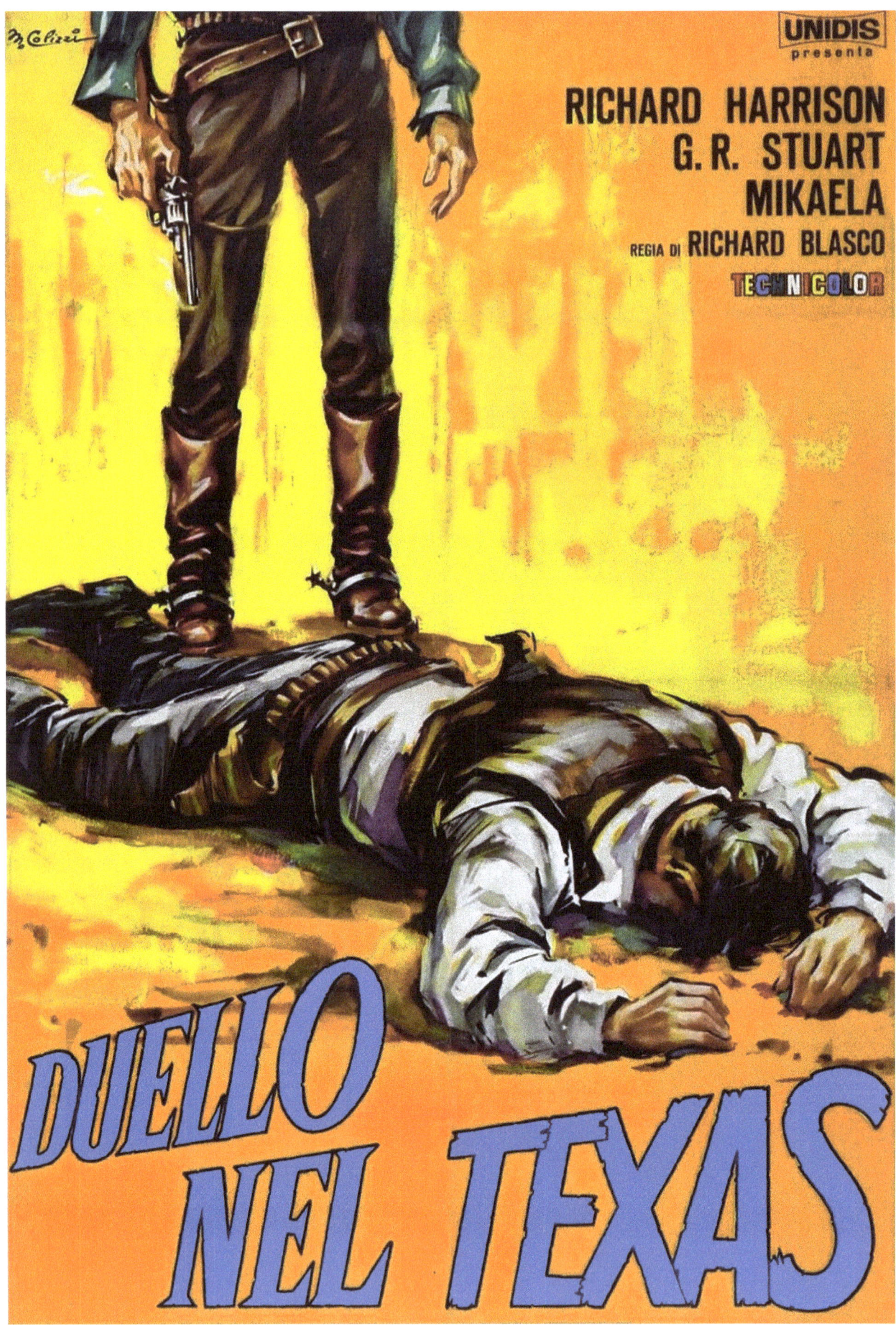

DUELLO NEL TEXAS

("Duel In Texas"). Artist: Mauro Colizzi. Original Title: **Duello Nel Texas** (1963, Italy).

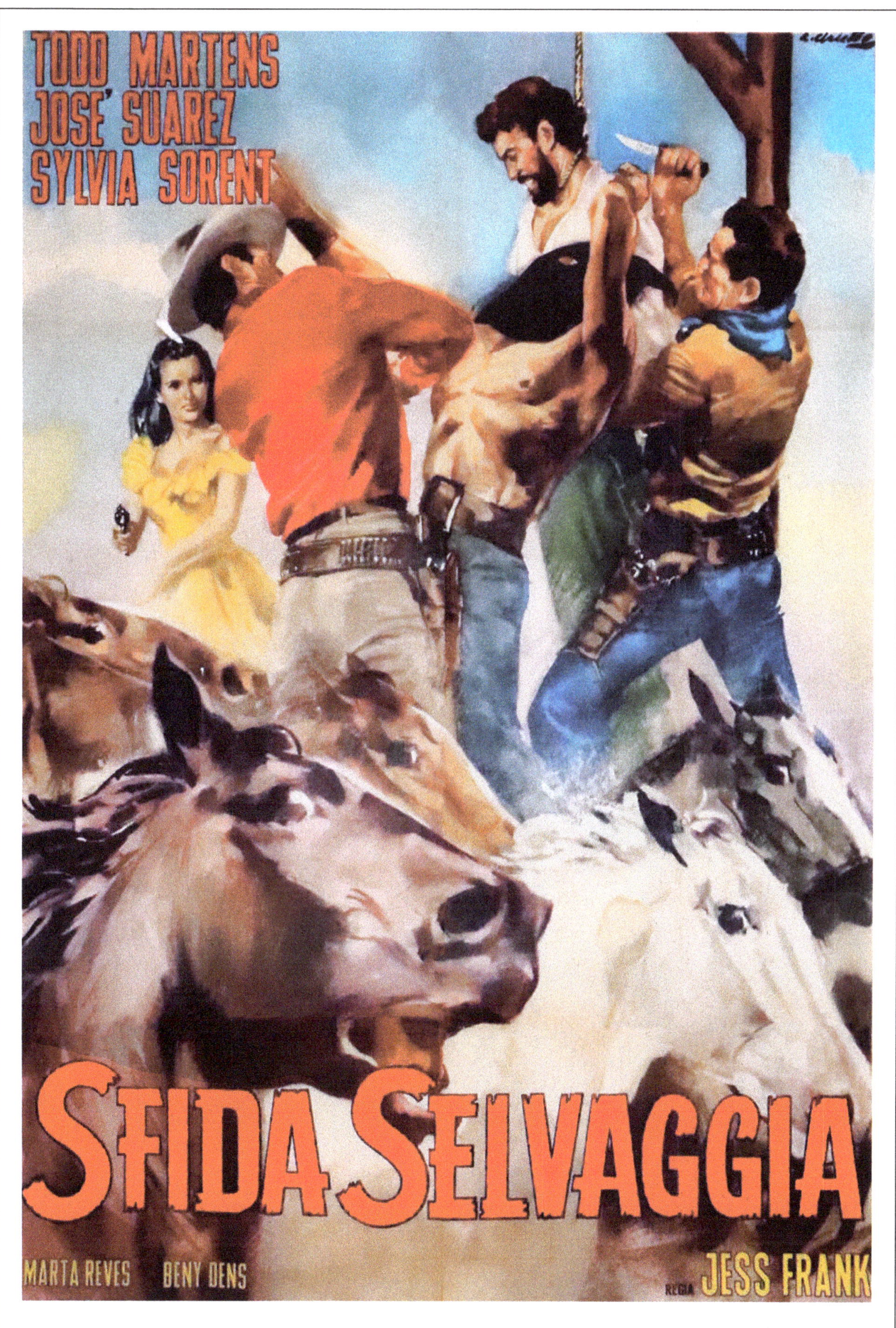

SFIDA SELVAGGIA

("Savage Challenge"). Artist: Averado Ciriello. Original Title: **El Llanero** (1963, Spain).

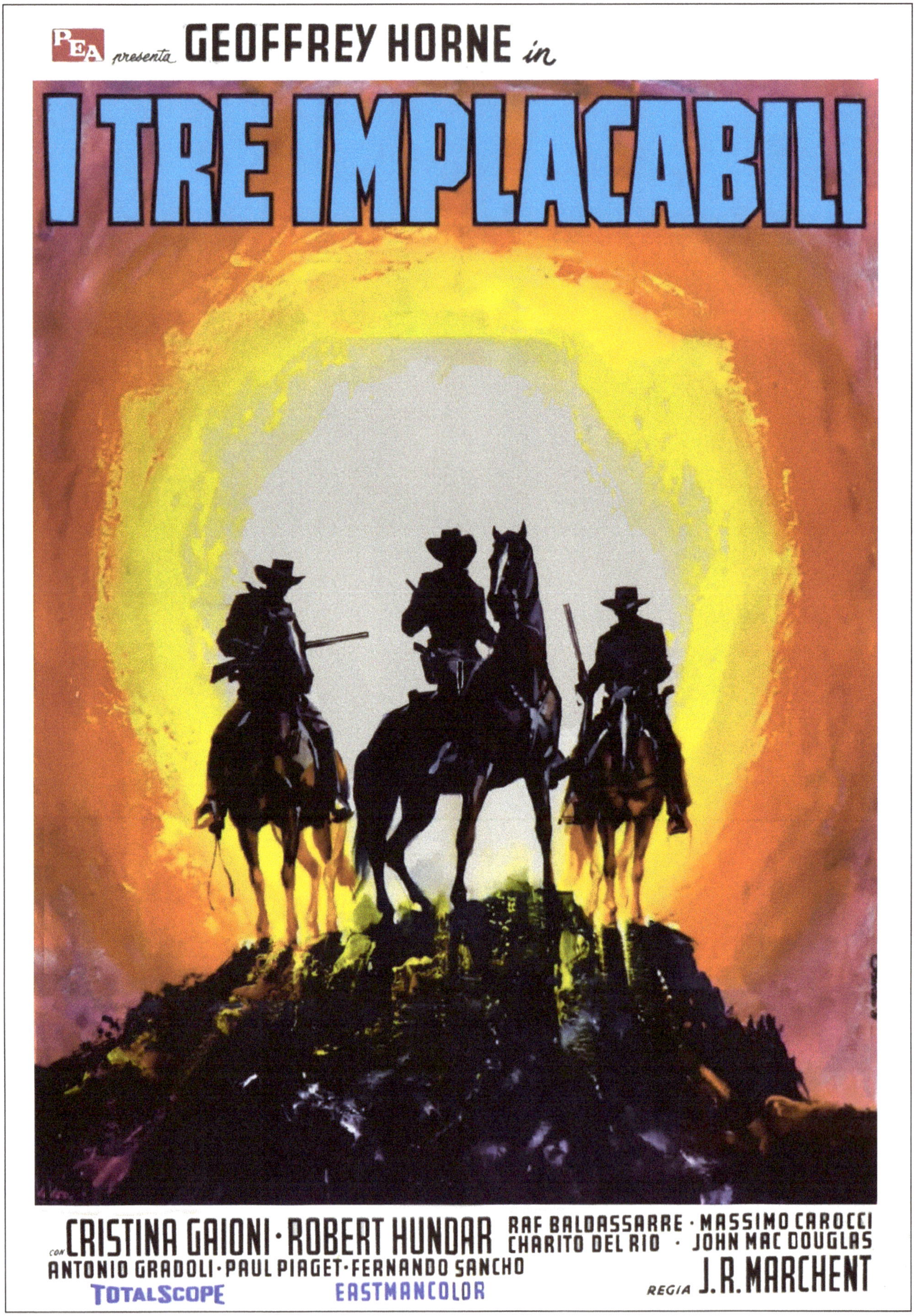

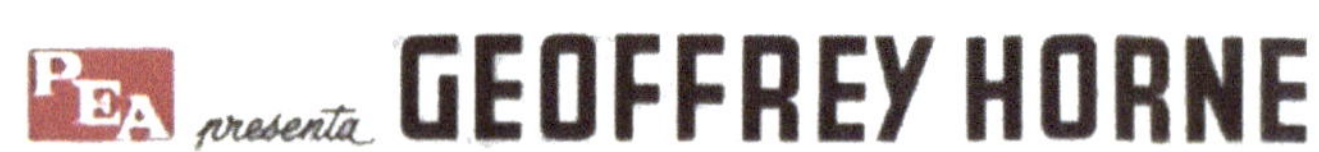

I TRE IMPLACABILI

con CRISTINA GAIONI · ROBERT HUNDAR
RAF BALDASSARRE · MASSIMO CAROCCI
CHARITO DEL RIO · JOHN MAC DOUGLAS
ANTONIO GRADOLI · PAUL PIAGET · FERNANDO SANCHO
TOTALSCOPE
EASTMANCOLOR
REGIA J.R. MARCHENT

I TRE IMPLACABILI

("The Remorseless Three"). Artist: Renato Casaro. Original Title: **Tres Hombres Buenos** (1963, Spain/Italy).

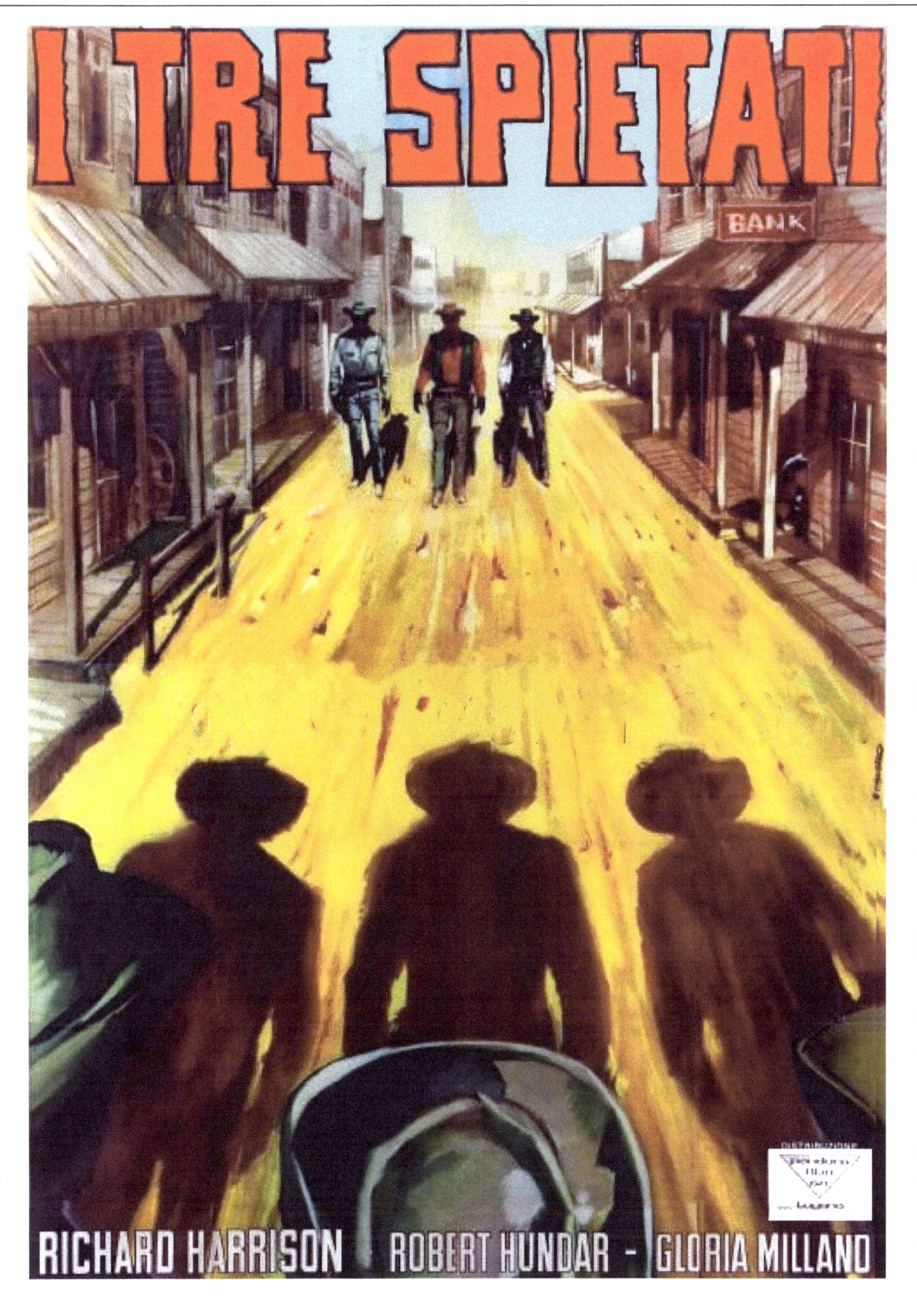

I TRE SPIETATI

("The Ruthless Three"). Artist: Renato Casaro. Original Title: **El Sabor De La Venganza** (1963, Spain/Italy).

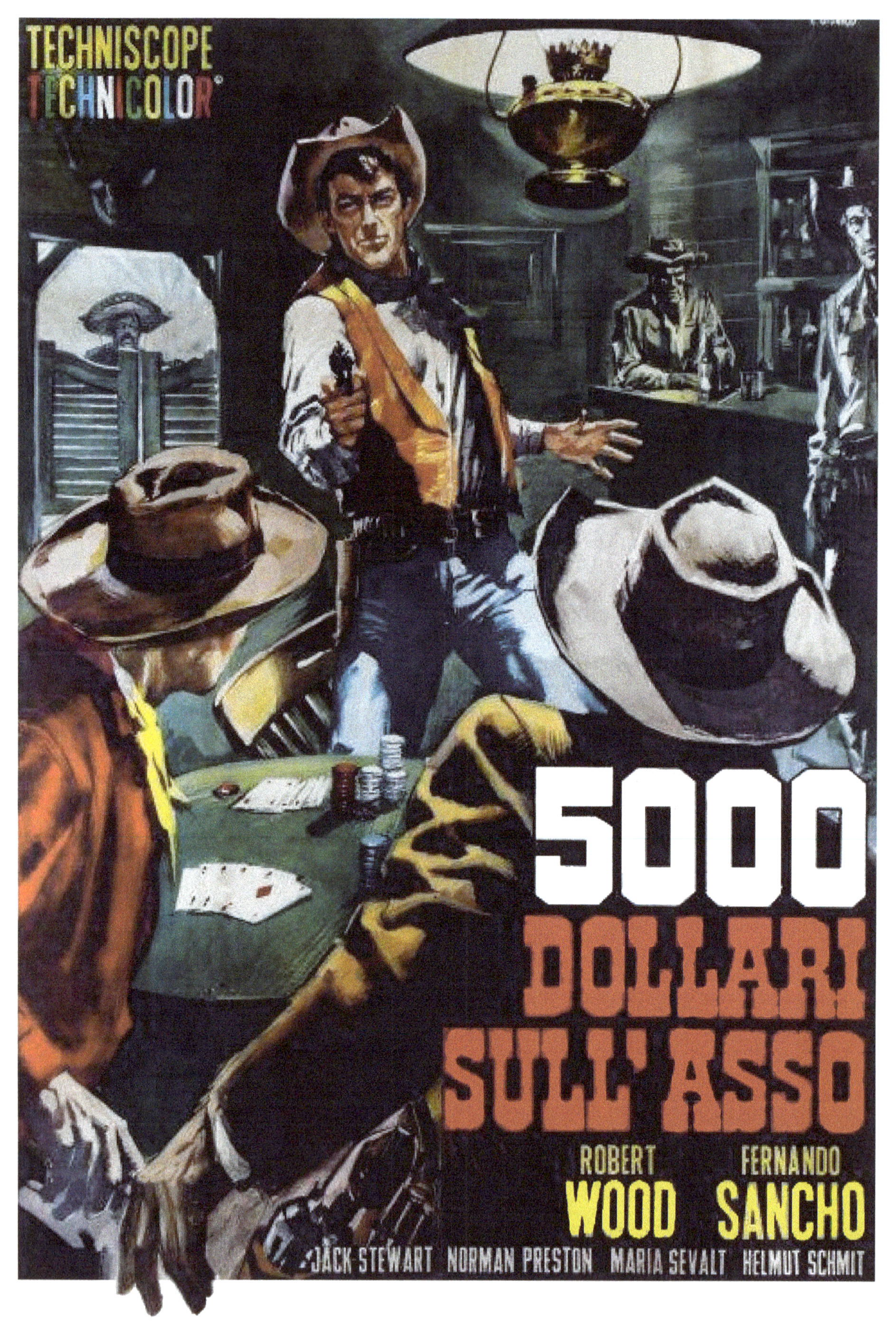

5.000 DOLLARI SULL'ASSO

("$5,000 On The Ace"). Artist: Renato Casaro. Original Title: **Pistoleros De Arizona** (1964, Spain/Italy).

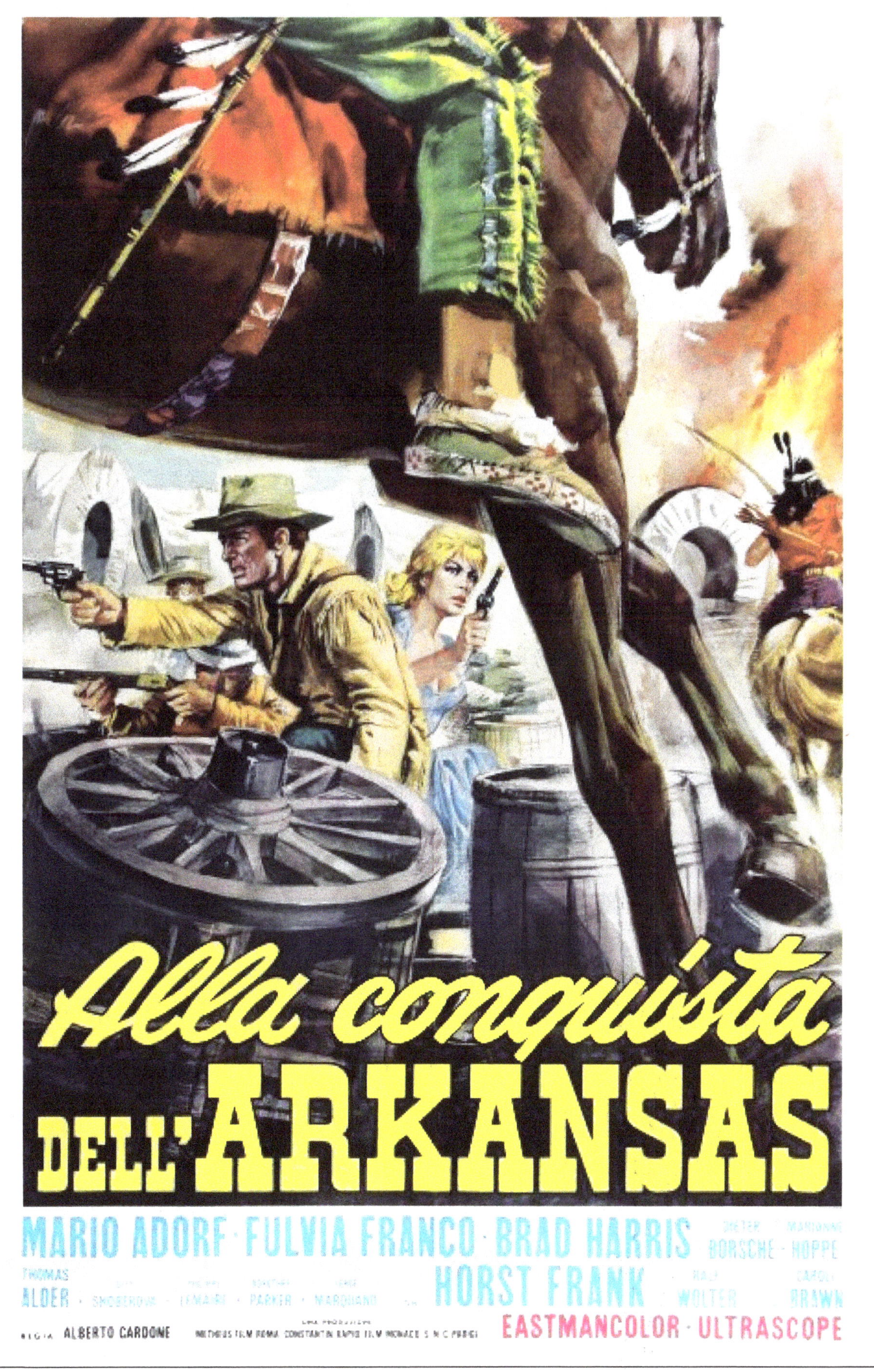

ALLA CONQUISTA DELL'ARKANSAS

("At The Conquest Of Arkansas"). Artist: unsigned. Original Title: **Die Goldsucher Von Arkansas** (1964, Germany/Italy/France).

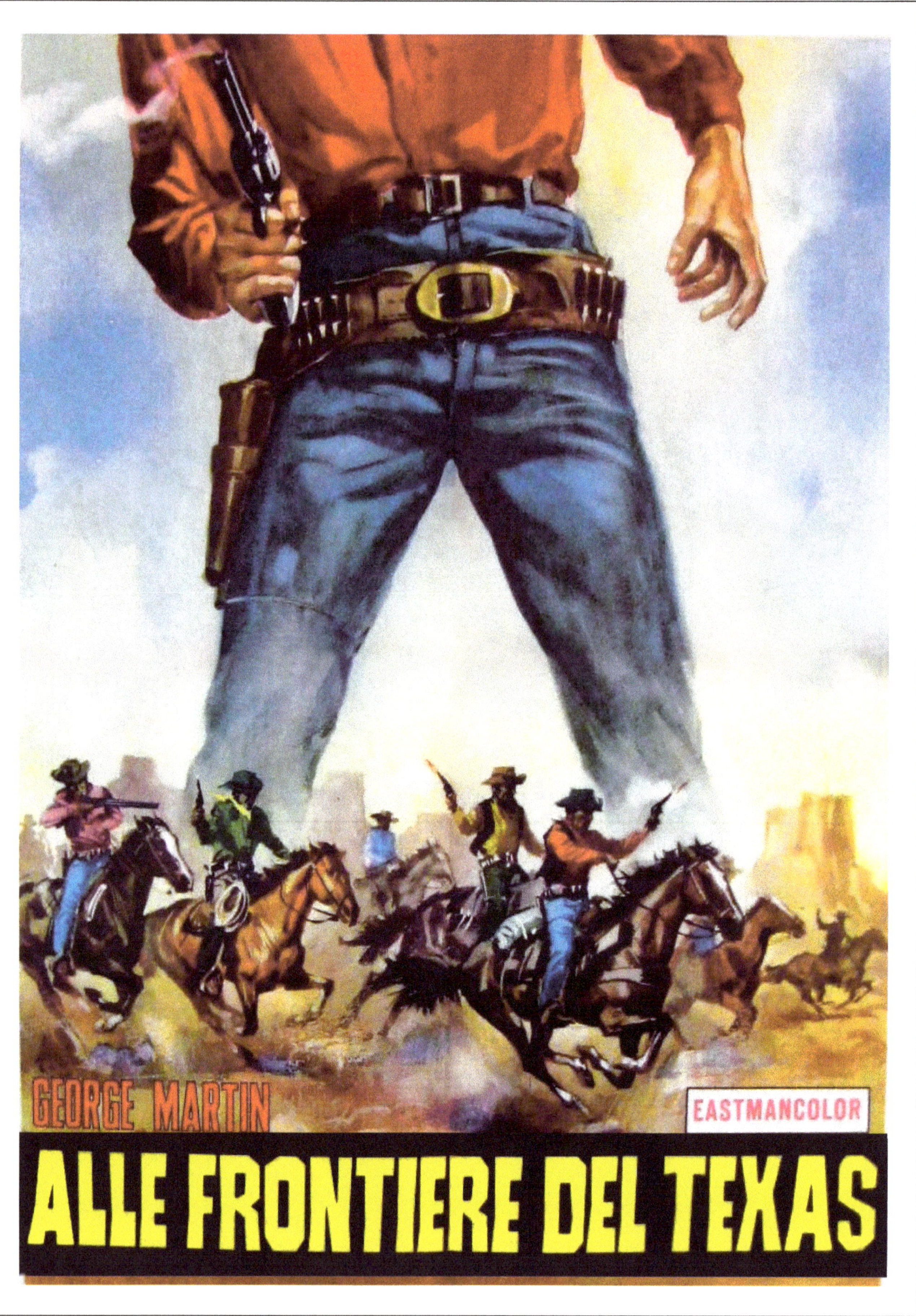

ALLE FRONTIERE DEL TEXAS

("At The Texas Frontier"). Artist: unsigned. Original Title: **Fuera De La Ley** (1964, Spain).

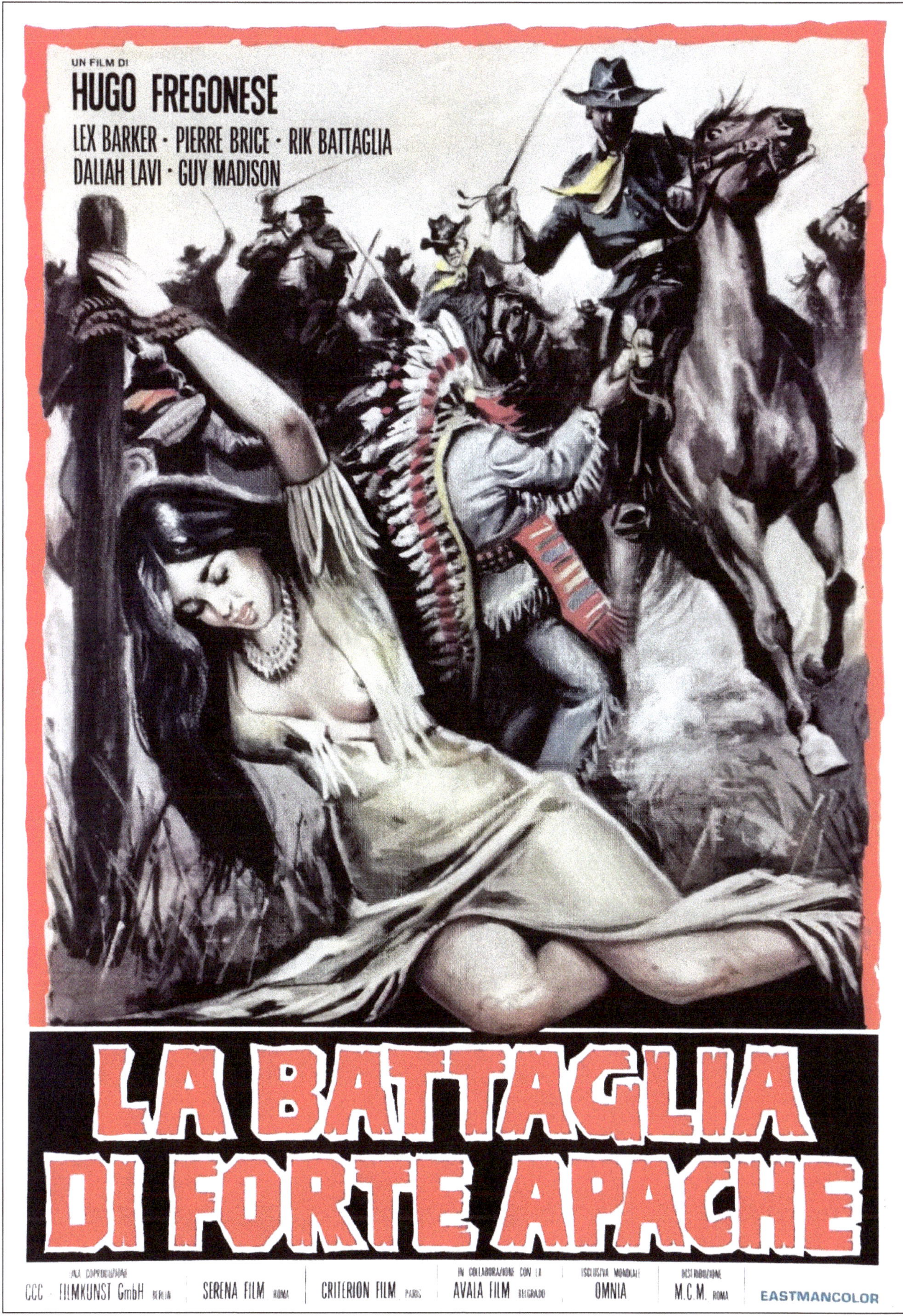

LA BATTAGLIA DI FORT APACHE

("The Battle Of Fort Apache"). Artist: unsigned. Original Title: **Old Shatterhand** (1964, Germany/Italy/France/Yugoslavia).

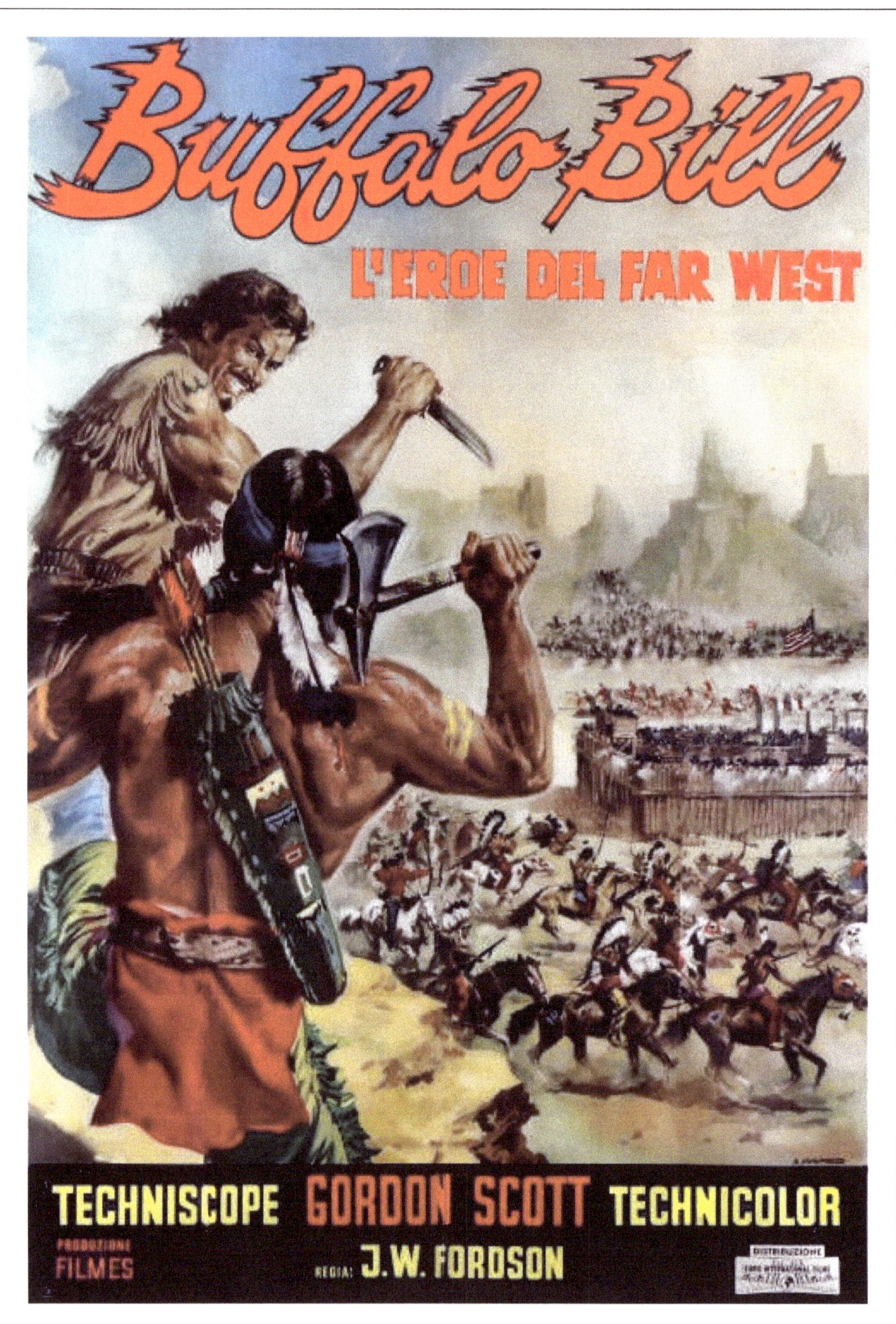

BUFFALO BILL, L'EROE DEL FAR WEST

("Buffalo Bill, Wild West Hero"). Artist: Renato Casaro. Original Title: **Buffalo Bill, L'Eroe Del Far West** (1964, Italy/France/Germany).

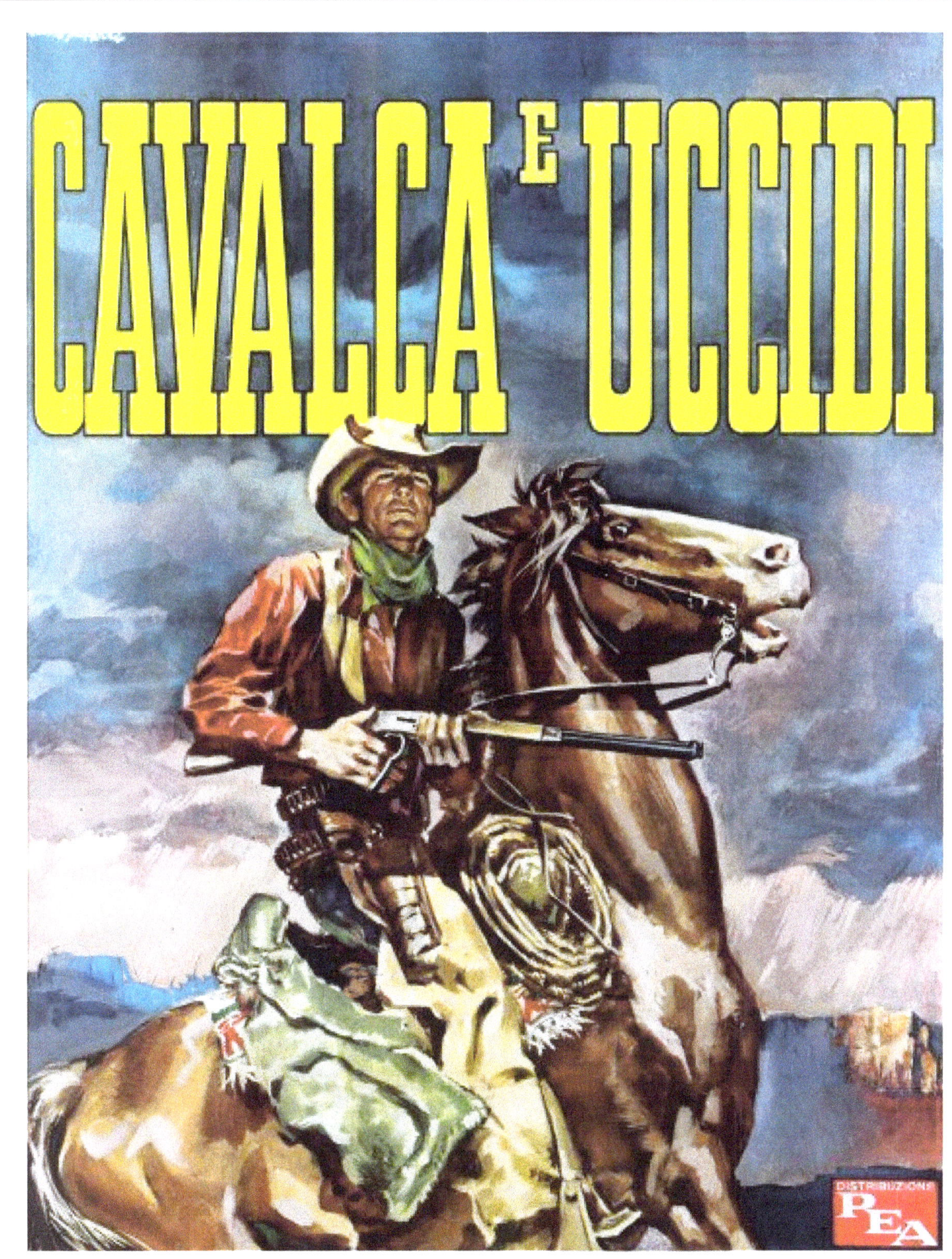

ALEX NICOL ROBERT HUNDAR MARGARET GRAYSON
LAWRENCE PALMER PAULINE BAARDS
REGIA J.L.BORAW

CAVALCA E UCCIDI

("Ride And Kill"). Artist: Rodlfo Gasparri. Original Title: **Cavalca E Uccidi** (1964, Italy/Spain).

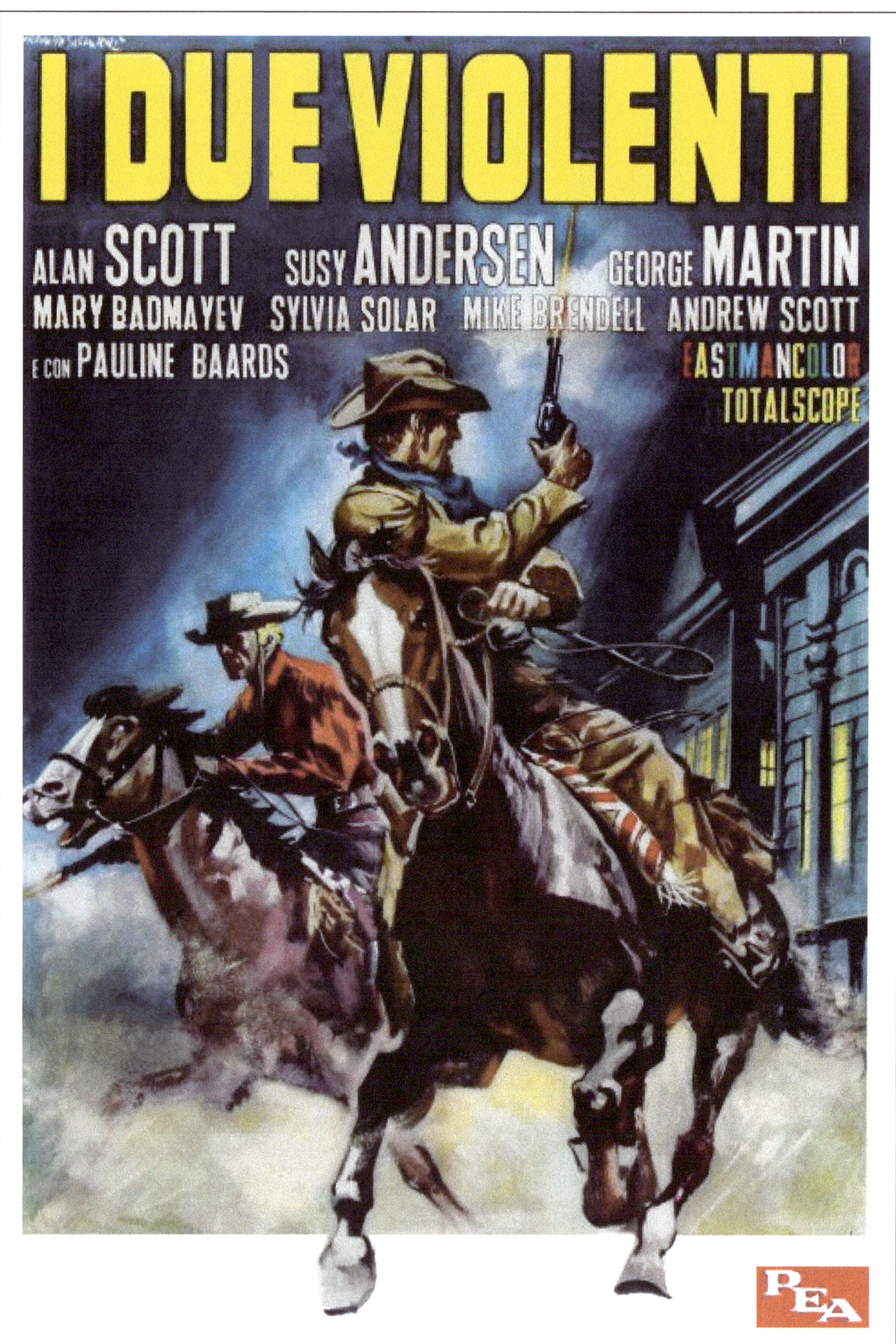

I DUE VIOLENTI

("Two Violent Men"). Artist: Rodolfo Gasparri. Original Title: **I Due Violenti** (1964, Italy/Spain).

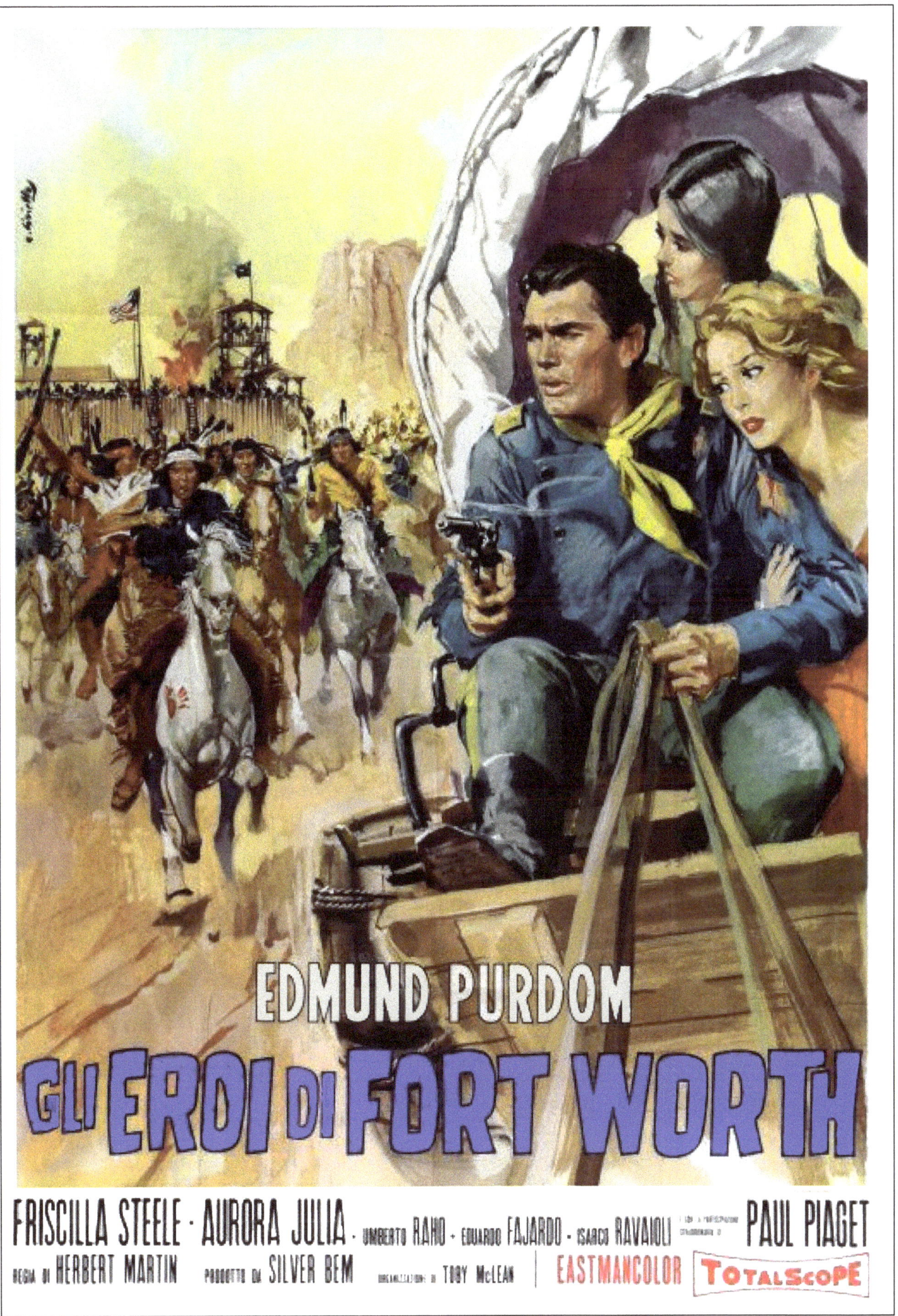

GLI EROI DI FORT WORTH

("Heroes Of Fort Worth"). Artist: Averado Ciriello. Original Title: **Gli Eroi Di Fort Worth** (1964, Italy/Spain).

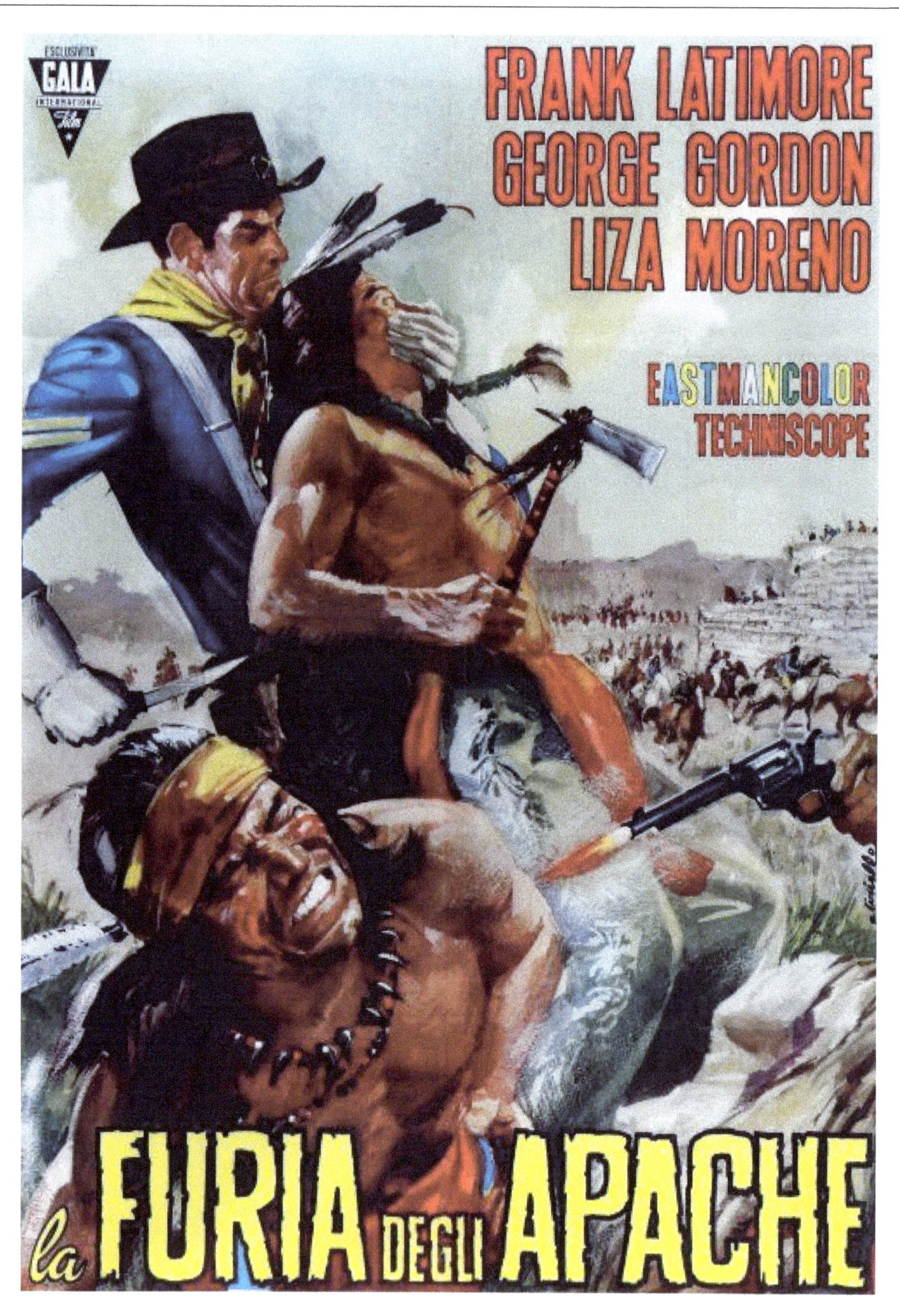

LA FURIA DEGLI APACHE

("Apache Rage"). Artist: Sverado Ciriello. Original Title: **El Hombre De La Diligencia** (1964, Spain).

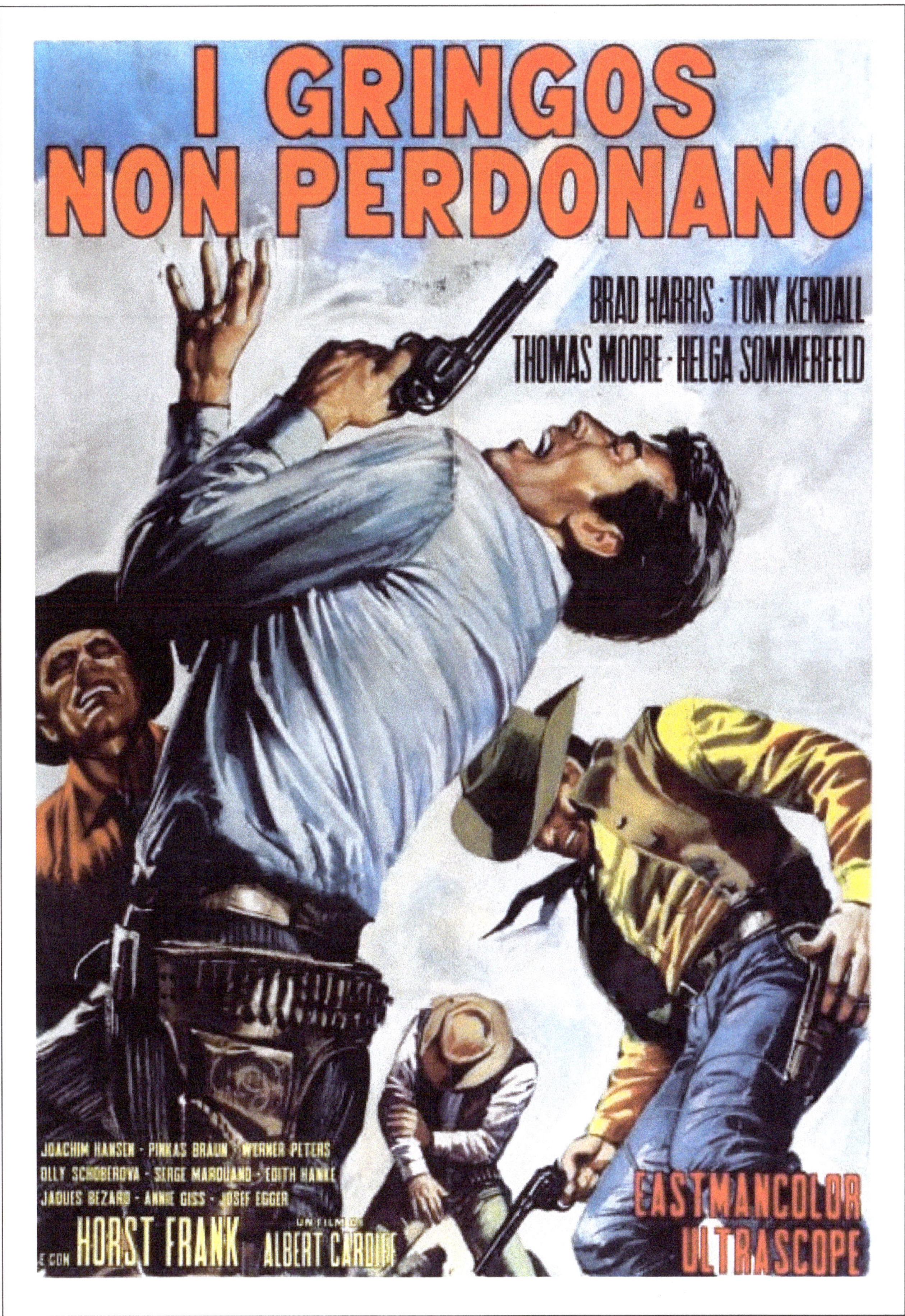

I GRINGOS NON PERDONANO

("Gringos Don't Forgive"). Artist: Renato Casaro. Original Title: **Die Schwarzen Adler Von Santa Fe** (1964, Germany/Italy/France).

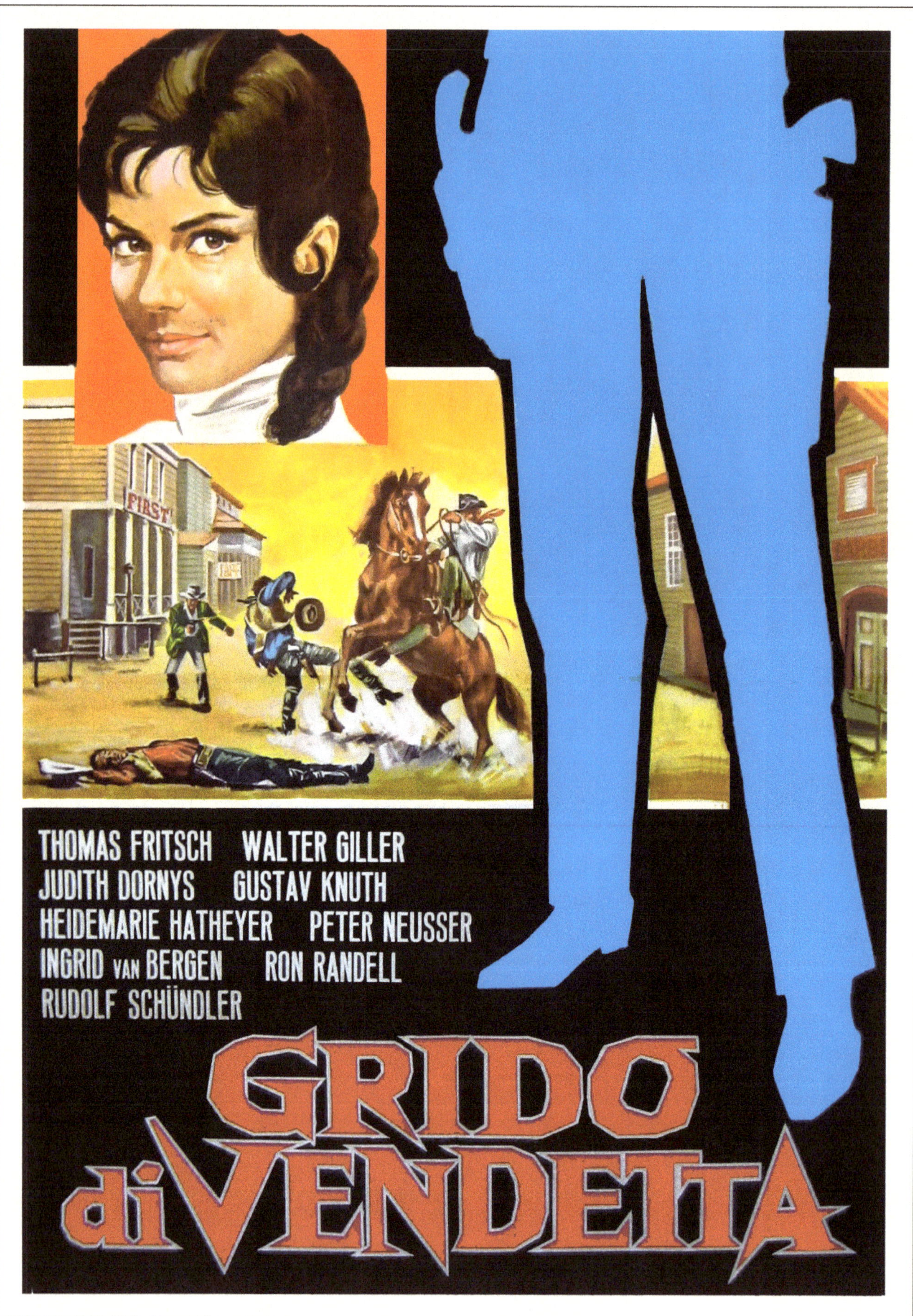

GRIDO DI VENDETTA

("Cry Of Vengeance"). Artist: unsigned. Original Title: **Heiß Weht Der Wind** (1964, Germany/Austria).

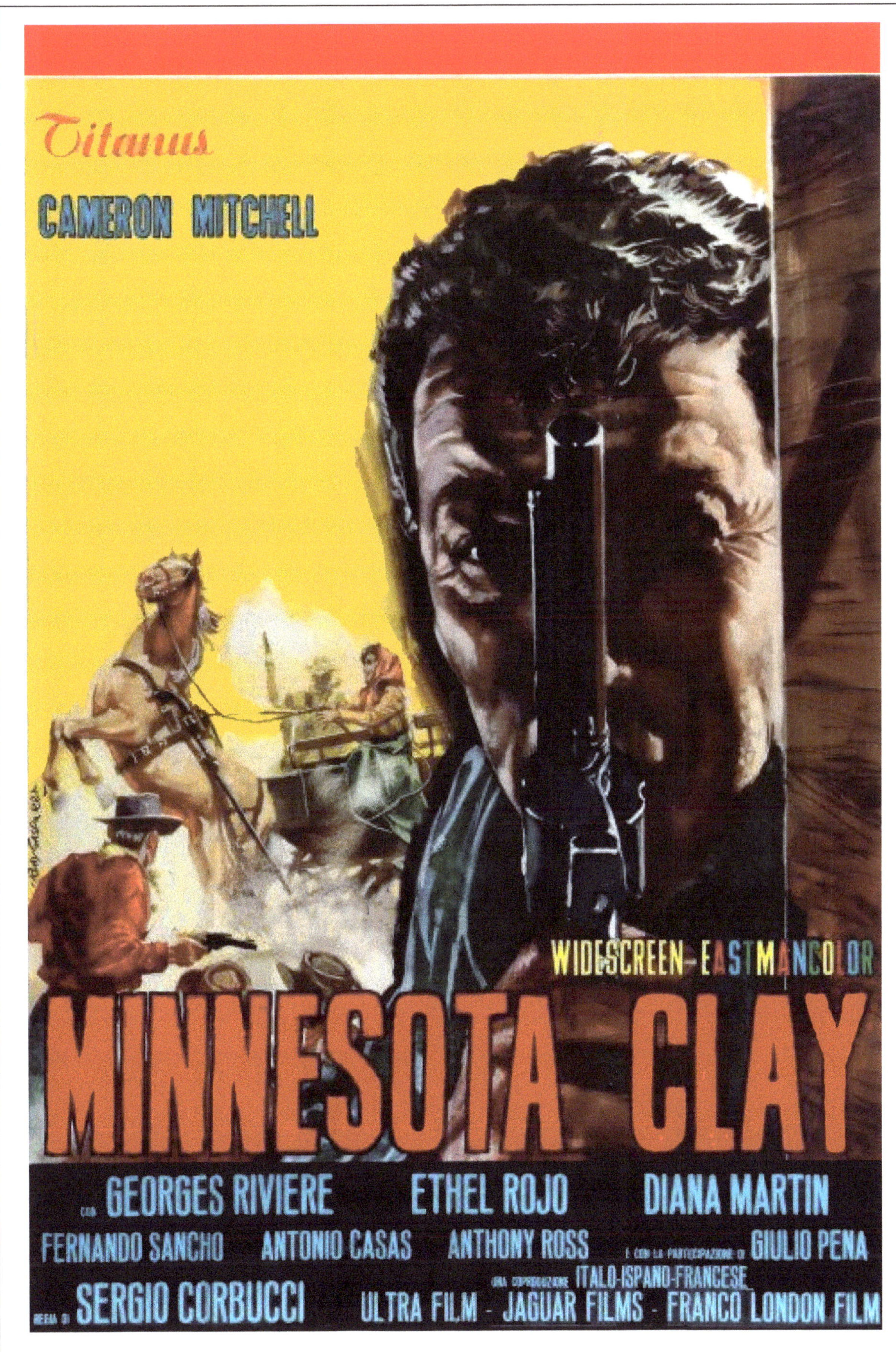

MINNESOTA CLAY

("Minnesota Clay"). Artist: Rodolfo Gasparri. Original Title: **Minnesota Clay** (1964, Italy/Spain/France).

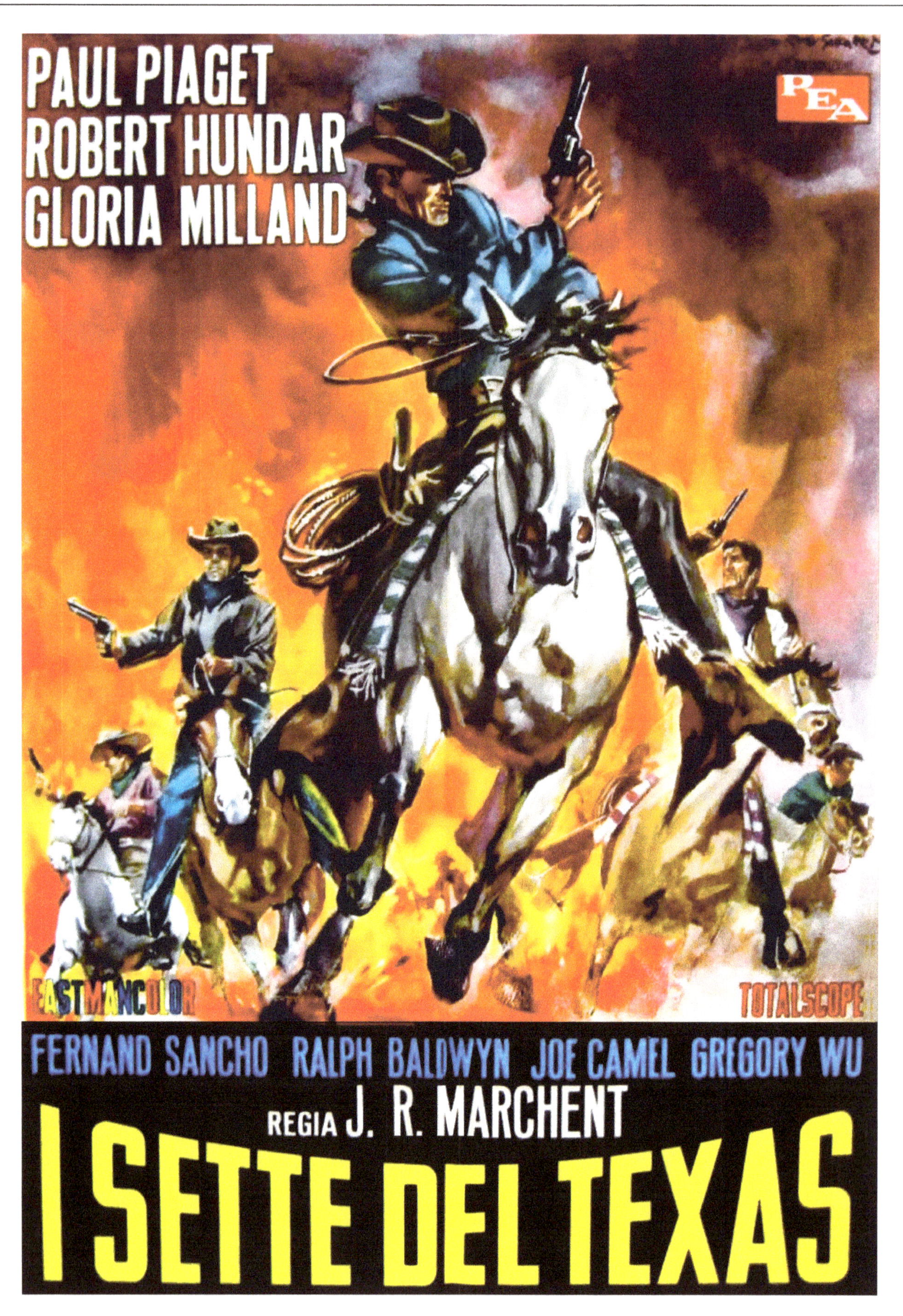

I SETTE DEL TEXAS

("The Texas Seven"). Artist: Rodlfo Gasparri. Original Title: **Antes Llega La muerte** (1964, Spain/Italy).

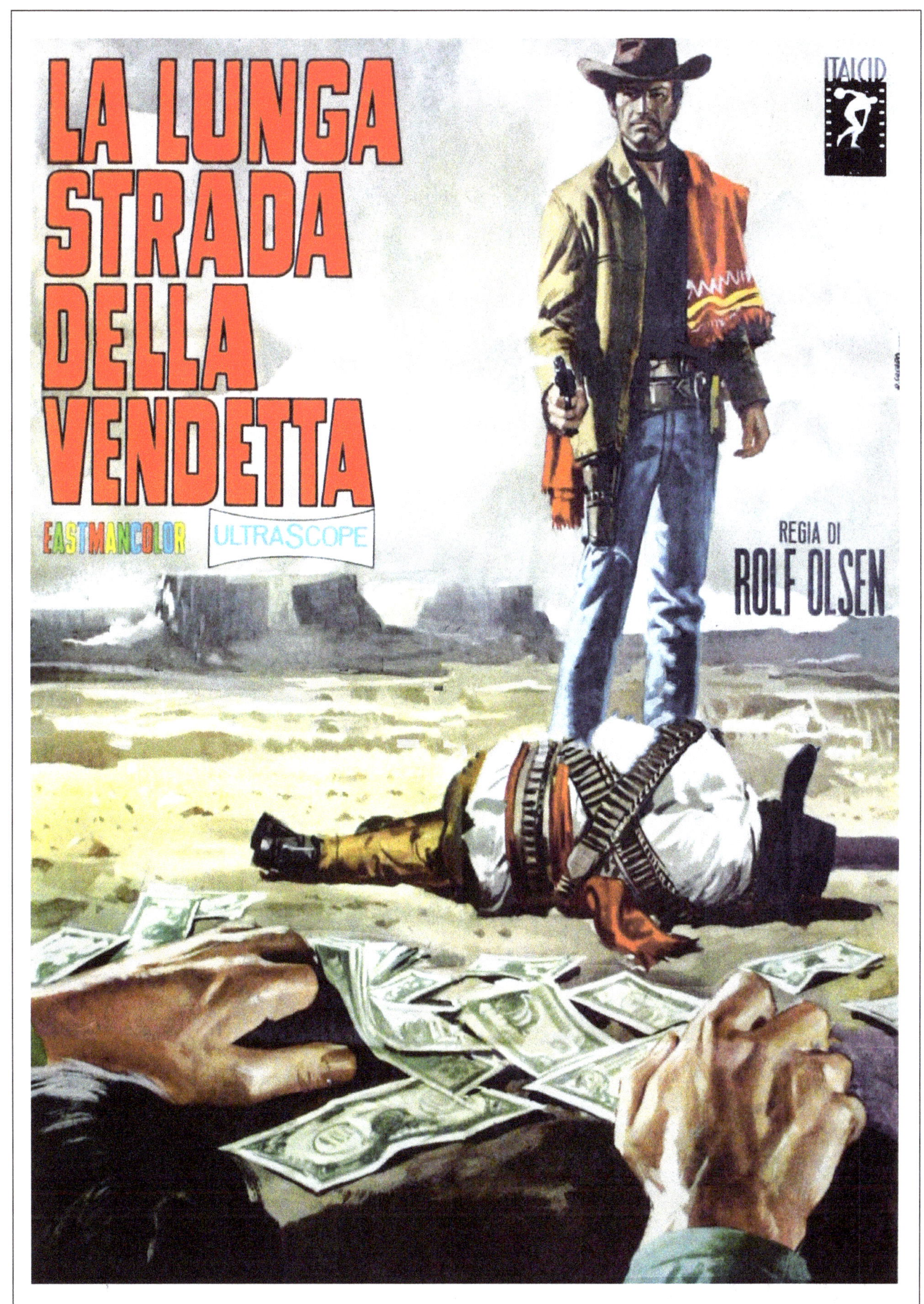

LA LUNGA STRADA DELLA VENDETTA

("The Long Road Of Vengeance"). Artist: Renato Casaro. Original Title: **Der Letzte Ritt Nach Santa Cruz** (1964, Austria/Germany).

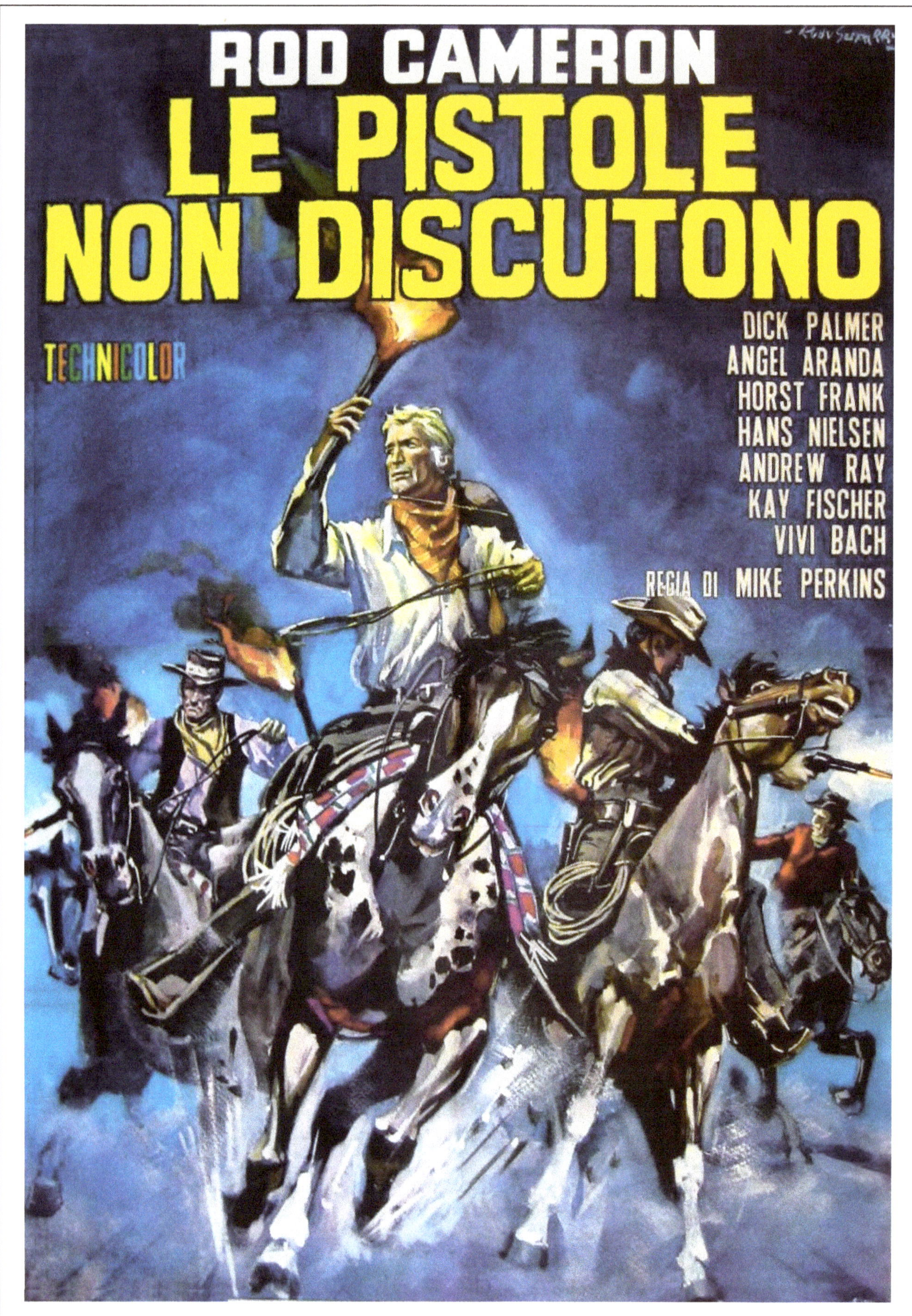

LE PISTOLE NON DISCUTONO

("Guns Don't Argue"). Artist: Rodlfo Gasparri. Original Title: **Le Pistole Non Discutono** (1964, Italy/Spain/Germany).

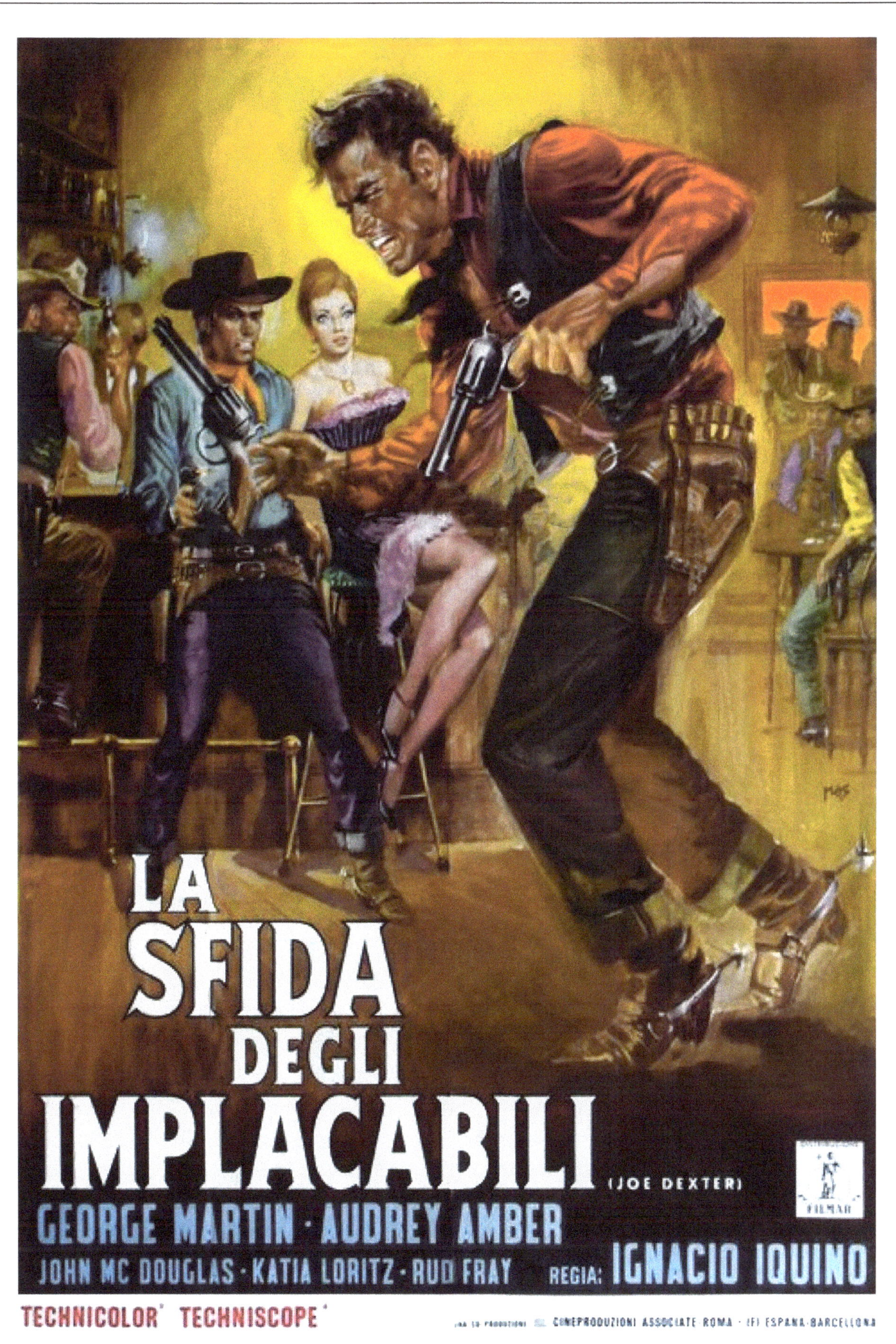

LA SFIDA DEGLI IMPLACABILI

("The Remorseless Ones' Challenge"). Artist: Moz. Original Title: **Oeste Nevada Joe** (1964, Spain/Italy).

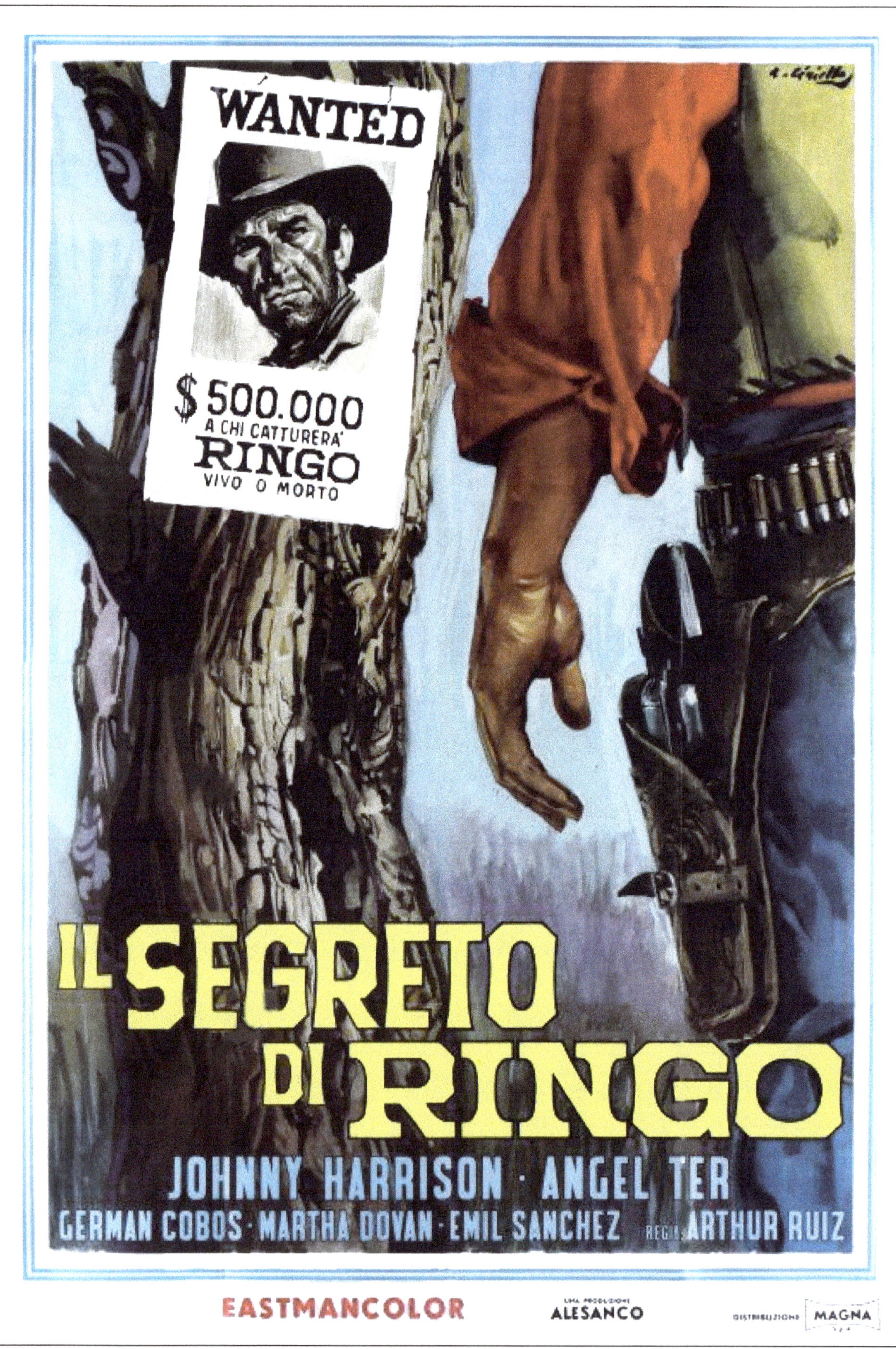

IL SEGRETO DI RINGO

("Ringo's Secret"). Artist: Averado Ciriello. Original Title: **El Secreto Del Capitan O'Hara** (1964, Spain).

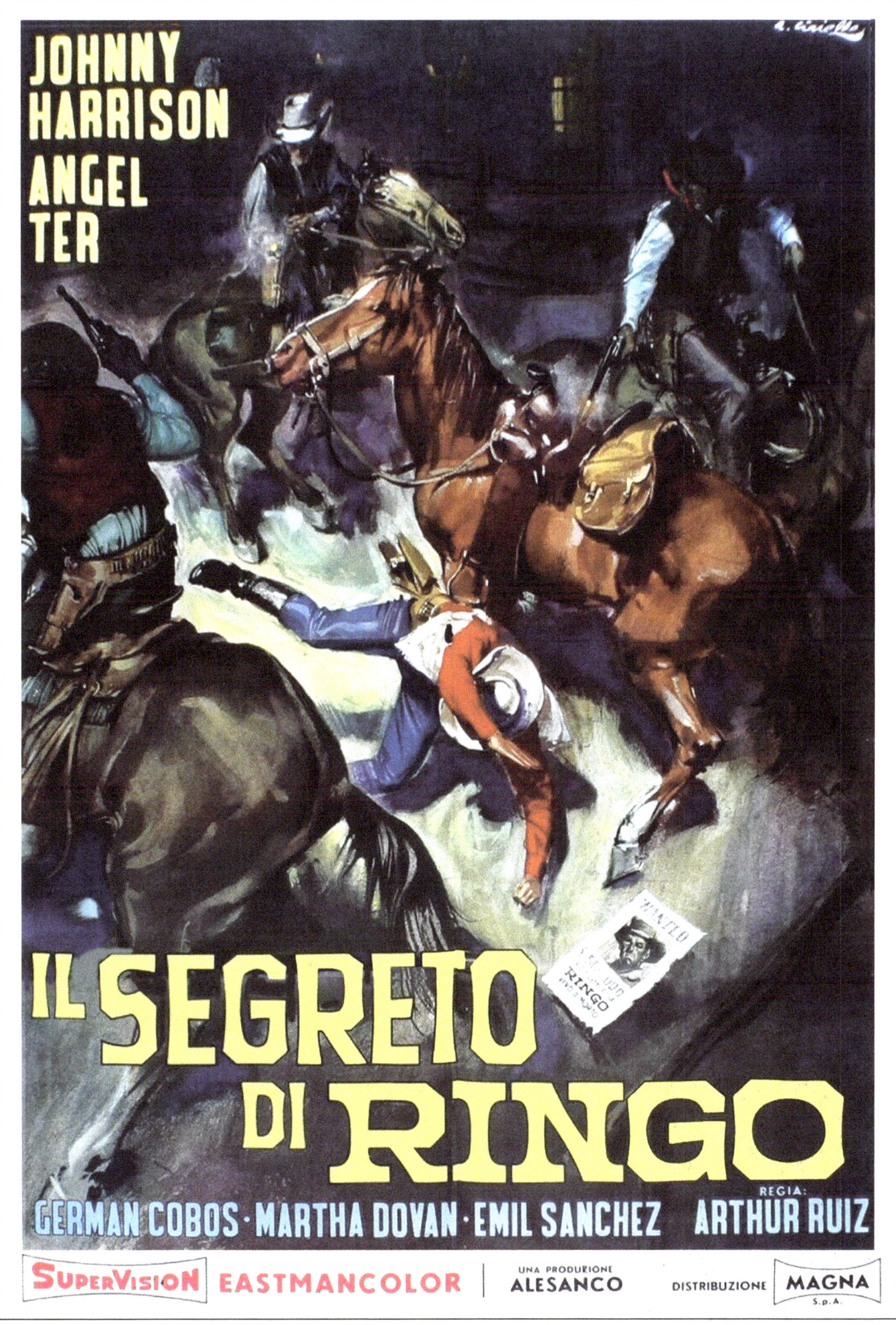

IL SEGRETO DI RINGO

("Ringo's Secret"). Artist: Averado Ciriello. Original Title: **El Secreto Del Capitan O'Hara** (1964, Spain).

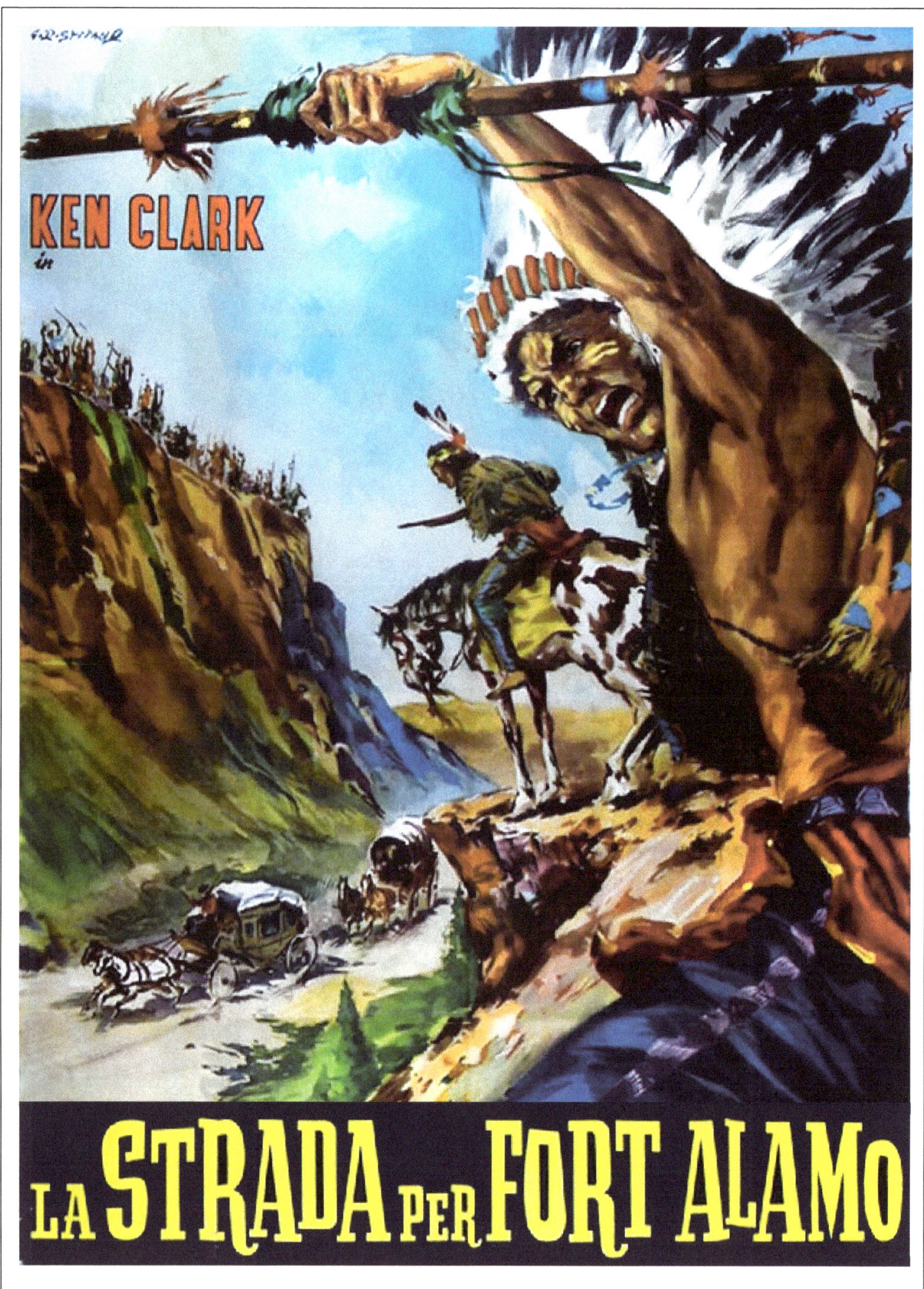

LA STRADA PER FORT ALAMO

("The Road To Fort Alamo"). Artist: G. Di Stefano. Original Title: **La Strada Per Fort Alamo** (1964, Italy/France).

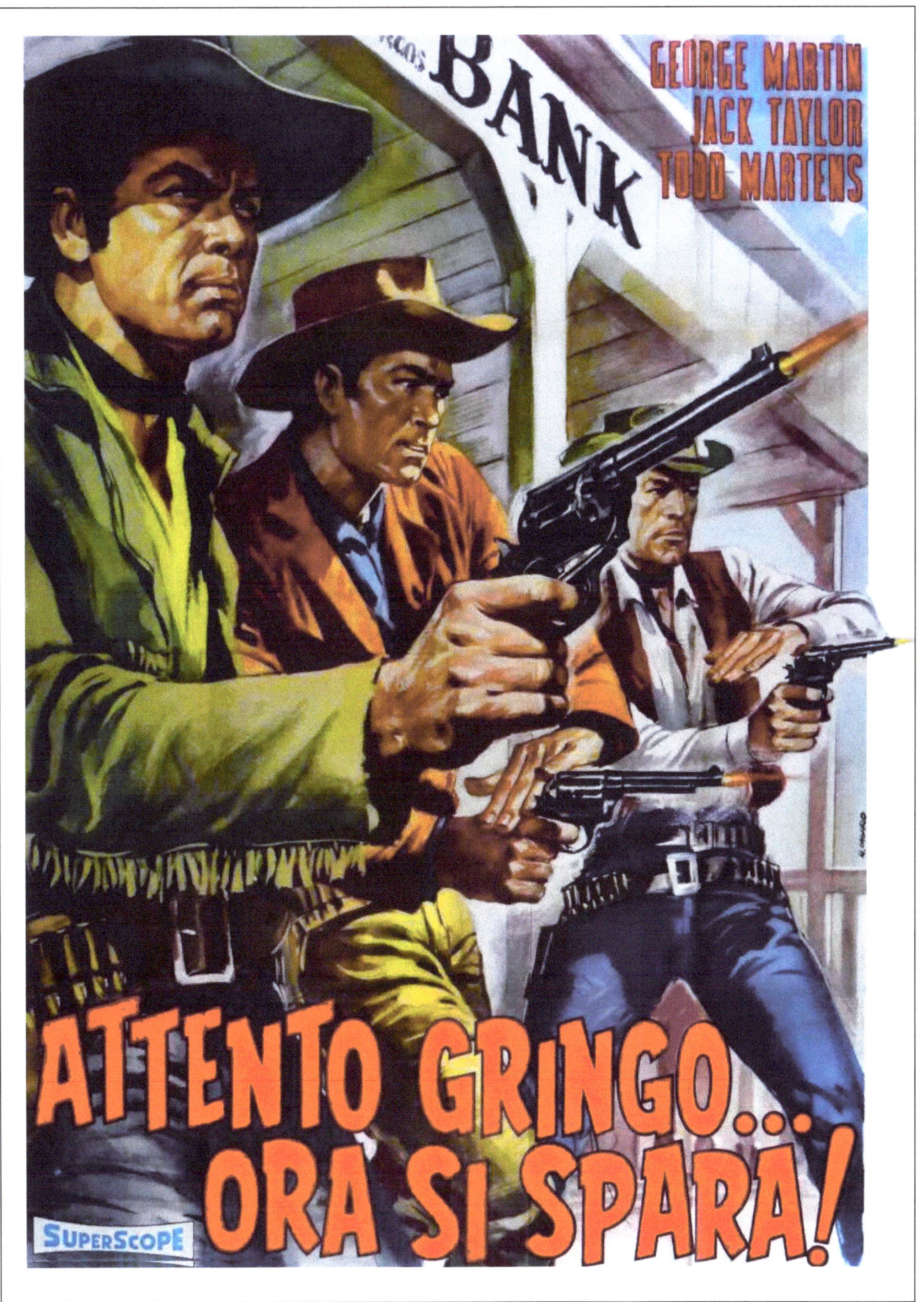

ATTENTO GRINGO... ORA SI SPARA!

("Watch Out Gringo... Now We Shoot!"). Artist: Renato Casaro. Original Title: **La Tumba Del Pistolero** (1964, Spain).

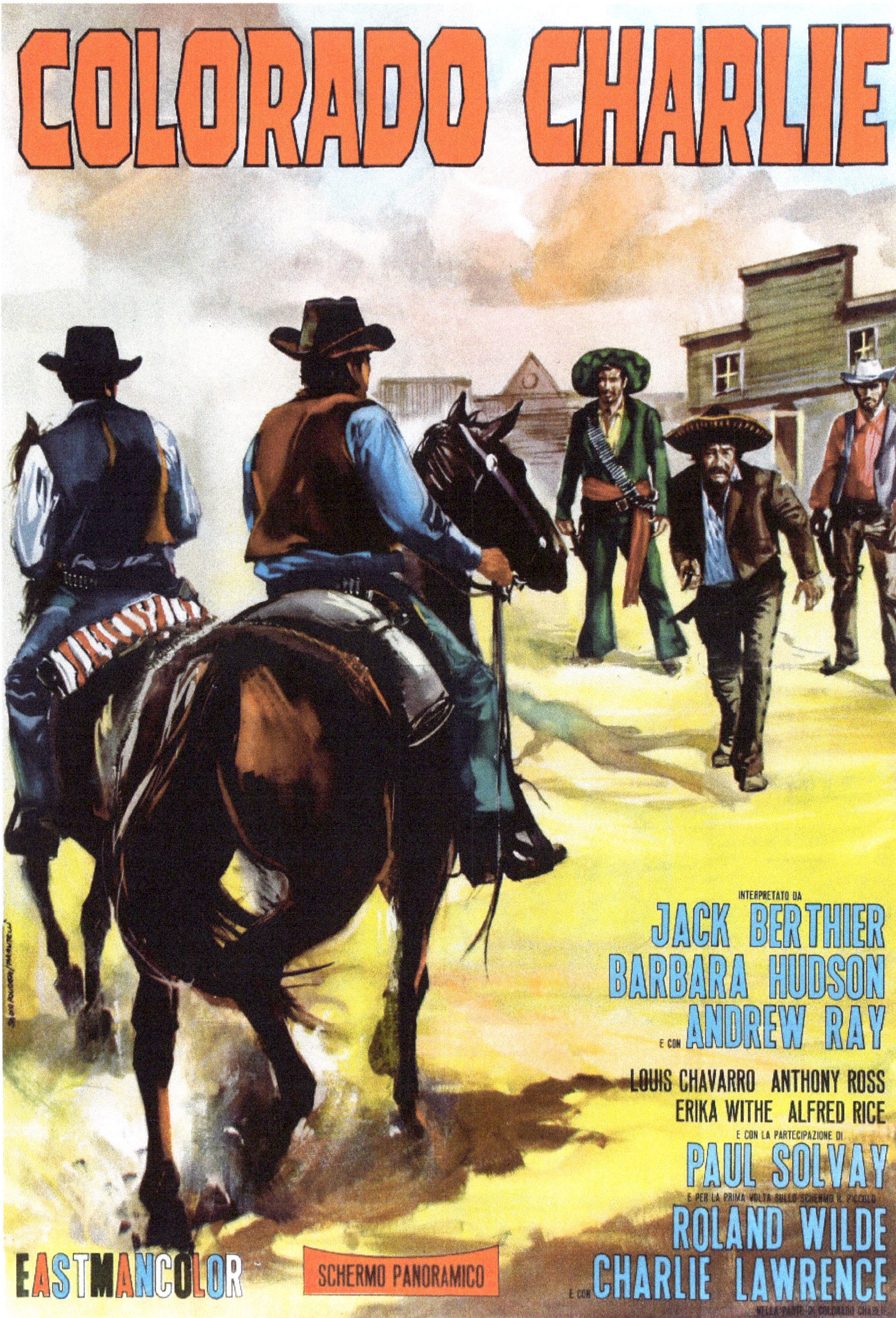

COLORADO CHARLIE

("Colorado Charlie"). Artist: Ezio Tarantelli. Original Title: **Colorado Charlie** (1965, Italy).

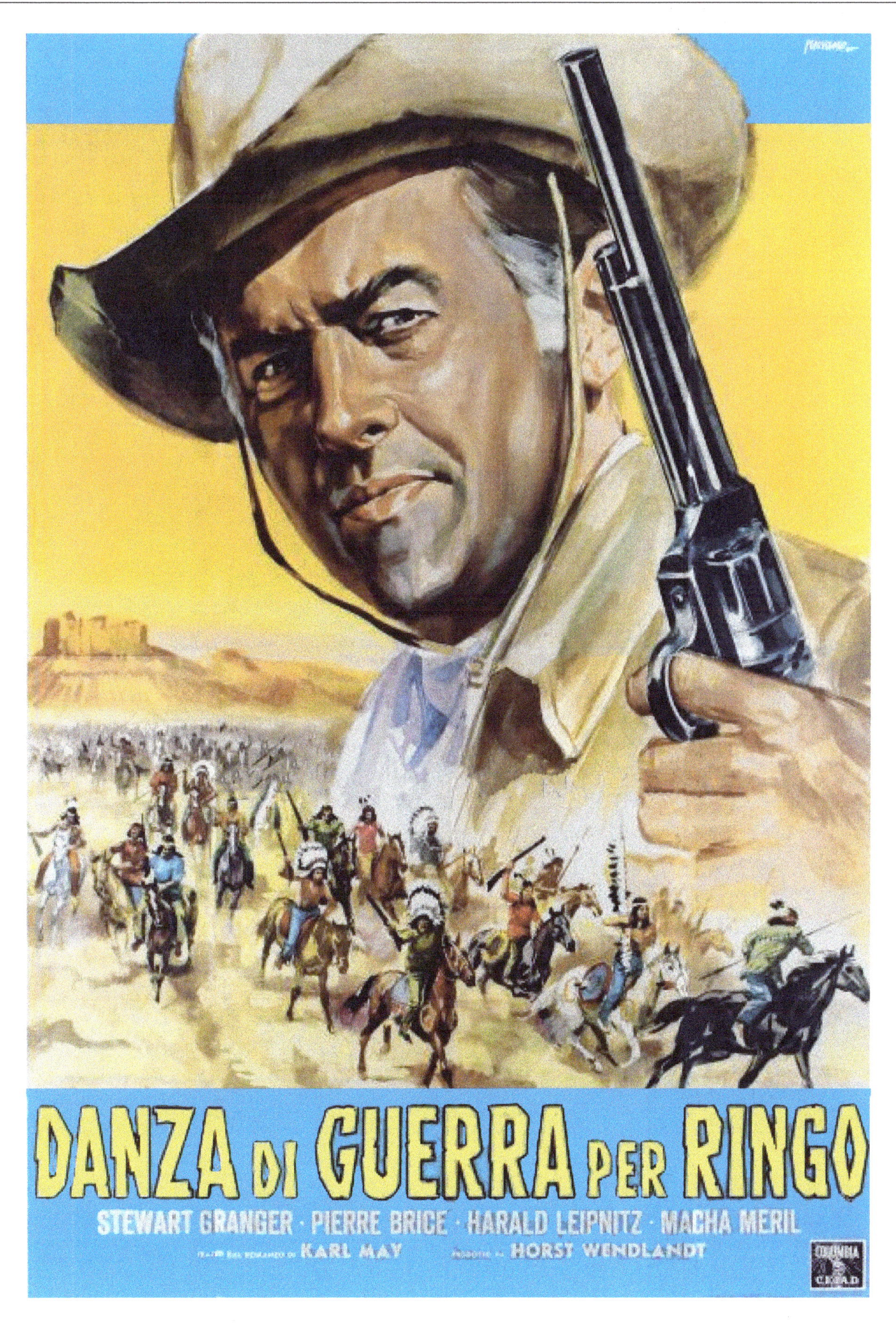

DANZA DI GUERRA PER RINGO

("War Dance For Ringo"). Artist: Mario Piovano. Original Title: **Der Ölprinz** (1965, Germany/Yugoslavia).

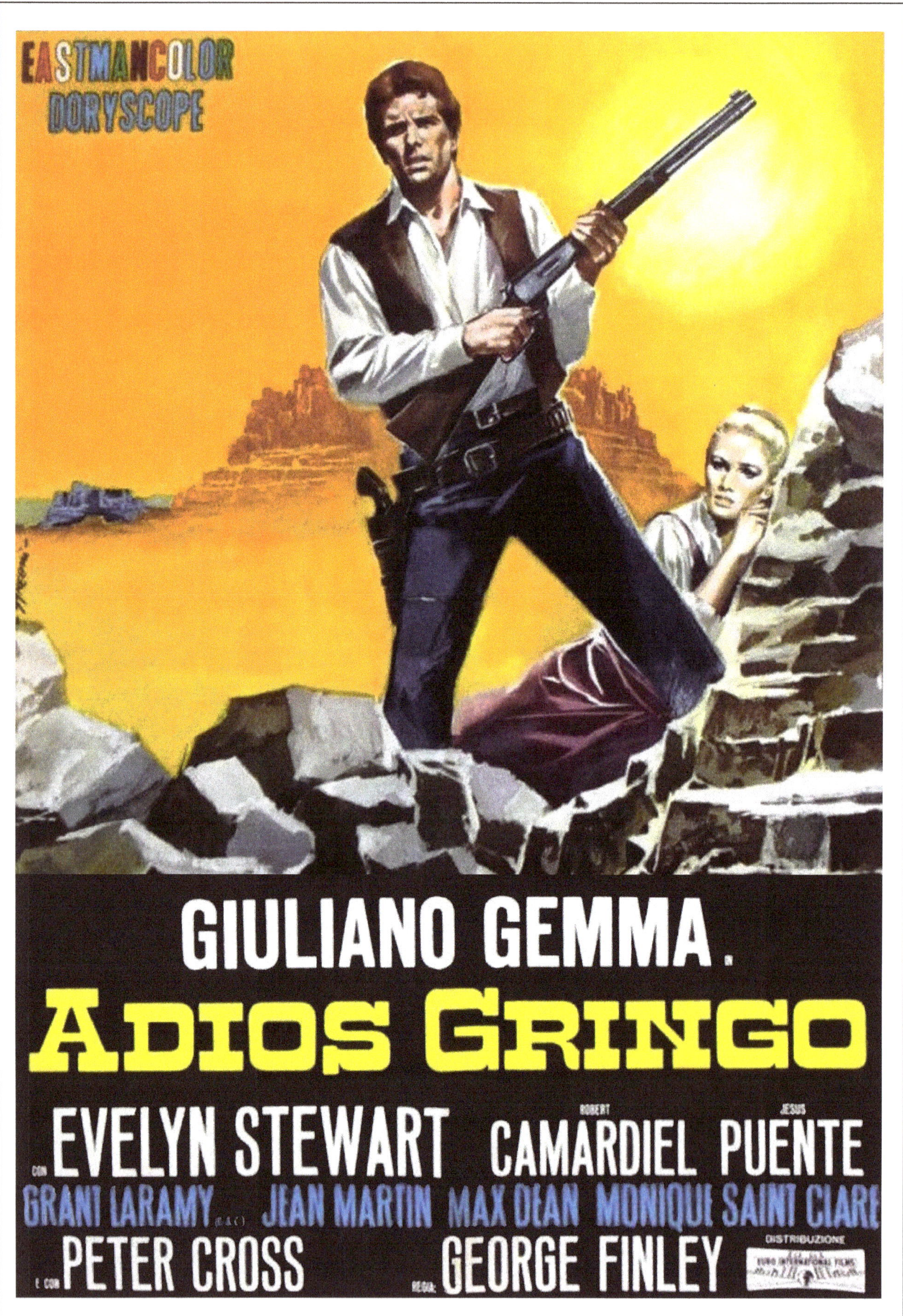

ADIOS GRINGO

("Farewell, Gringo"). Artist: Sandro Symeoni. Original Title: **Adios Gringo** (1965, Italy/France/Spain).

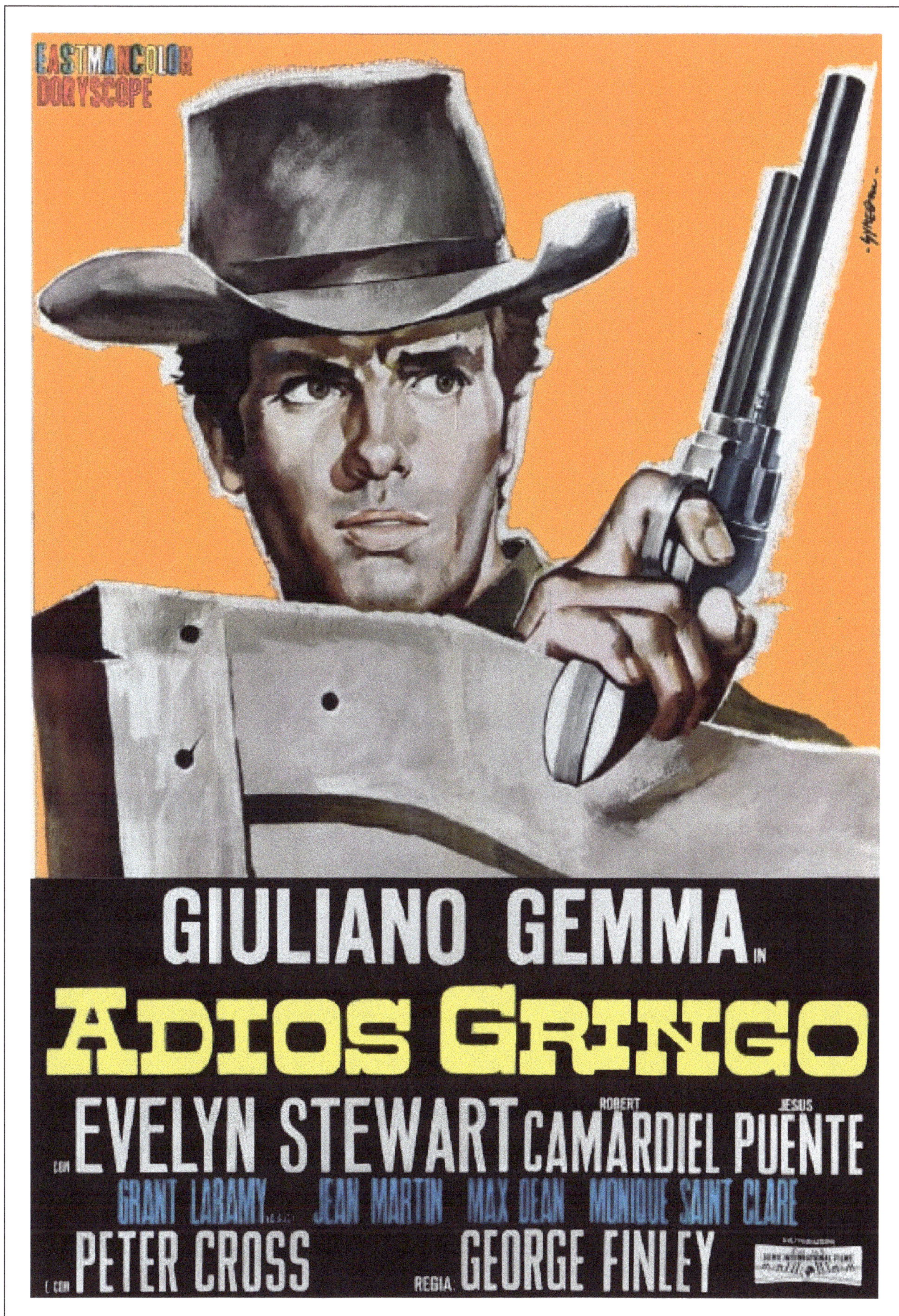

ADIOS GRINGO

("Farewell, Gringo"). Artist: Sandro Symeoni. Original Title: **Adios Gringo** (1965, Italy/France/Spain).

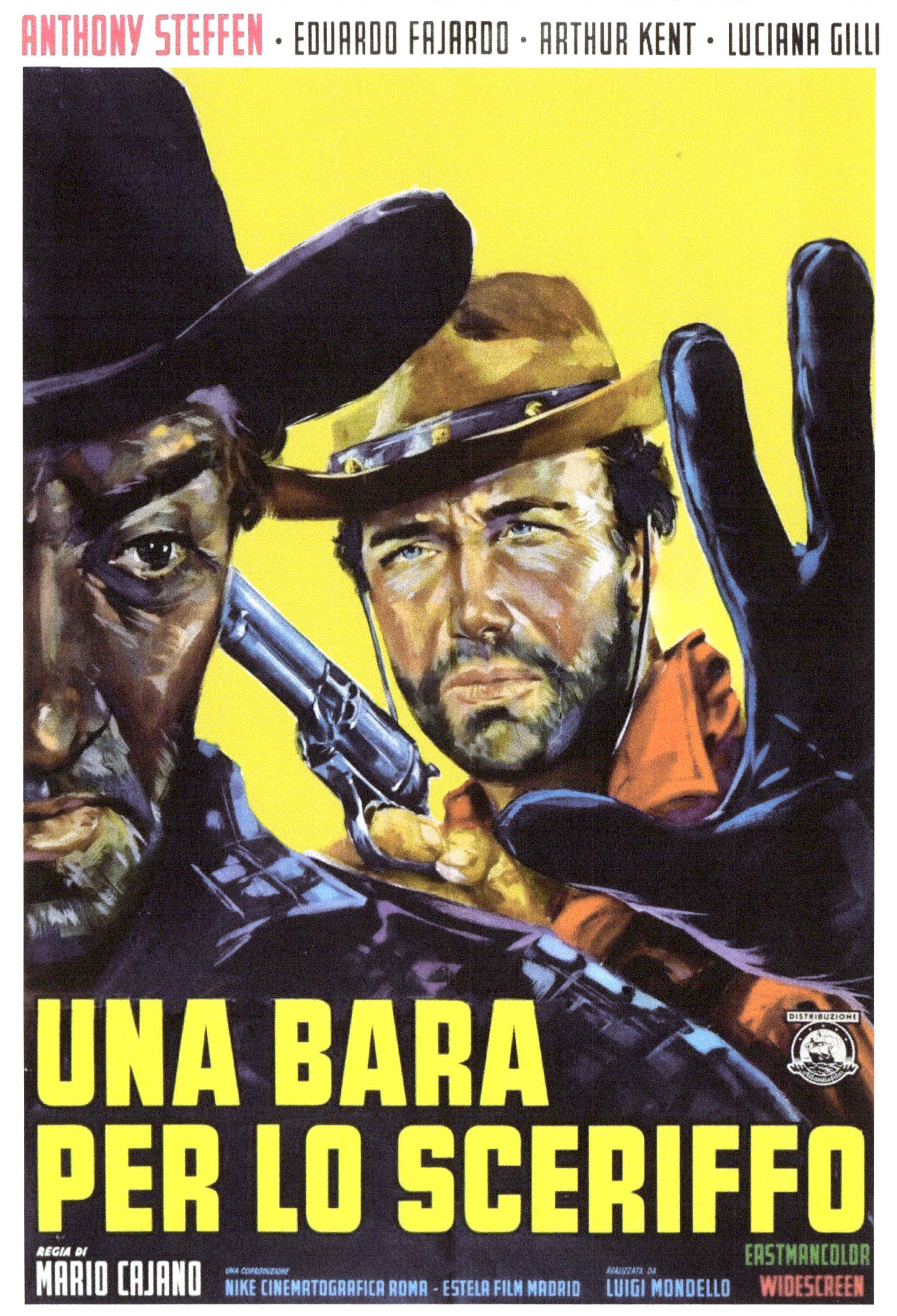

UNA BARA PER LO SCERIFFO

("A Coffin For The Sheriff"). Artist: A. Rena. Original Title: **Una Bara Per Lo Sceriffo** (1965, Italy/Spain).

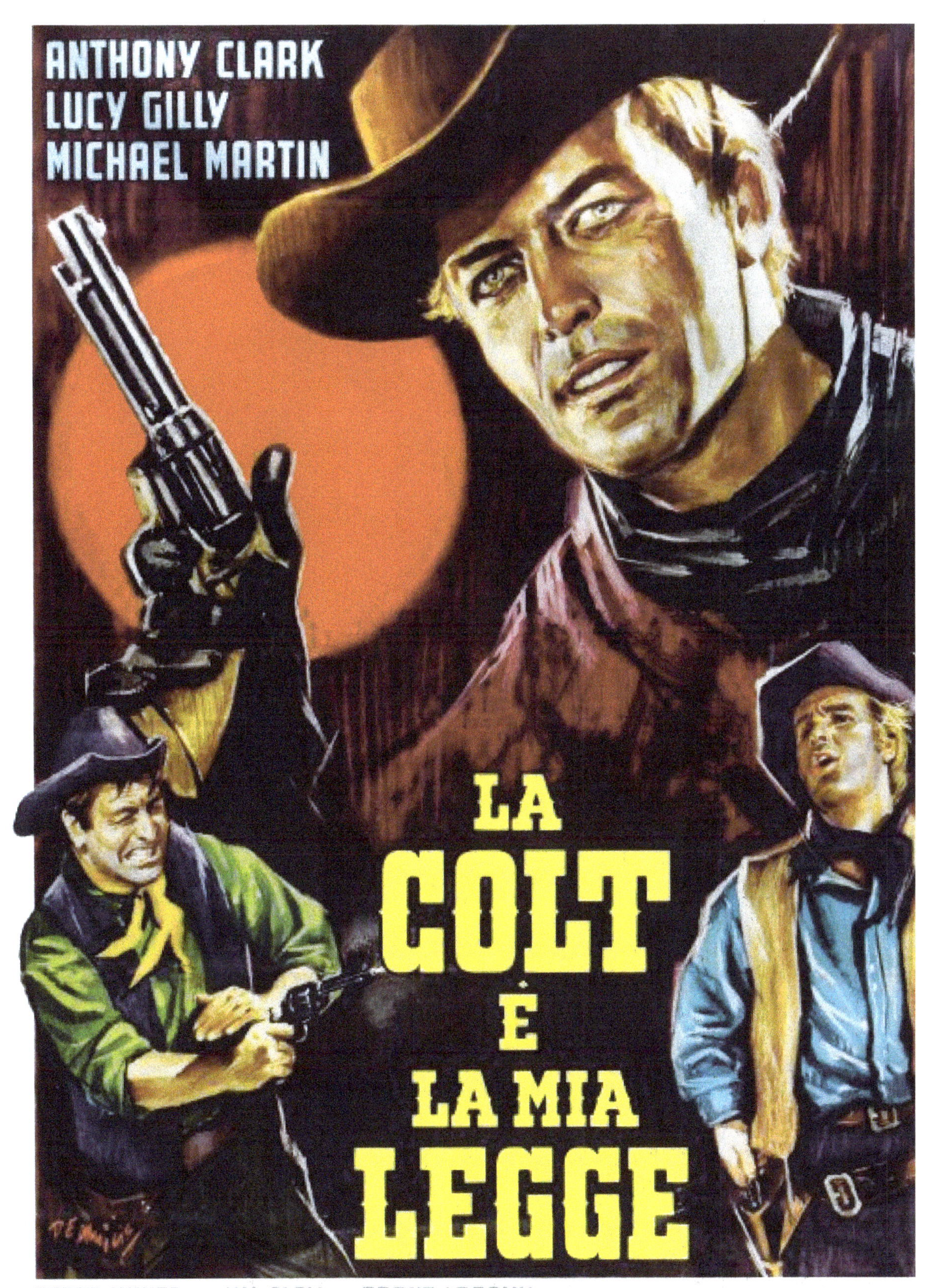

LA COLT È LA MIA LEGGE

("The Colt Is My Law"). Artist: De Amicis. Original Title: **La Colt È La Mia Legge** (1965, Italy/Spain).

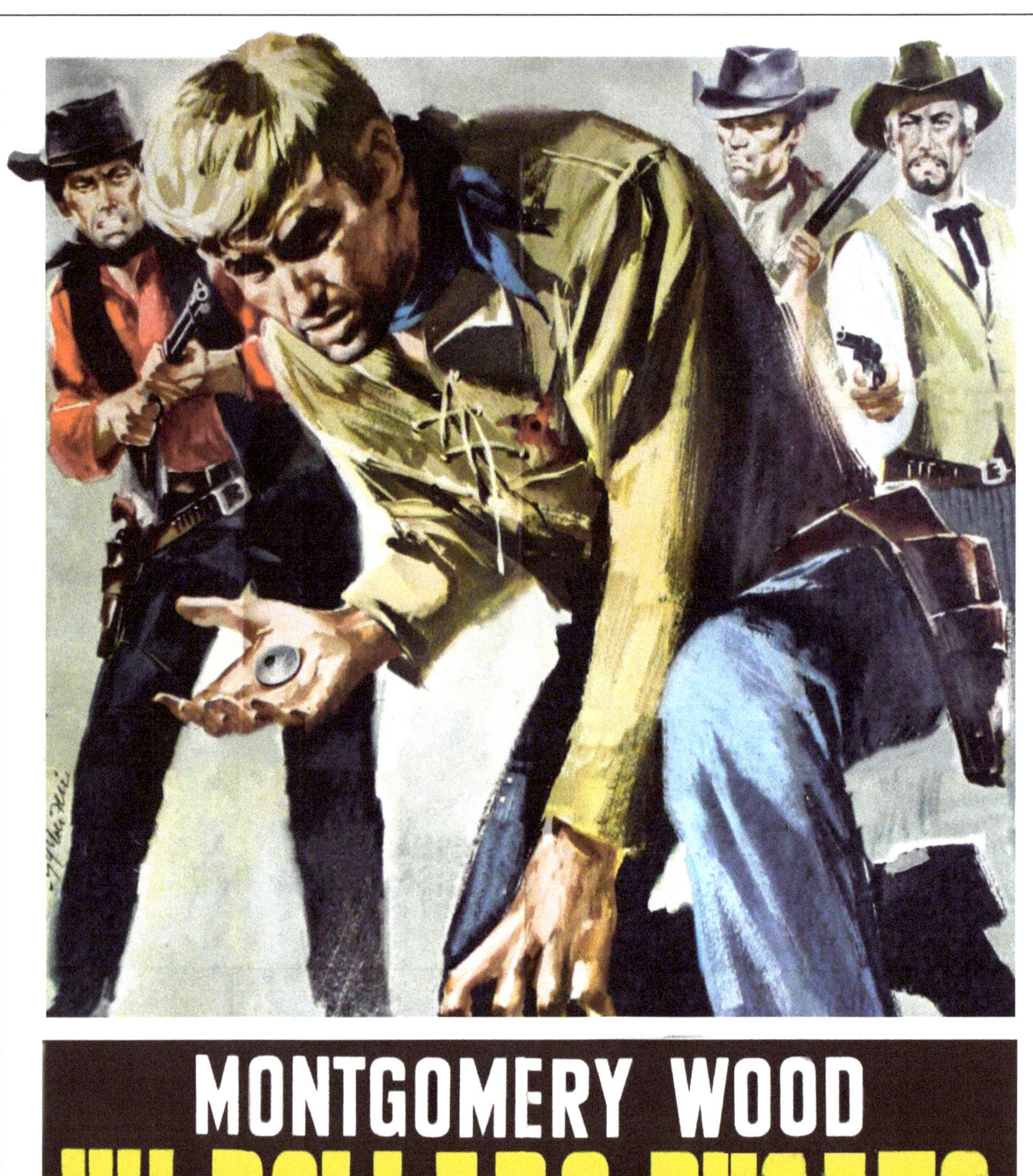

UN DOLLARO BUCATO

("A Plugged Dollar"). Artist: Sandro Symeoni. Original Title: **Un Dollaro Bucato** (1965, Italy/France).

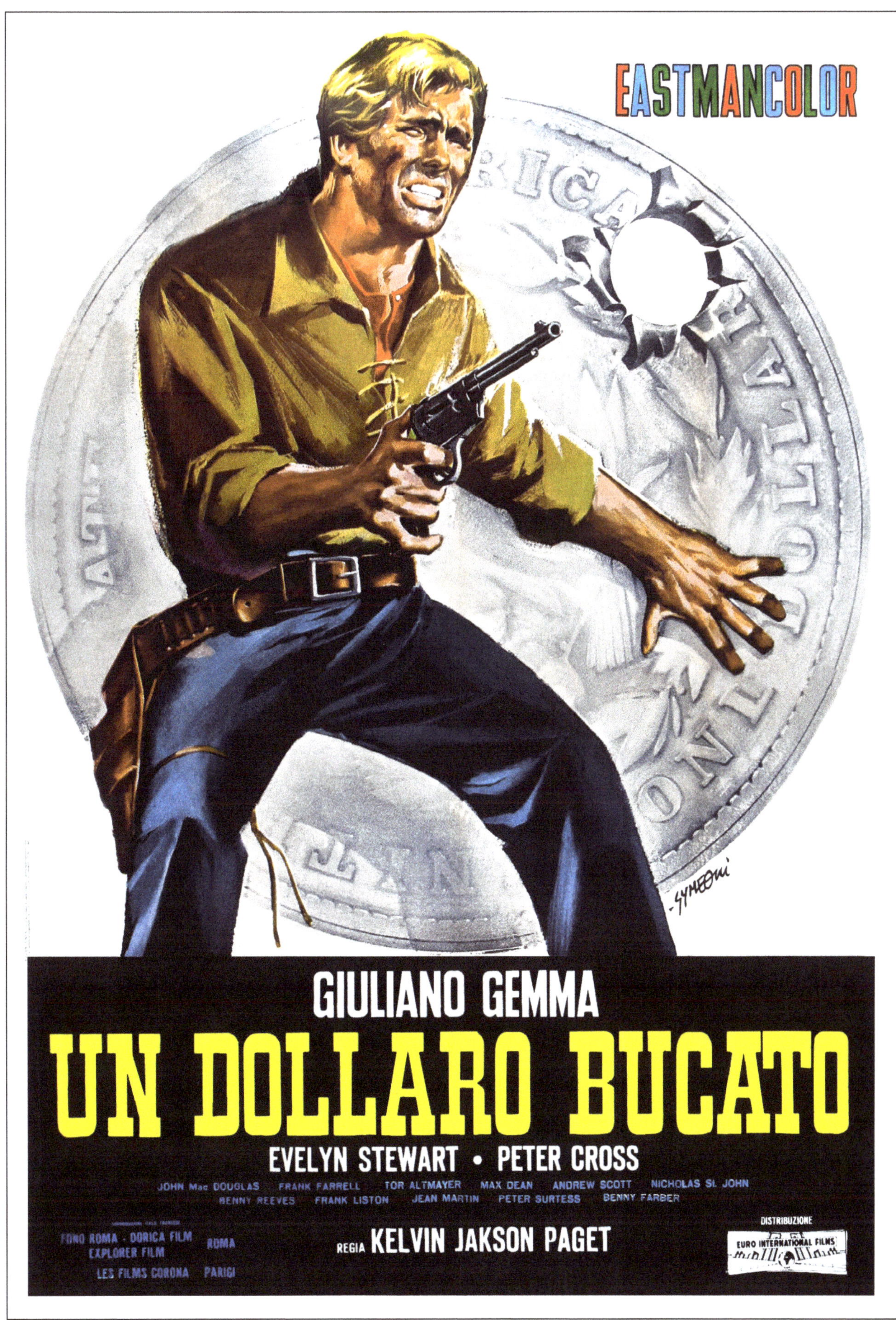

UN DOLLARO BUCATO

("A Plugged Dollar"). Artist: Sandro Symeoni. Original Title: **Un Dollaro Bucato** (1965, Italy/France).

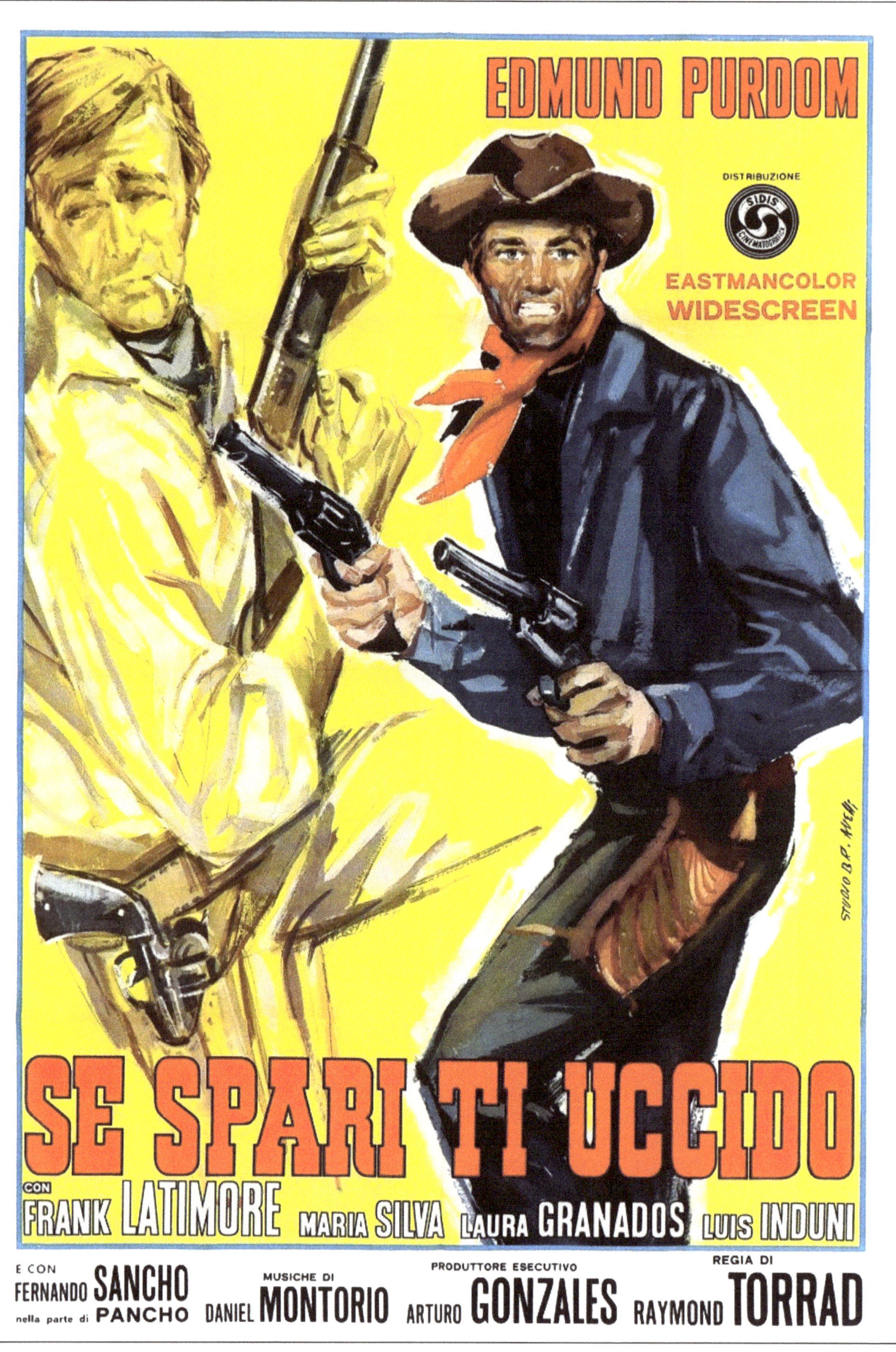

SE SPARI TI UCCIDO

("If You Shoot I'll Kill You"). Artist: Tino Avelli. Original Title: **Los Cuatreros** (1965, Spain).

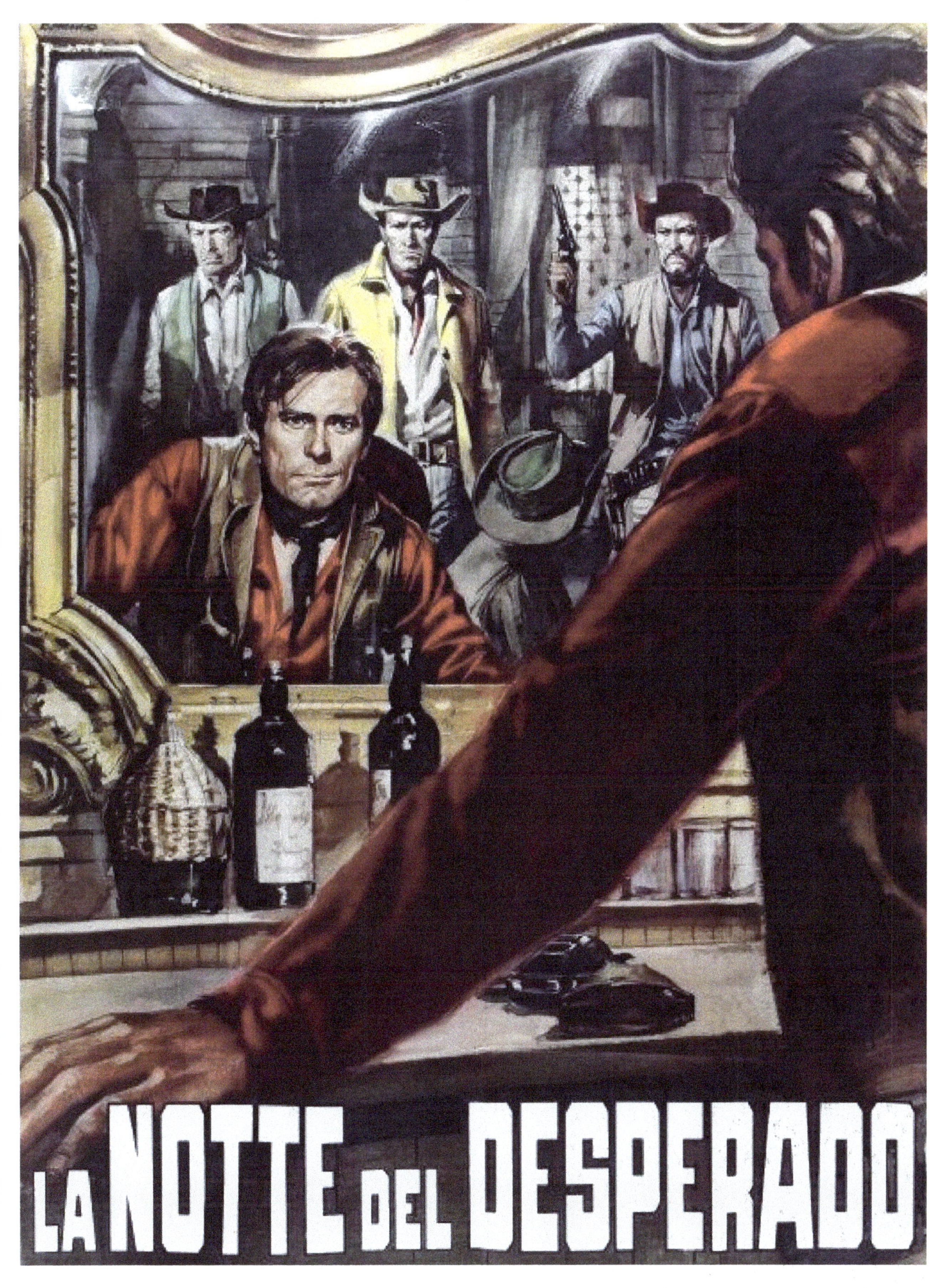

LA NOTTE DEL DESPERADO

("Night Of The Desperado"). Artist: Renato Casaro. Original Title: **La Grande Notte Di Ringo** (1965, Italy/Spain).

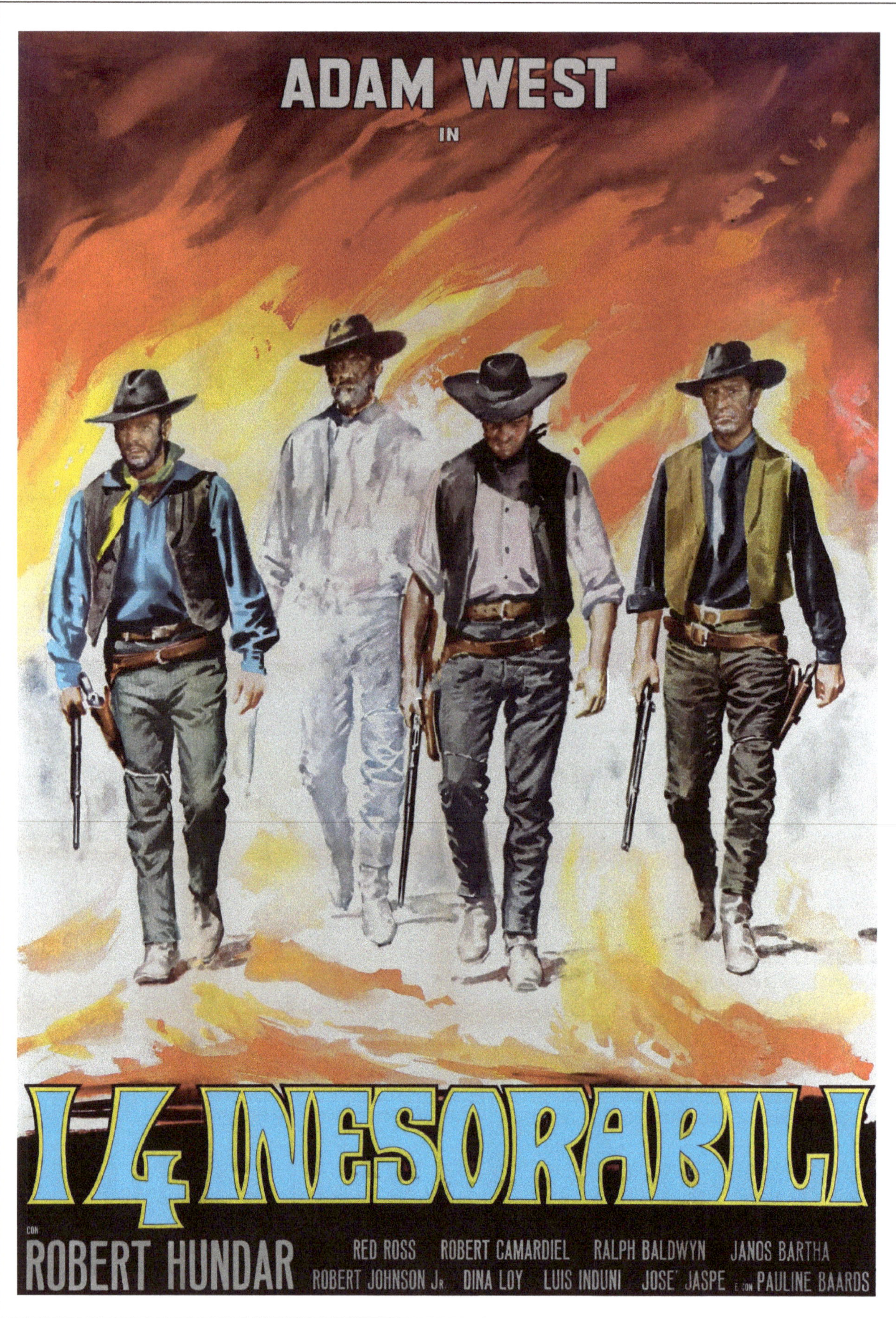

I QUATTRO INESORABILI

("The Inexorable Four"). Artist: Rodlfo Gasparri. Original Title: **I Quattro Inesorabili** (1965, Italy/Spain).

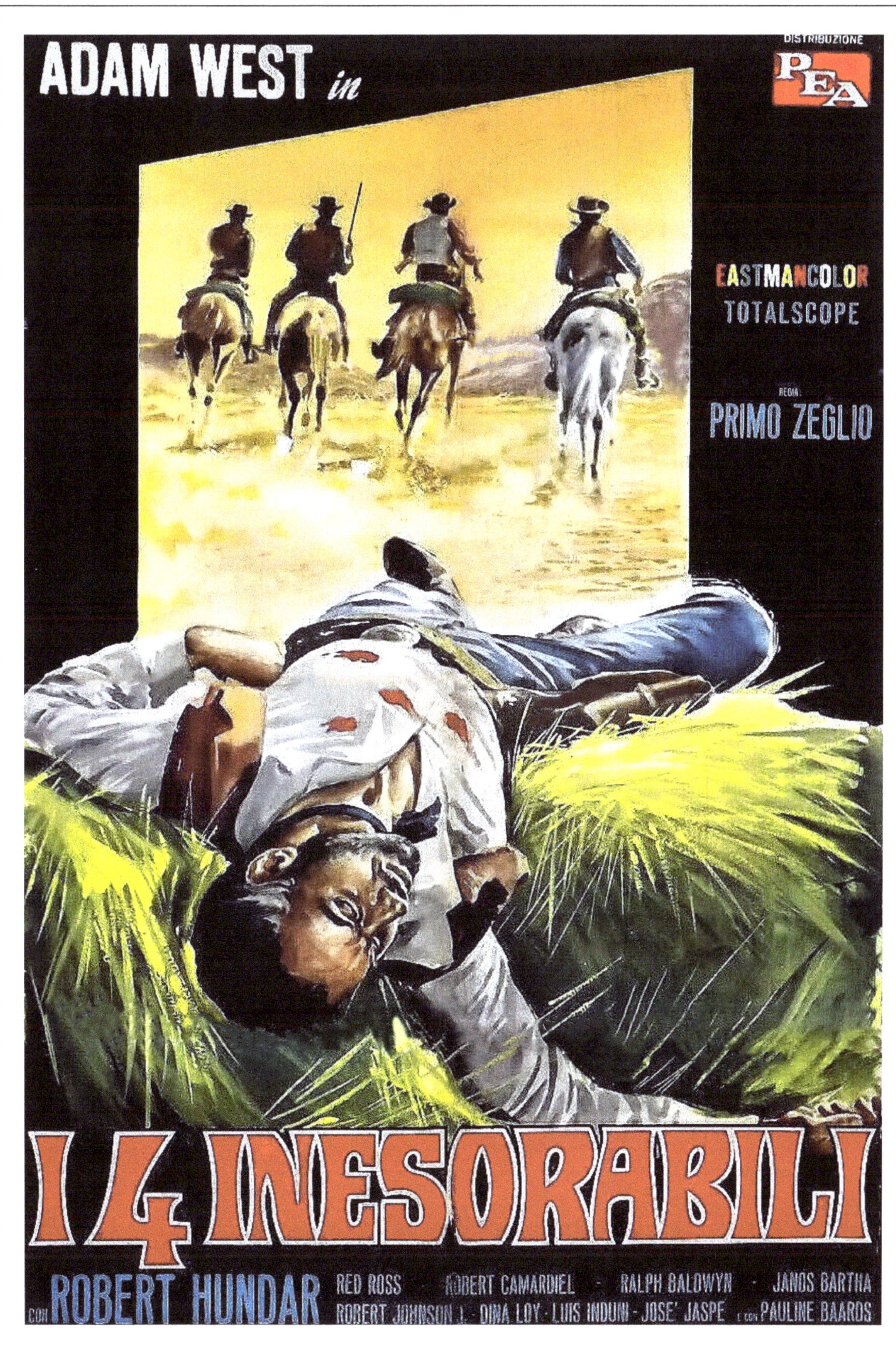

I QUATTRO INESORABILI

("The Inexorable Four"). Artist: Rodlfo Gasparri. Original Title: **I Quattro Inesorabili** (1965, Italy/Spain).

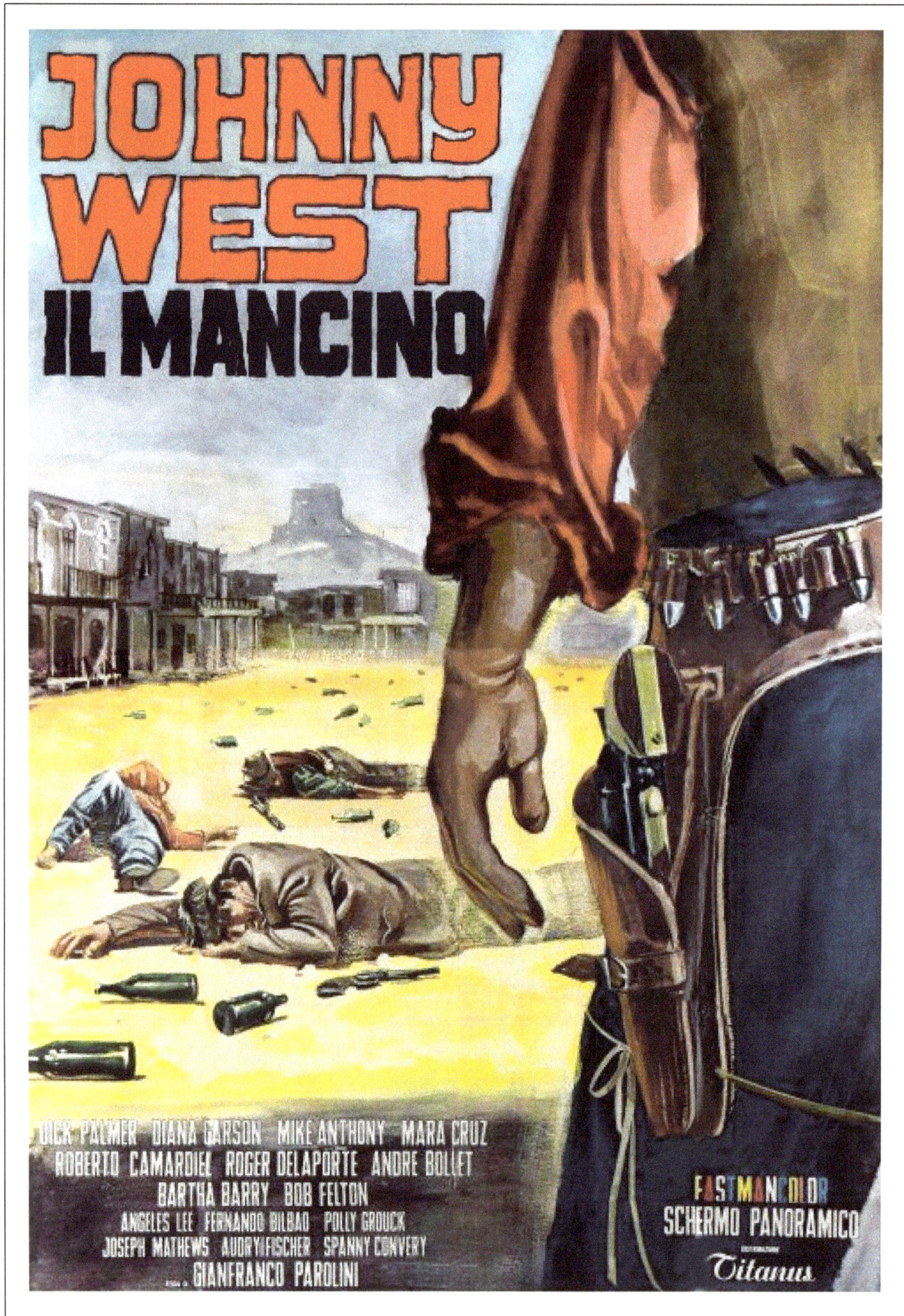

JOHNNY WEST IL MANCINO

("Left-Hand Johnny West"). Artist: unsigned. Original Title: **Johnny West Il Mancino** (1965, Italy/Spain/France).

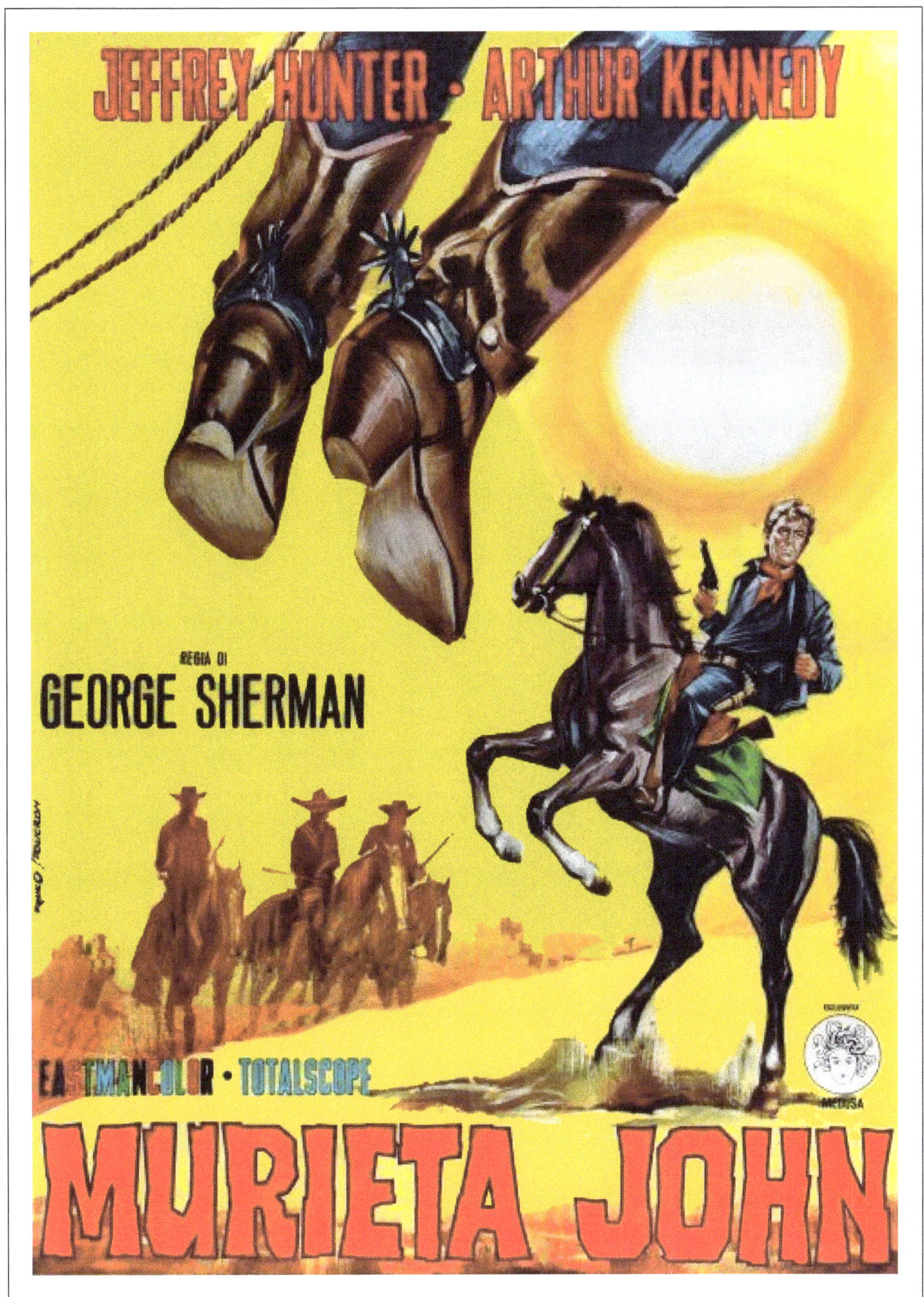

MURIETA JOHN

("John Murieta"). Artist: P. Franco/Policrom. Original Title: **Joaquin Murrieta** (1965, Spain).

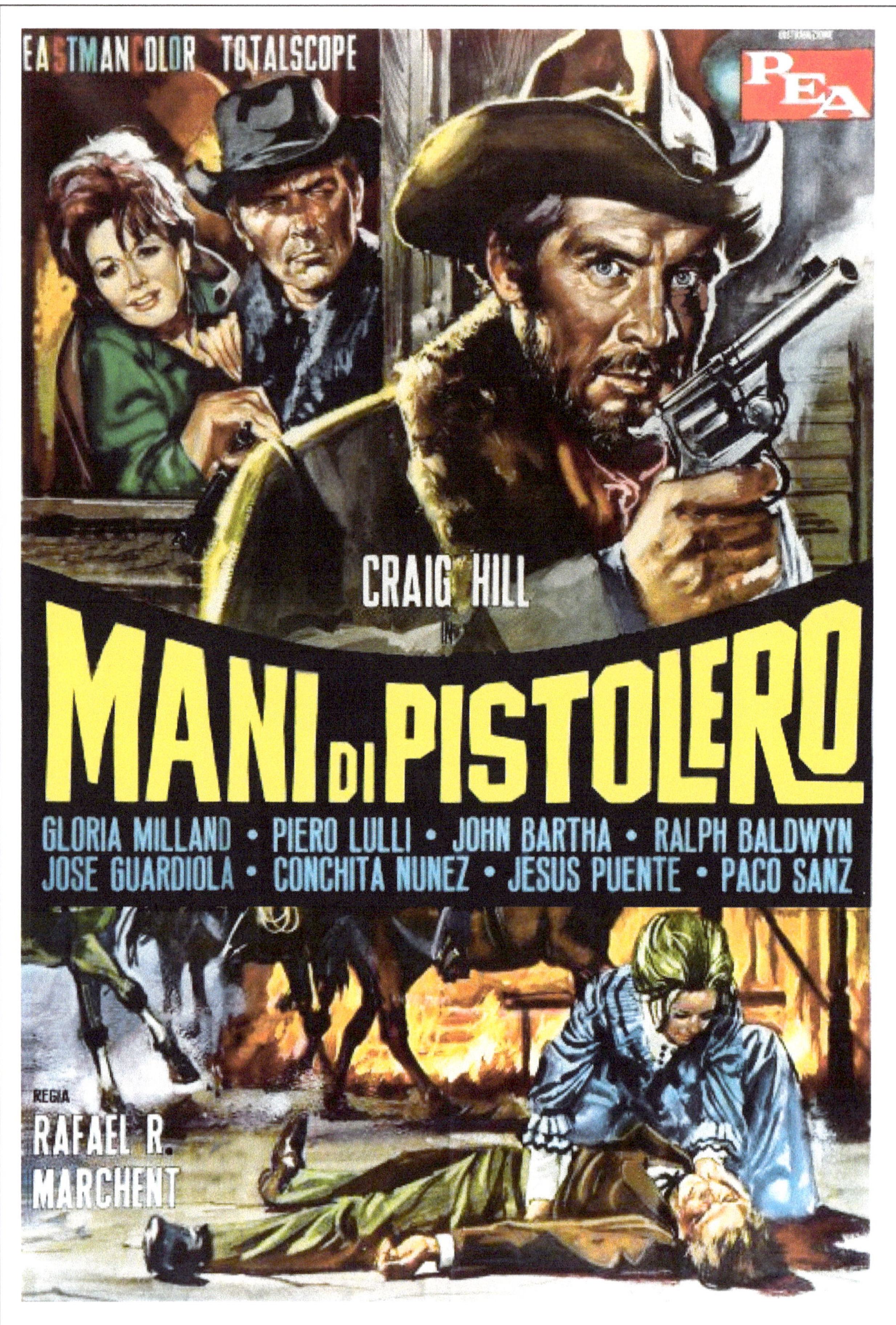

MANI DI PISTOLERO

("Hands Of A Gunslinger"). Artist: unsigned. Original Title: **Ocaso de un pistolero** (1965, Spain/Italy).

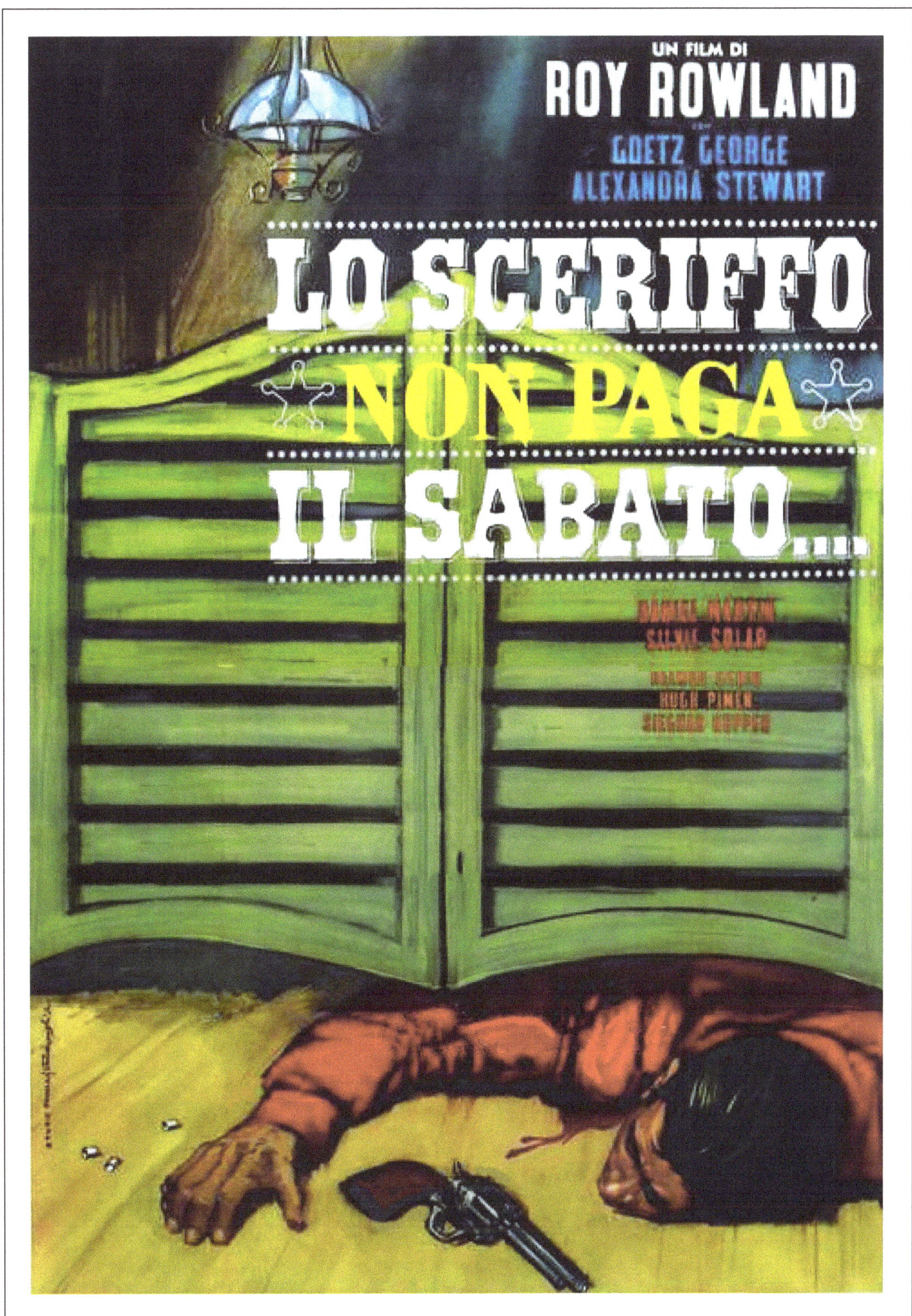

LO SCERIFFO NON PAGA IL SABATO

("The Sheriff Doesn't Pay On Saturdays"). Artist: Studio Favalli. Original Title: **Sie Nannten Ihn Gringo** (1965, Germany/Spain).

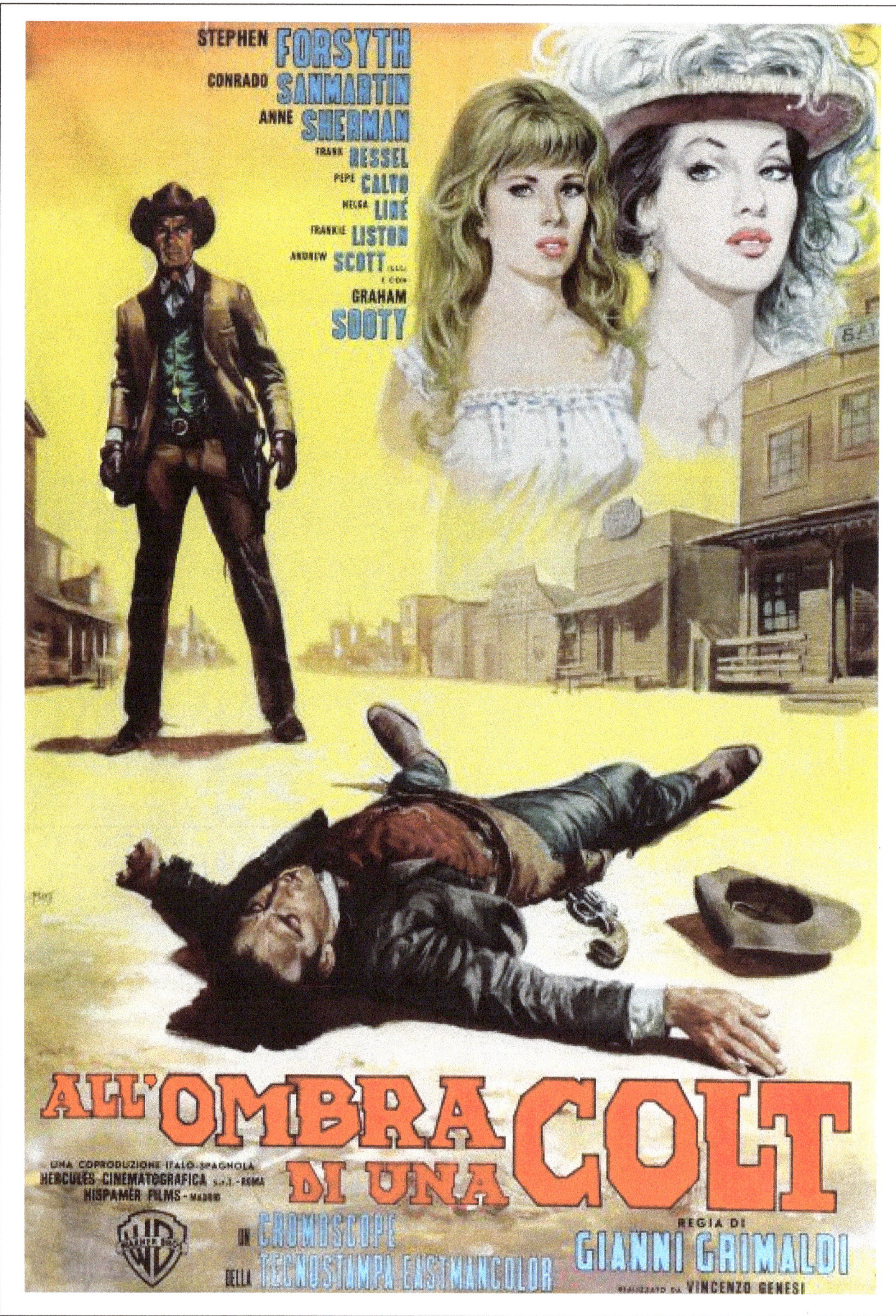

ALL'OMBRA DI UNA COLT

("In The Shadow Of A Colt"). Artist: Moz. Original Title: **All'Ombra Di Una Colt** (1965, Italy/Spain).

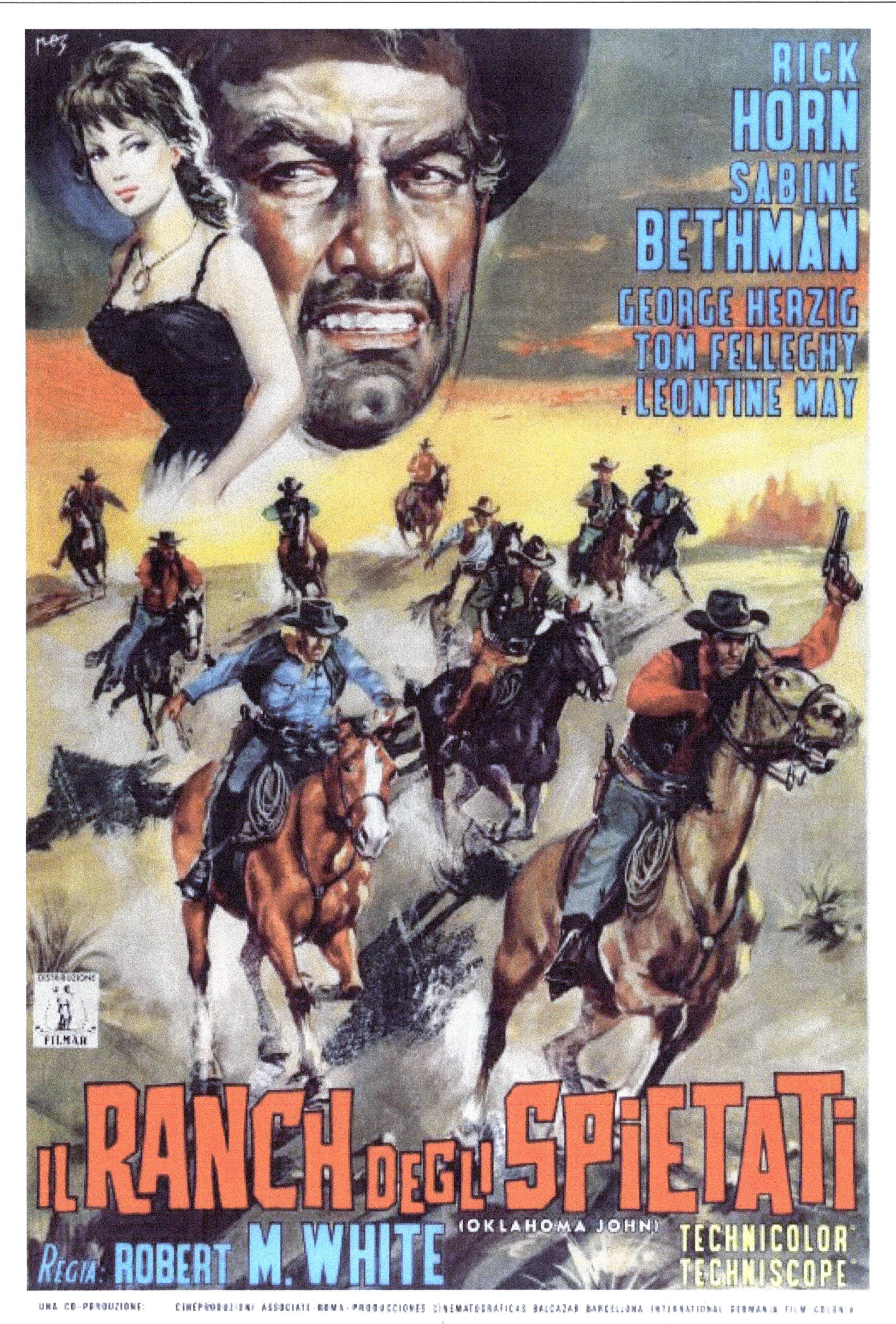

IL RANCH DEGLI SPIETATI

("Ranch Of The Ruthless"). Artist: Moz. Original Title: **Oklahoma John** (1965, Spain/Italy/Germany).

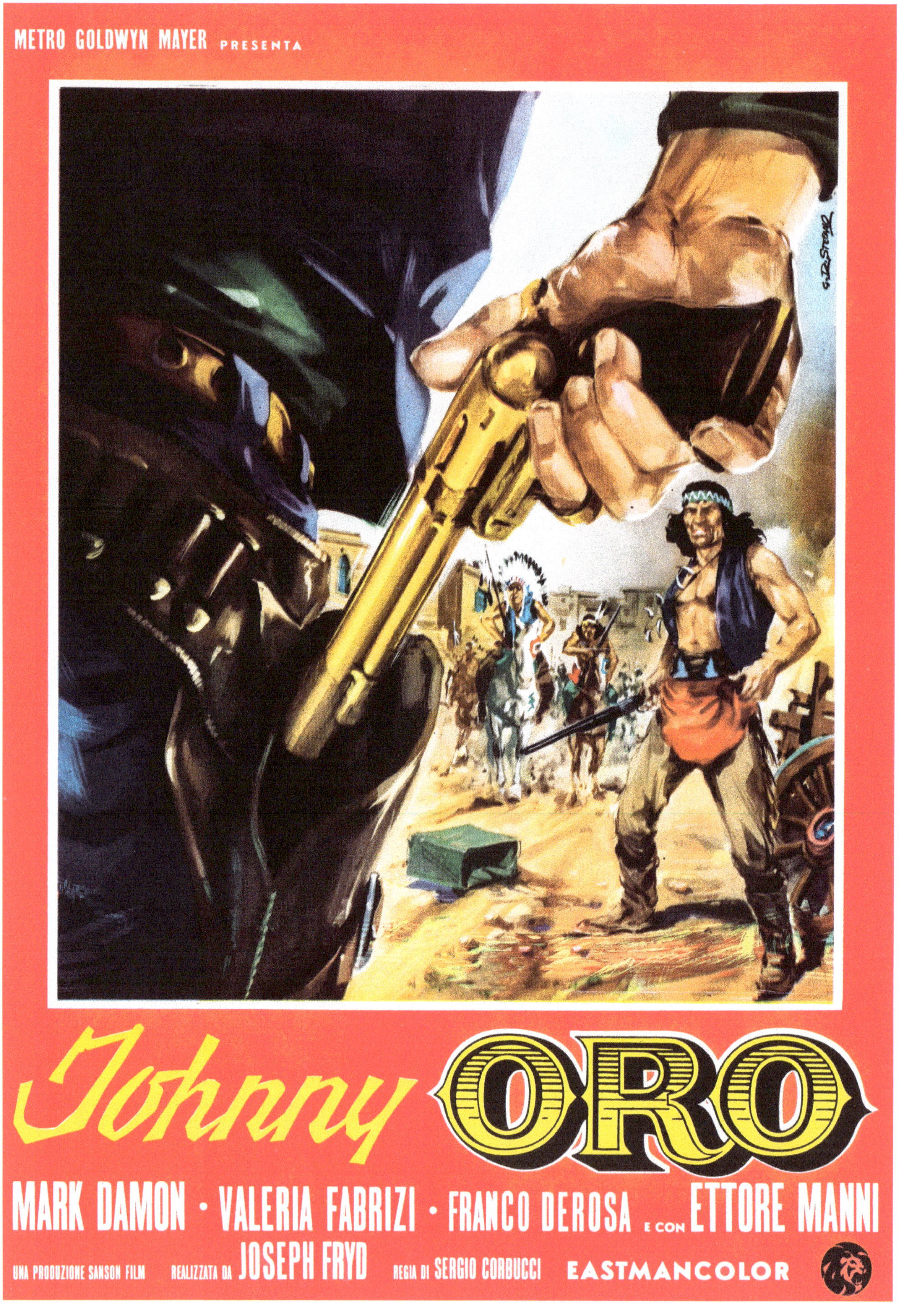

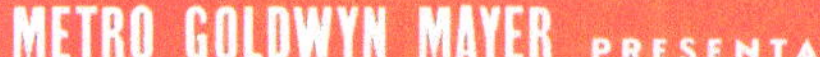

Johnny ORO

MARK DAMON · VALERIA FABRIZI · FRANCO DEROSA E CON ETTORE MANNI

UNA PRODUZIONE SANSON FILM REALIZZATA DA JOSEPH FRYD REGIA DI SERGIO CORBUCCI EASTMANCOLOR

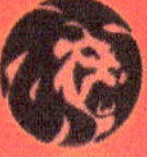

JOHNNY ORO

("Johnny Gold"). Artist: G. Di Stefano. Original Title: **Johnny Oro** (1965, Italy).

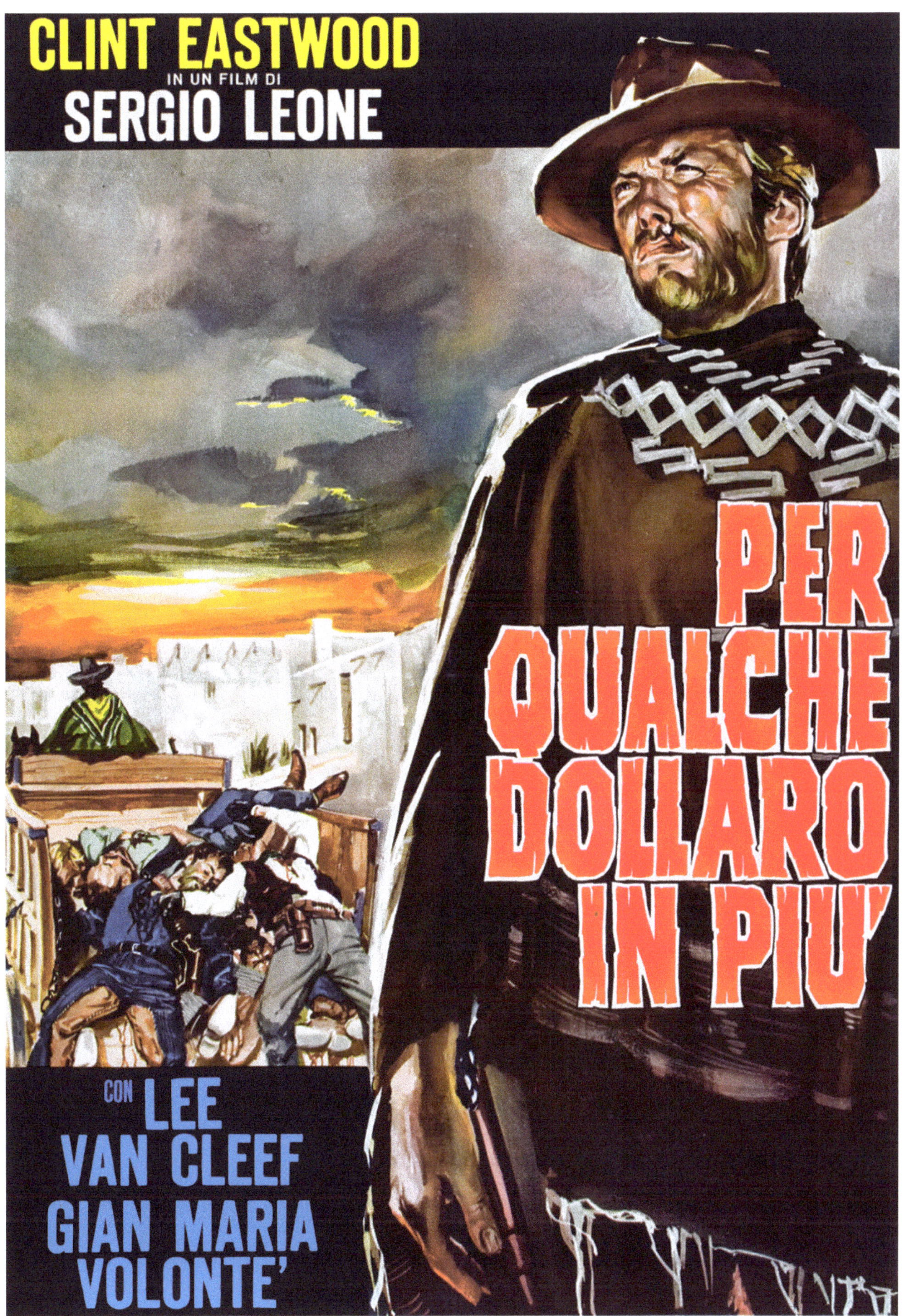

PER QUALCHE DOLLARO IN PIÙ

("For A Few Dollras More"). Artist: unsigned. Original Title: **Per Qualche Dollaro In Più** (1965, Italy/Spain/Germany).

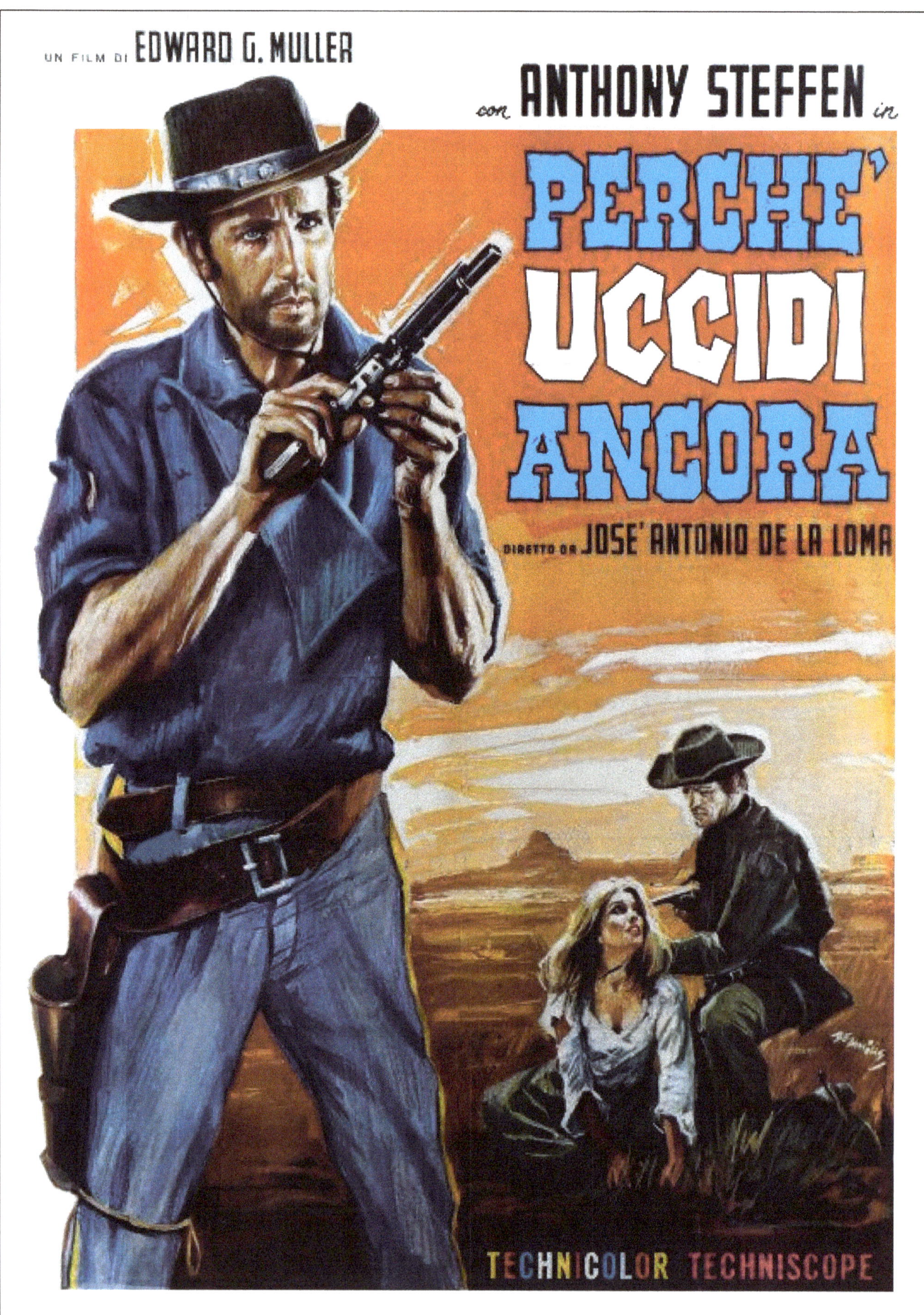

PERCHÉ UCCIDI ANCORA?

("Why Kill Again?"). Artist: De Amicis. Original Title: **Perché Uccidi Ancora?** (1965, Italy/Spain).

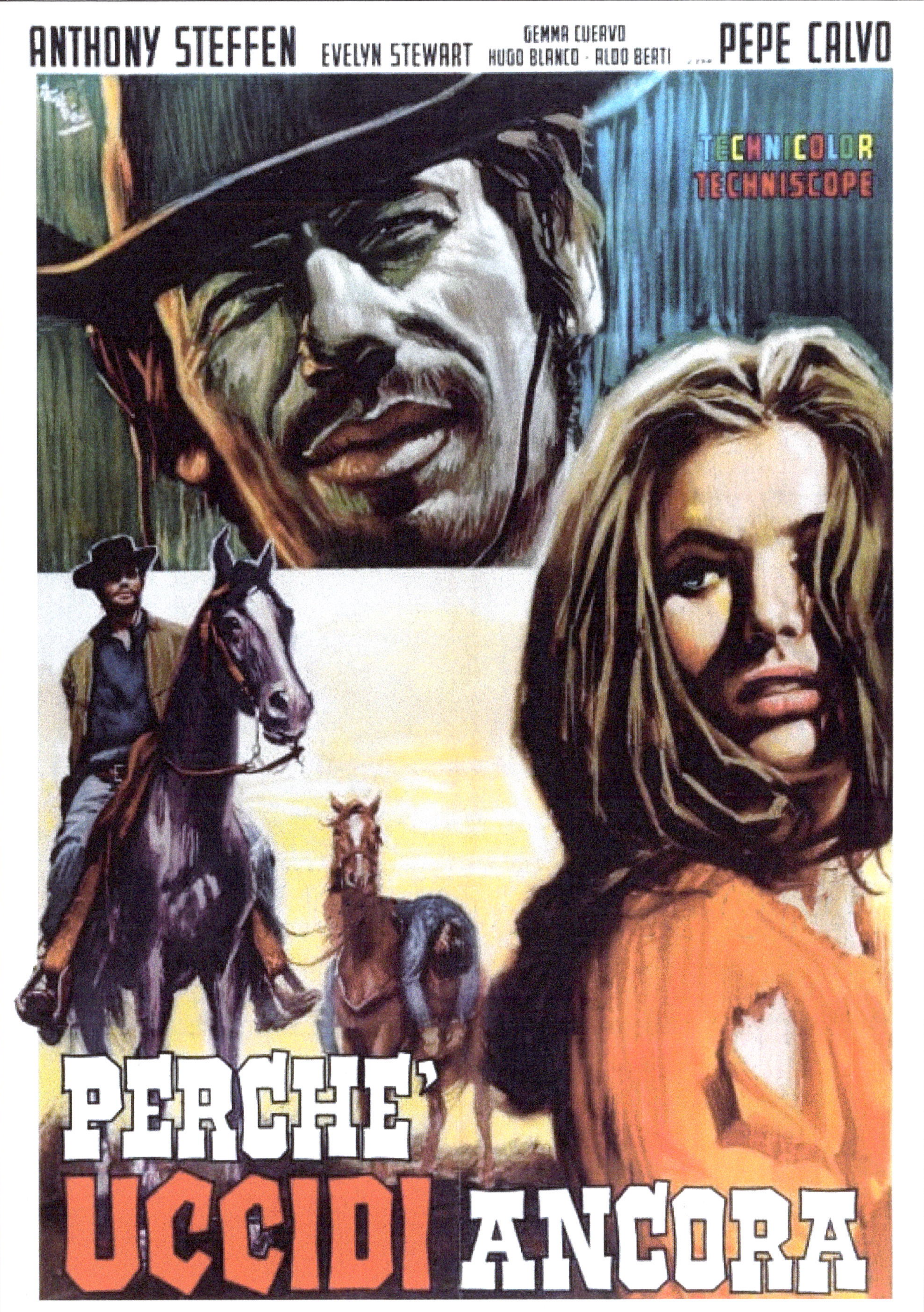

PERCHÉ UCCIDI ANCORA?

("Why Kill Again?"). Artist: De Amicis. Original Title: **Perché Uccidi Ancora?** (1965, Italy/Spain).

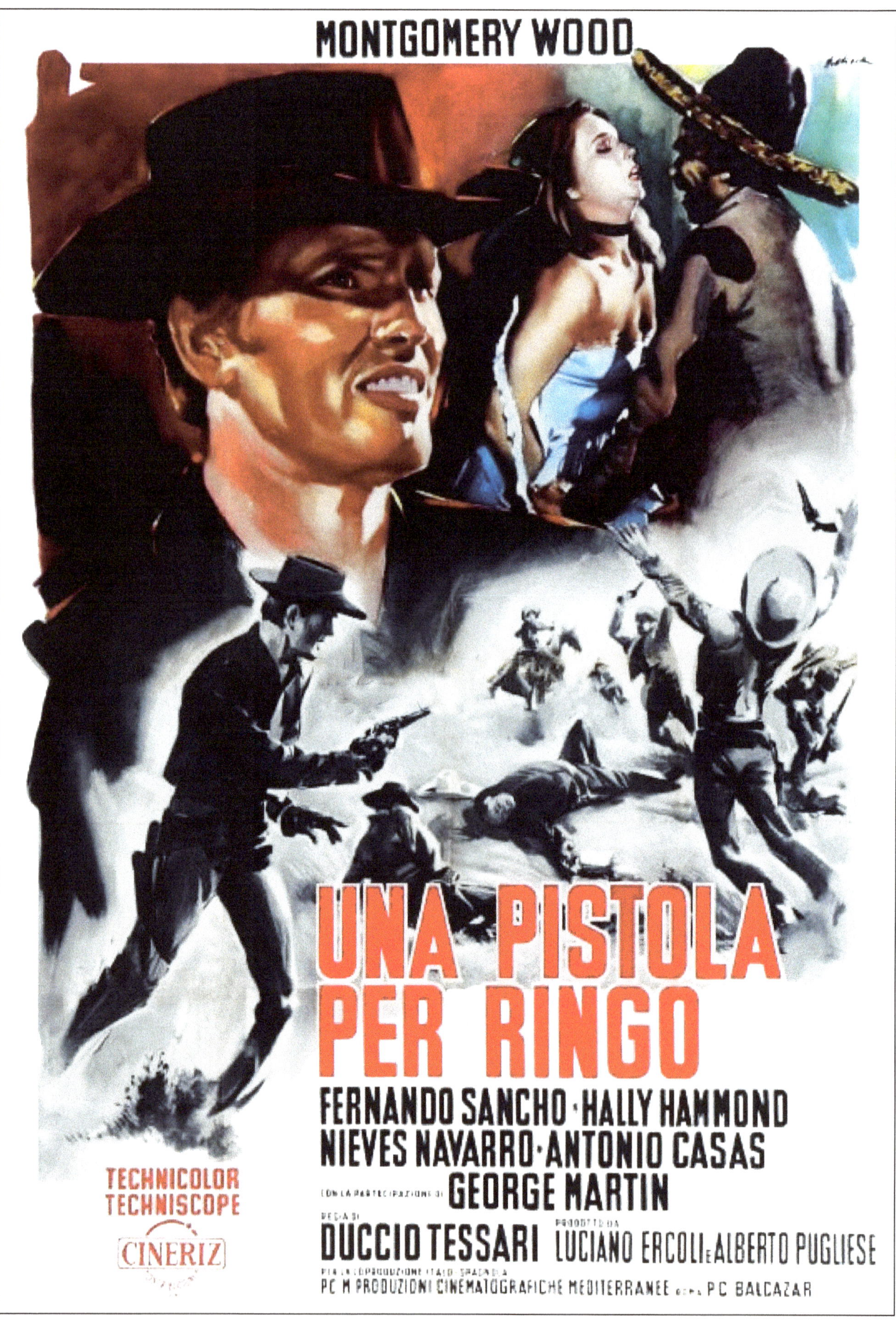

UNA PISTOLA PER RINGO

("A Pistol For Ringo"). Artist: Giorgio Olivetti. Original Title: **Una Pistola Per Ringo** (1965, Italy/Spain).

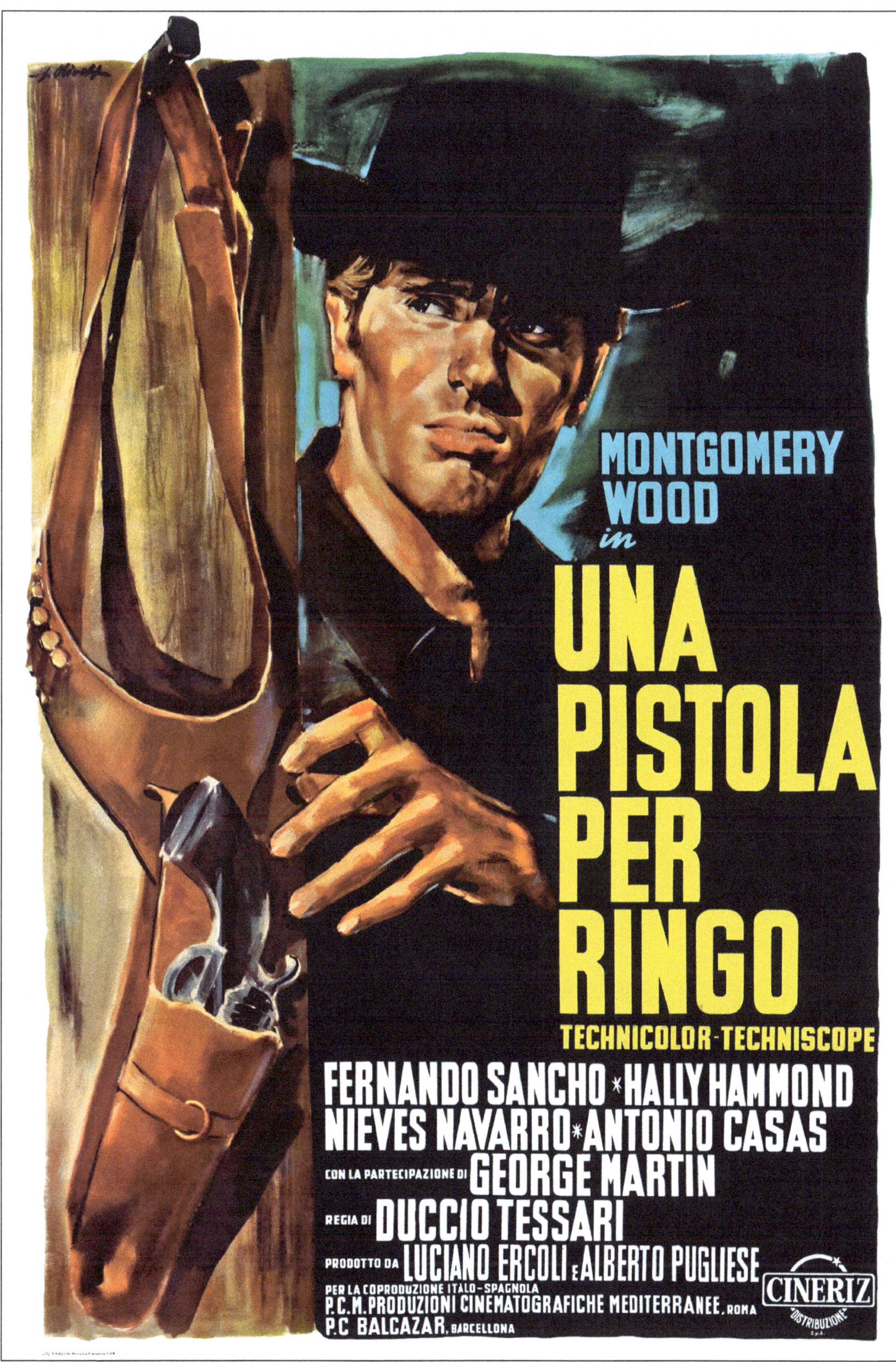

UNA PISTOLA PER RINGO

("A Pistol For Ringo"). Artist: Giorgio Olivetti. Original Title: **Una Pistola Per Ringo** (1965, Italy/Spain).

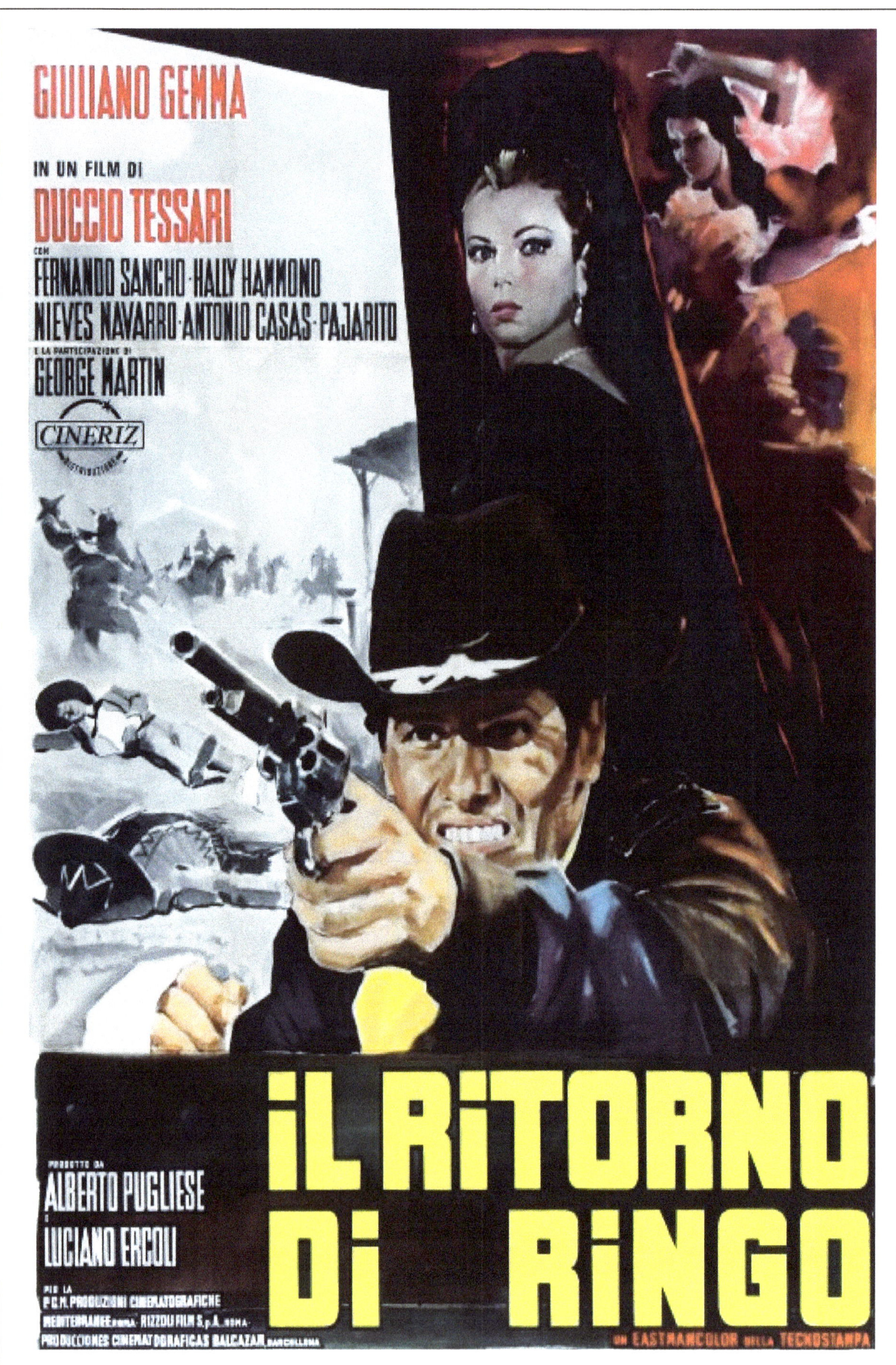

IL RITORNO DI RINGO

("Ringo's Return"). Artist: Giorgio Olivetti. Original Title: **Il Ritorno Di Ringo** (1965, Italy/Spain).

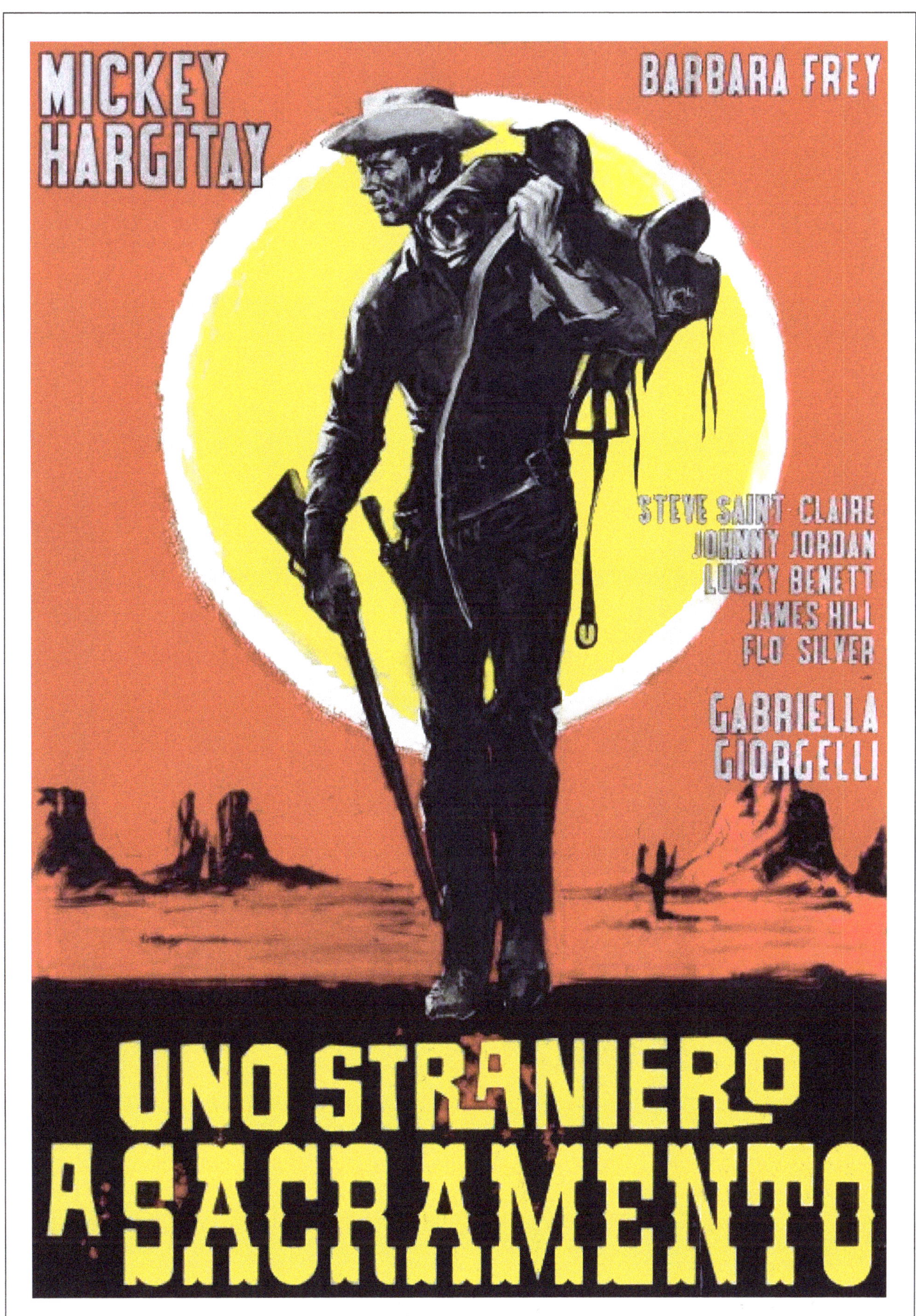

UNO STRANIERO A SACRAMENTO

("A Stranger In Sacramento"). Artist: unsigned. Original Title: **Uno Straniero A Sacramento** (1965, Italy).

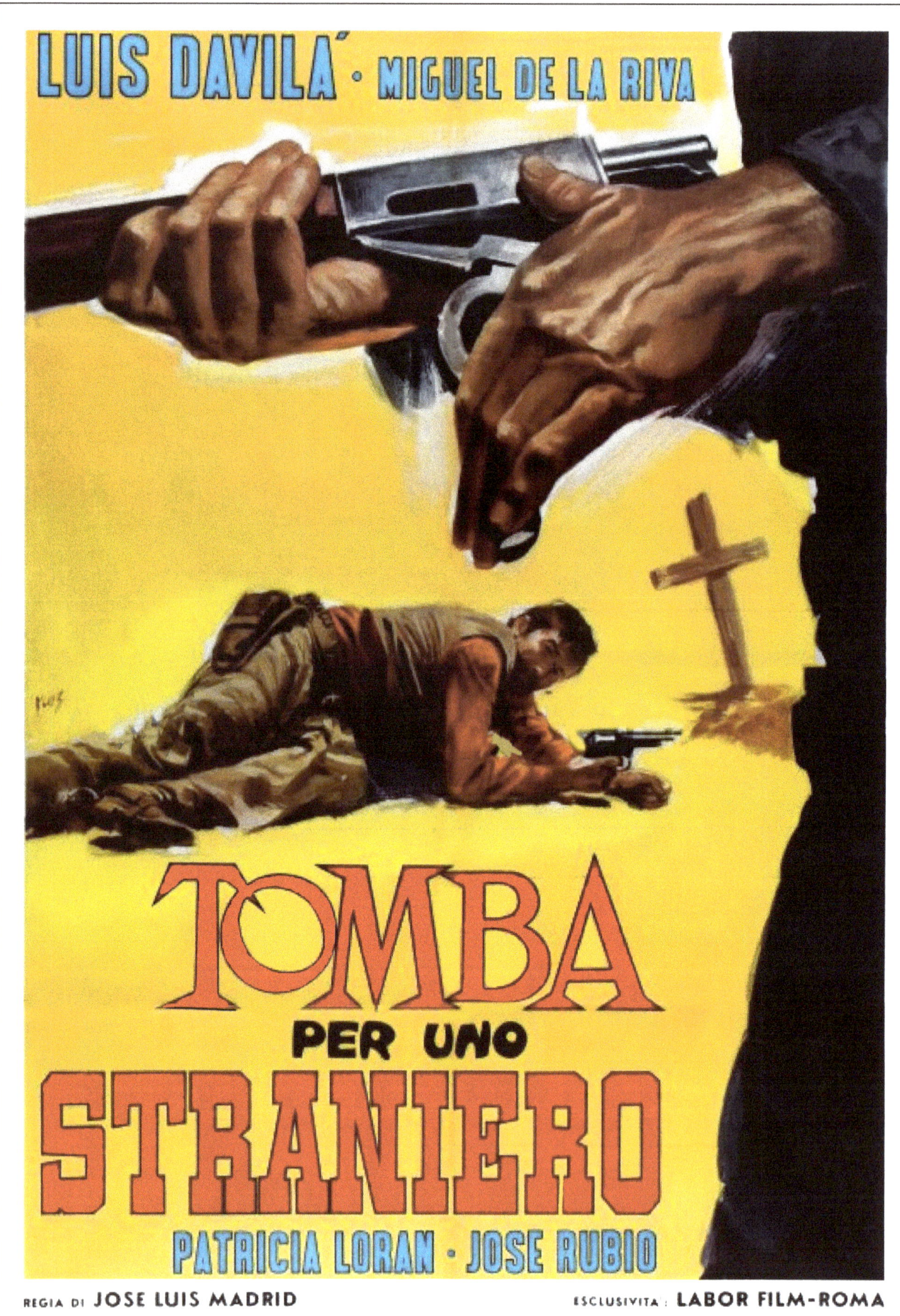

TOMBA PER UNO STRANIERO

("Tomb For A Stranger"). Artist: Moz. Original Title: **Tumba Para Un Forajido** (1965, Spain).

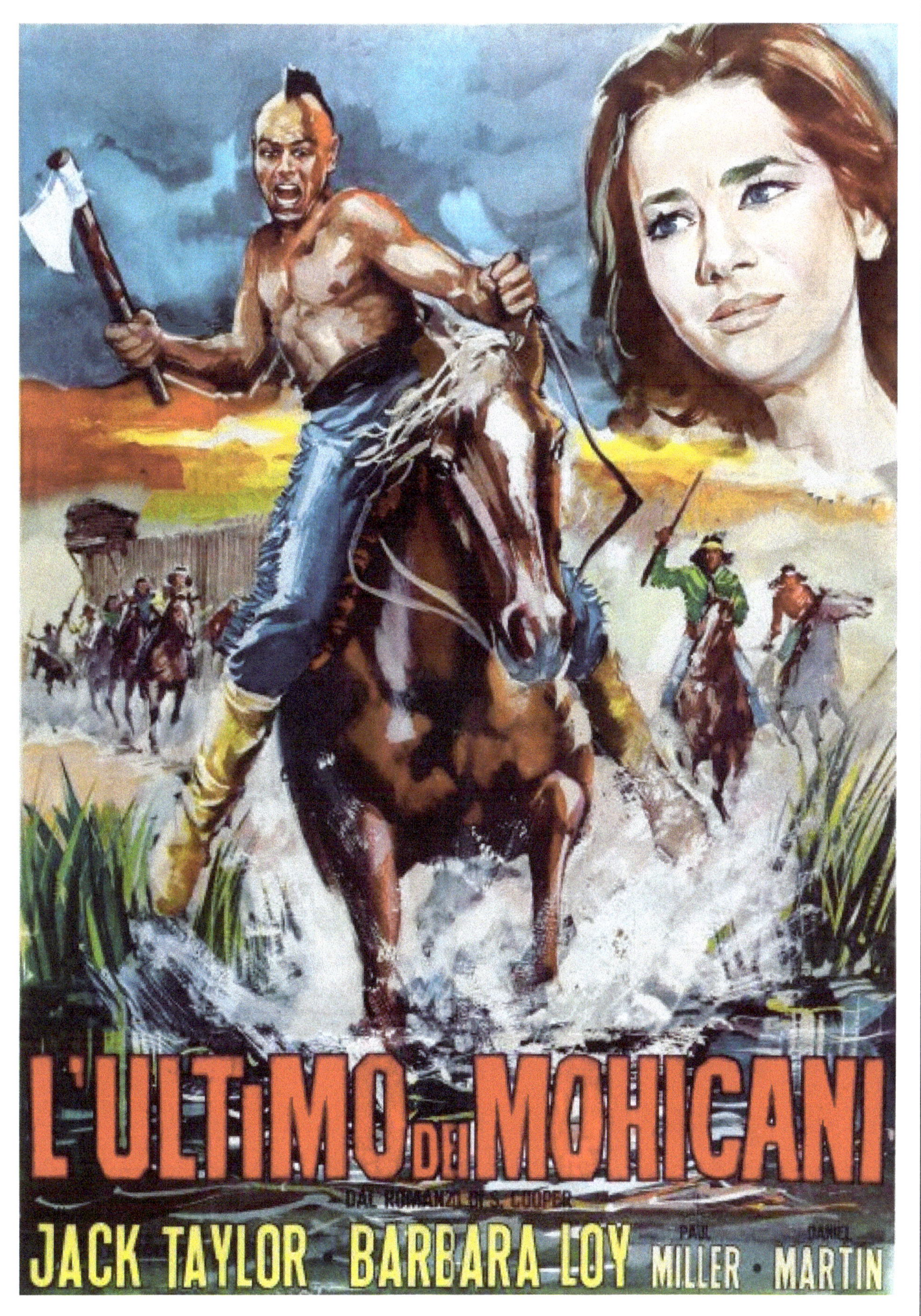

L'ULTIMO DEI MOHICANI

("Last Of The Mohicans"). Artist: unsigned. Original Title: **Uncas, El Fin De Una Raza** (1965, Spain/Italy).

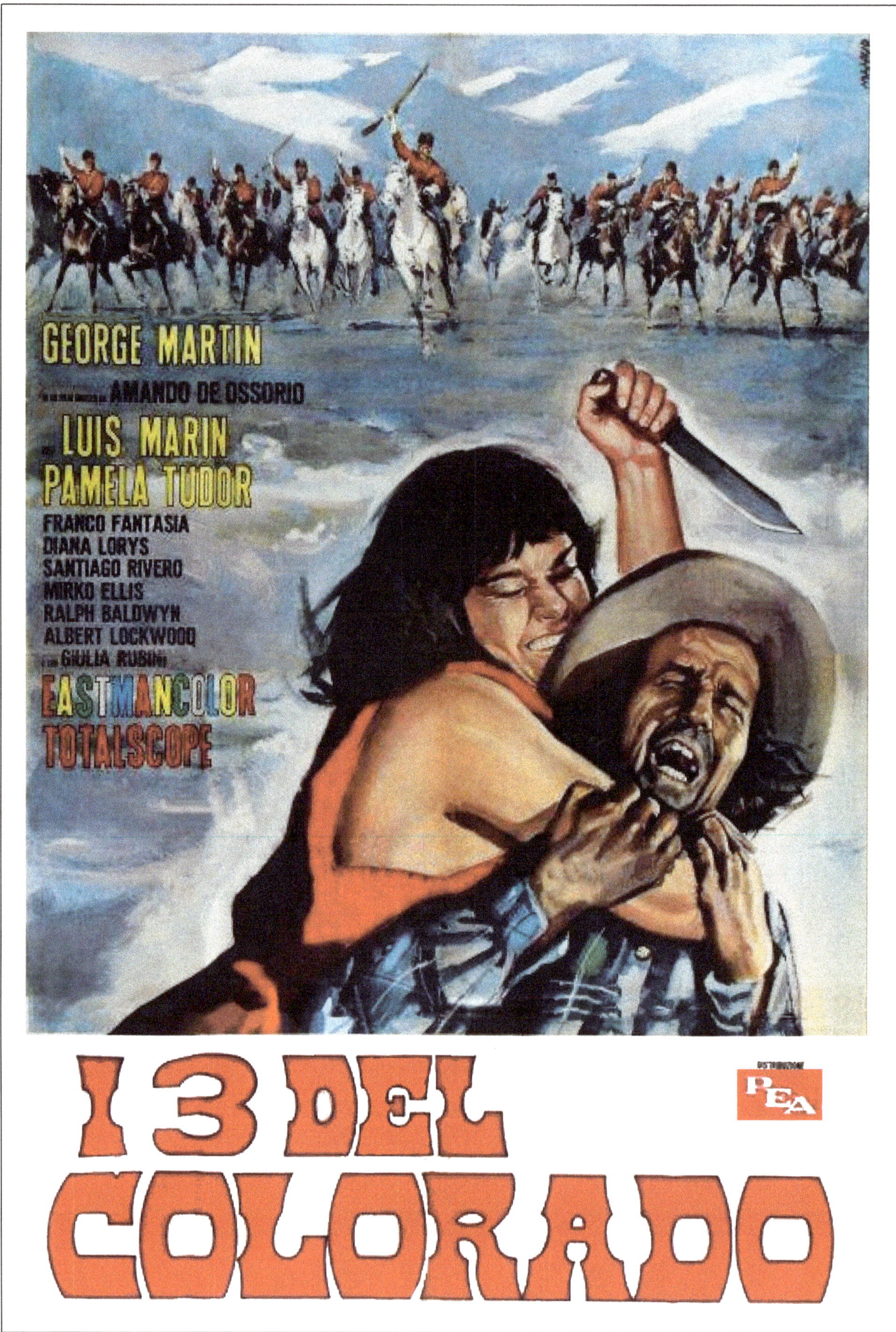

I TRE DEL COLORADO

("The Colorado Three"). Artist: Dante Manno. Original Title: **Rebeldes En Canadá** (1965, Spain/Italy).

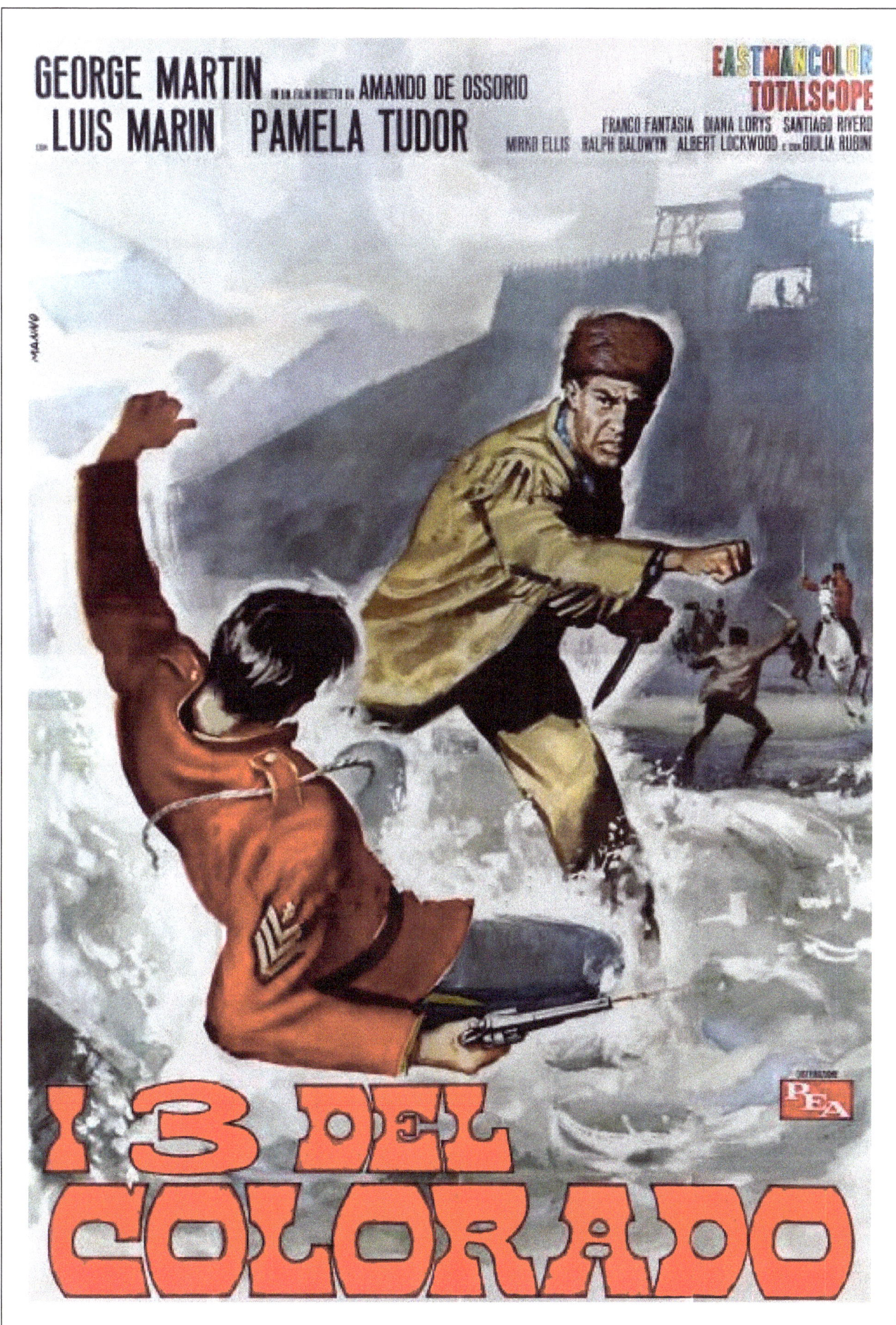

I TRE DEL COLORADO

("The Colorado Three"). Artist: Dante Manno. Original Title: **Rebeldes En Canadá** (1965, Spain/Italy).

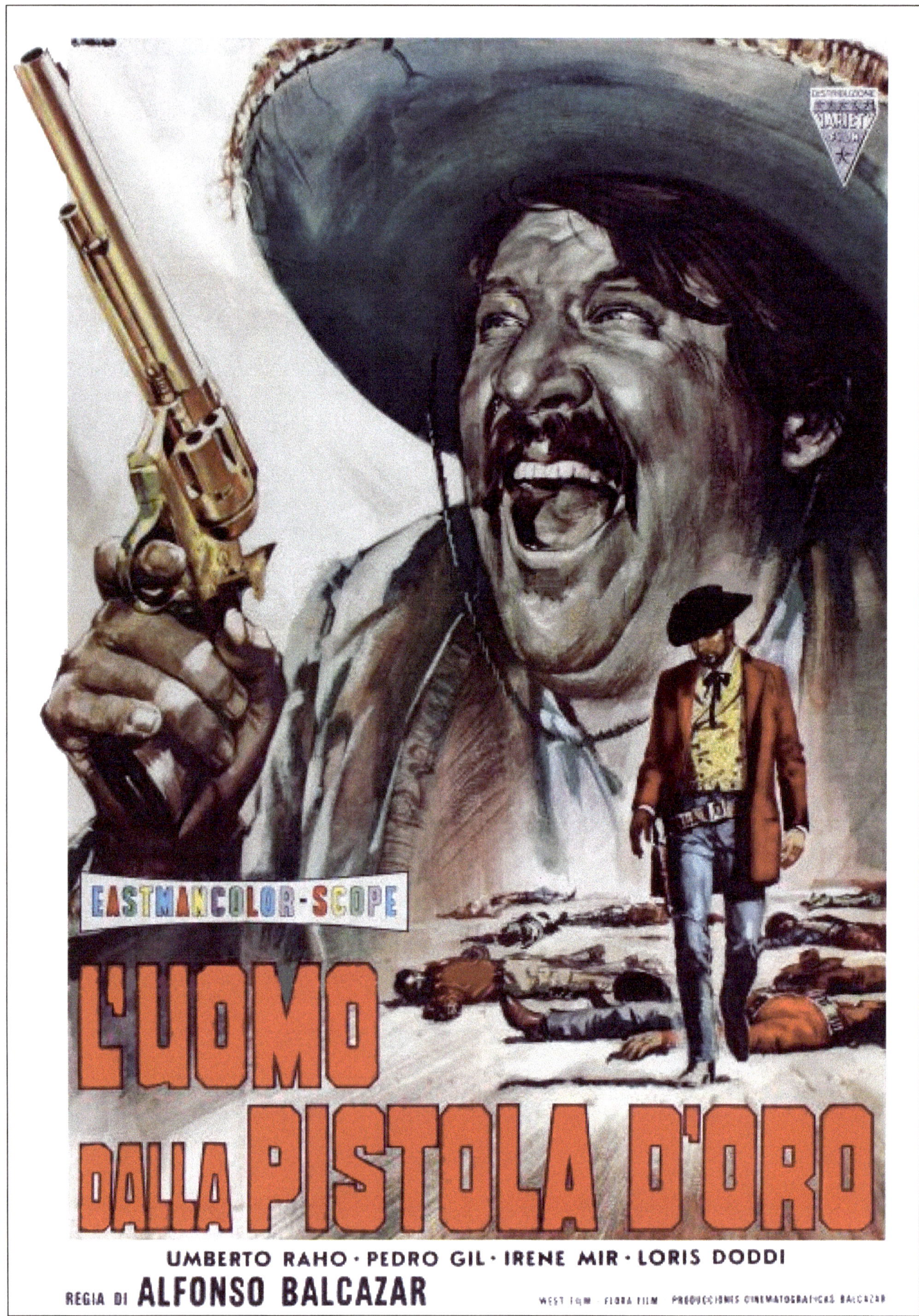

L'UOMO DALLA PISTOLA D'ORO

("The Man With The Golden Pistol"). Artist: Renato Casaro. Original Title: **L'Uomo Dalla Pistola D'Oro** (1965, Italy/Spain).

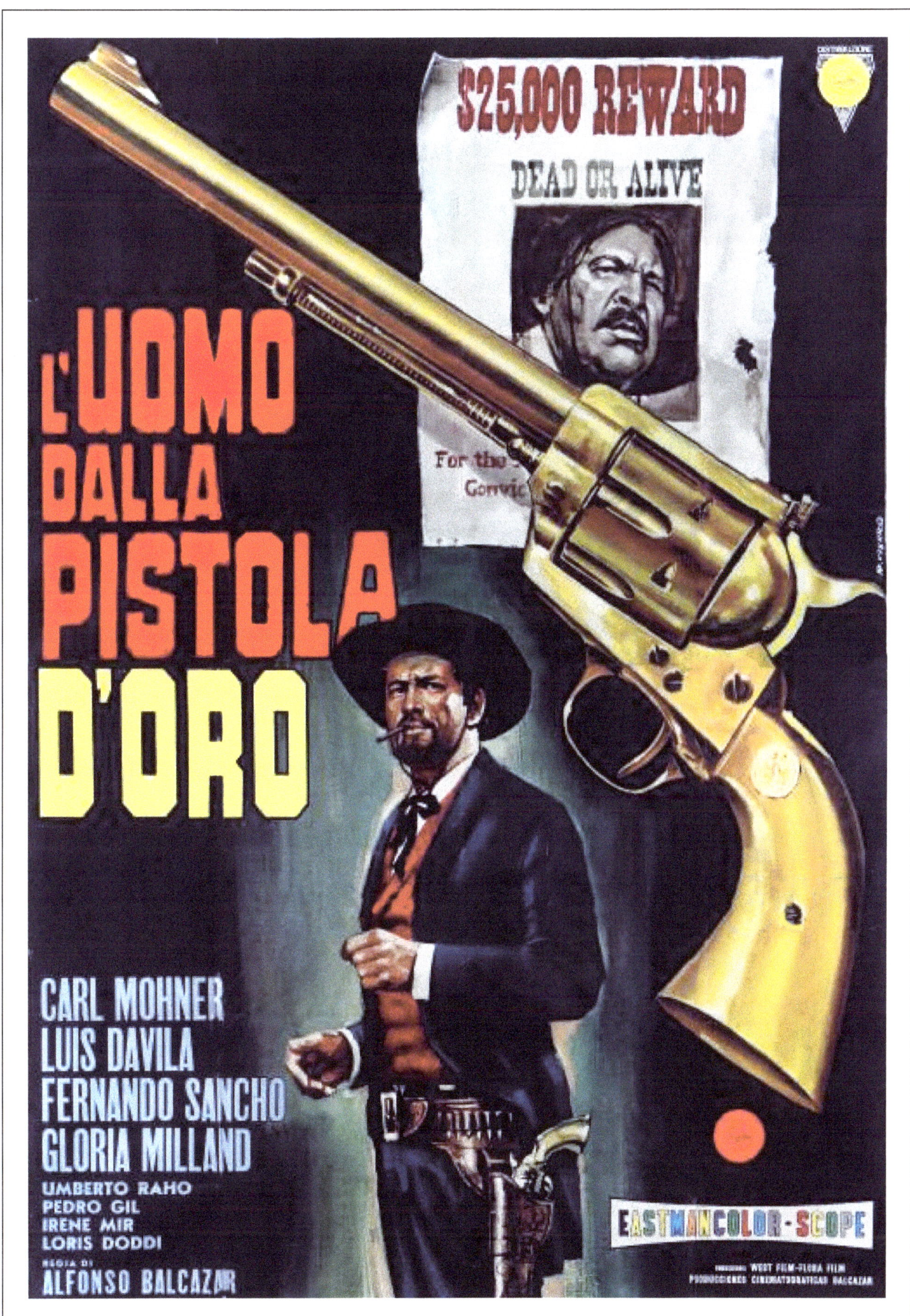

L'UOMO DALLA PISTOLA D'ORO

("The Man With The Golden Pistol"). Artist: Renato Casaro. Original Title: **L'Uomo Dalla Pistola D'Oro** (1965, Italy/Spain).

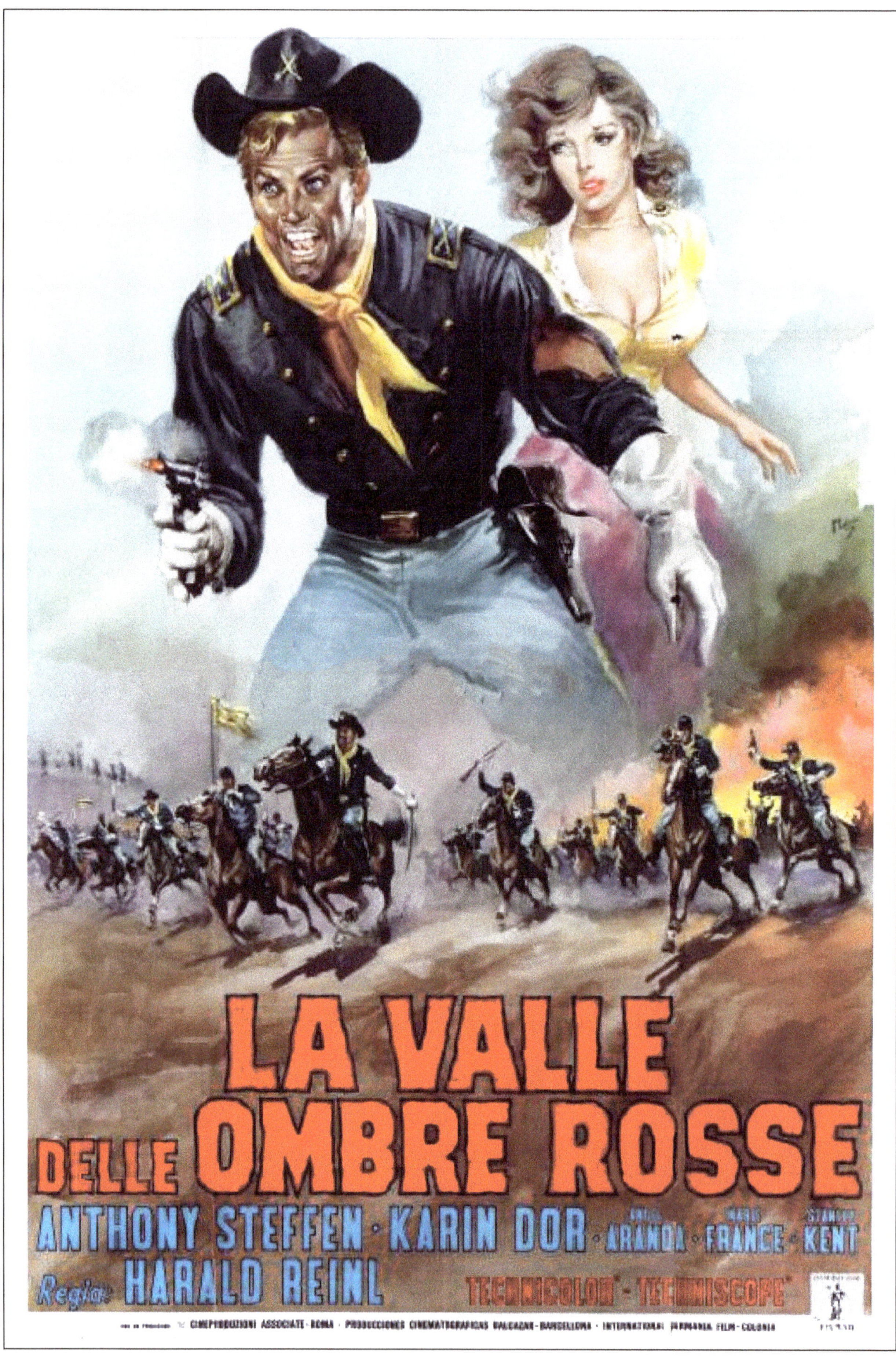

LA VALLE DELLE OMBRE ROSSE

("valley Of Red Shadows"). Artist: Moz. Original Title: **Der Letzte Mohikaner** (1965, Germany/Italy/Spain).

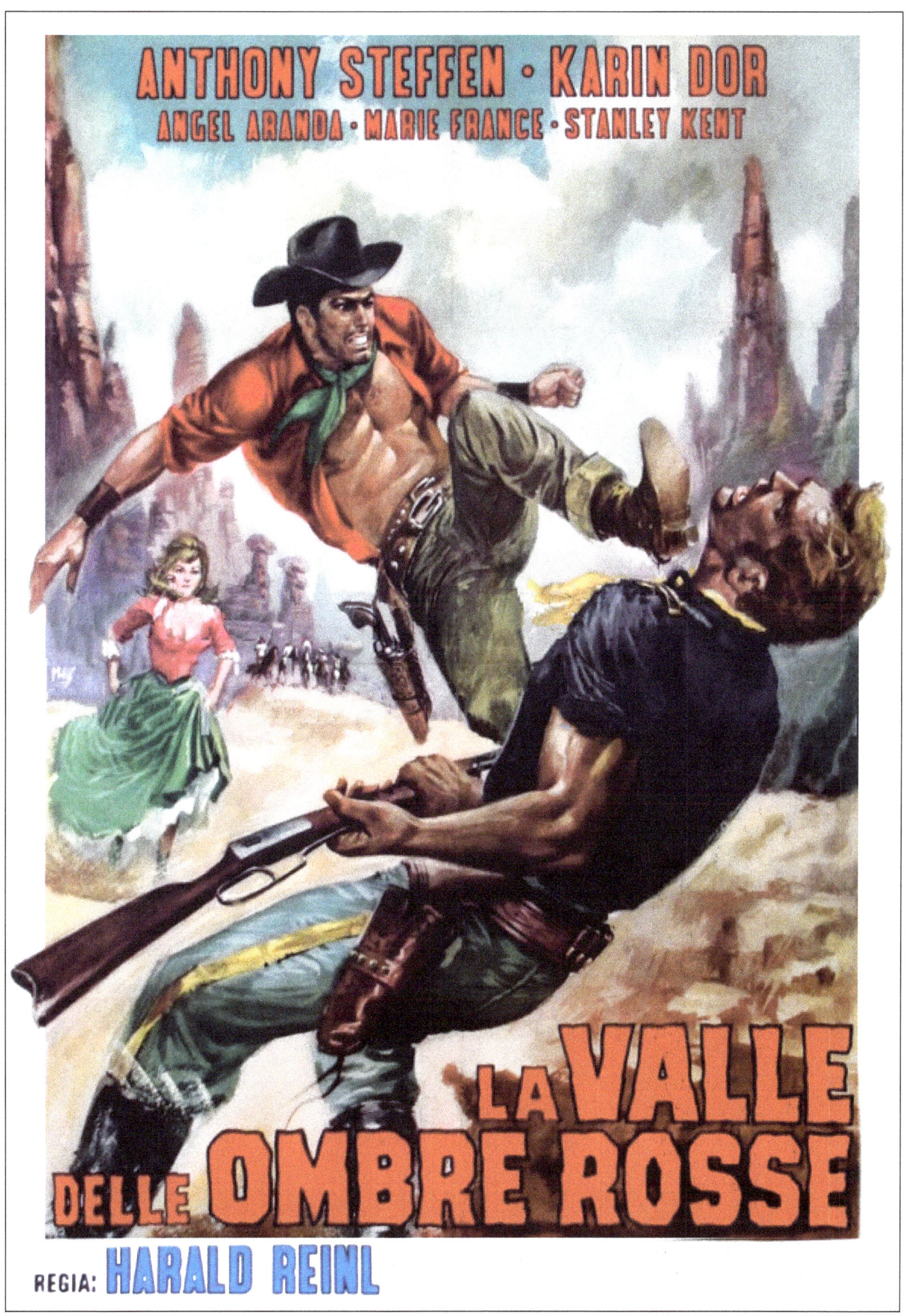

LA VALLE DELLE OMBRE ROSSE

("valley Of Red Shadows"). Artist: Moz. Original Title: **Der Letzte Mohikaner** (1965, Germany/Italy/Spain).

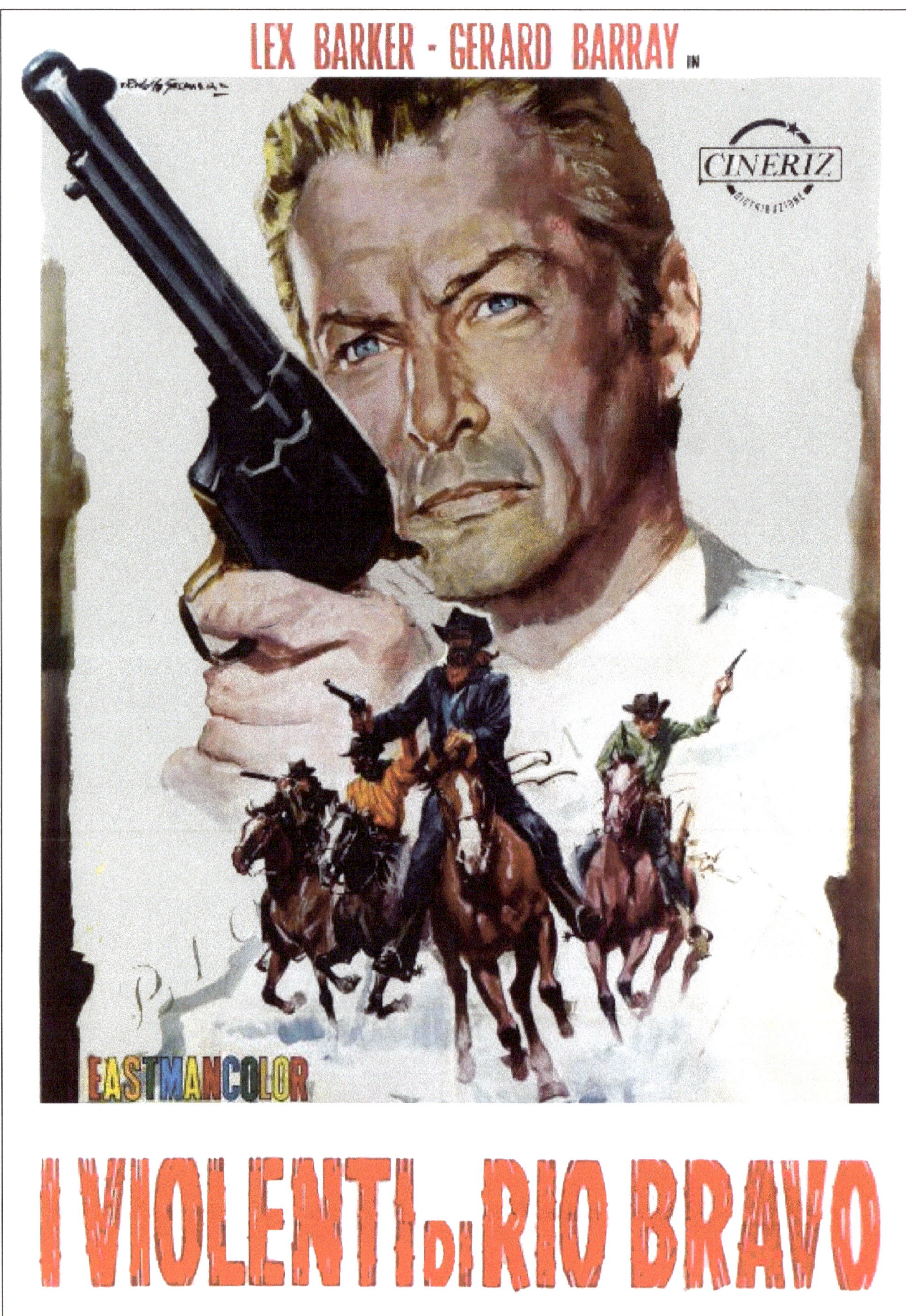

I VIOLENTI DI RIO BRAVO

("The Violent Ones From Rio Bravo"). Artist: Rodolfo Gasparri. Original Title: **Die Pyramide Des Sonnengottes** (1965, Germany/Italy/France).

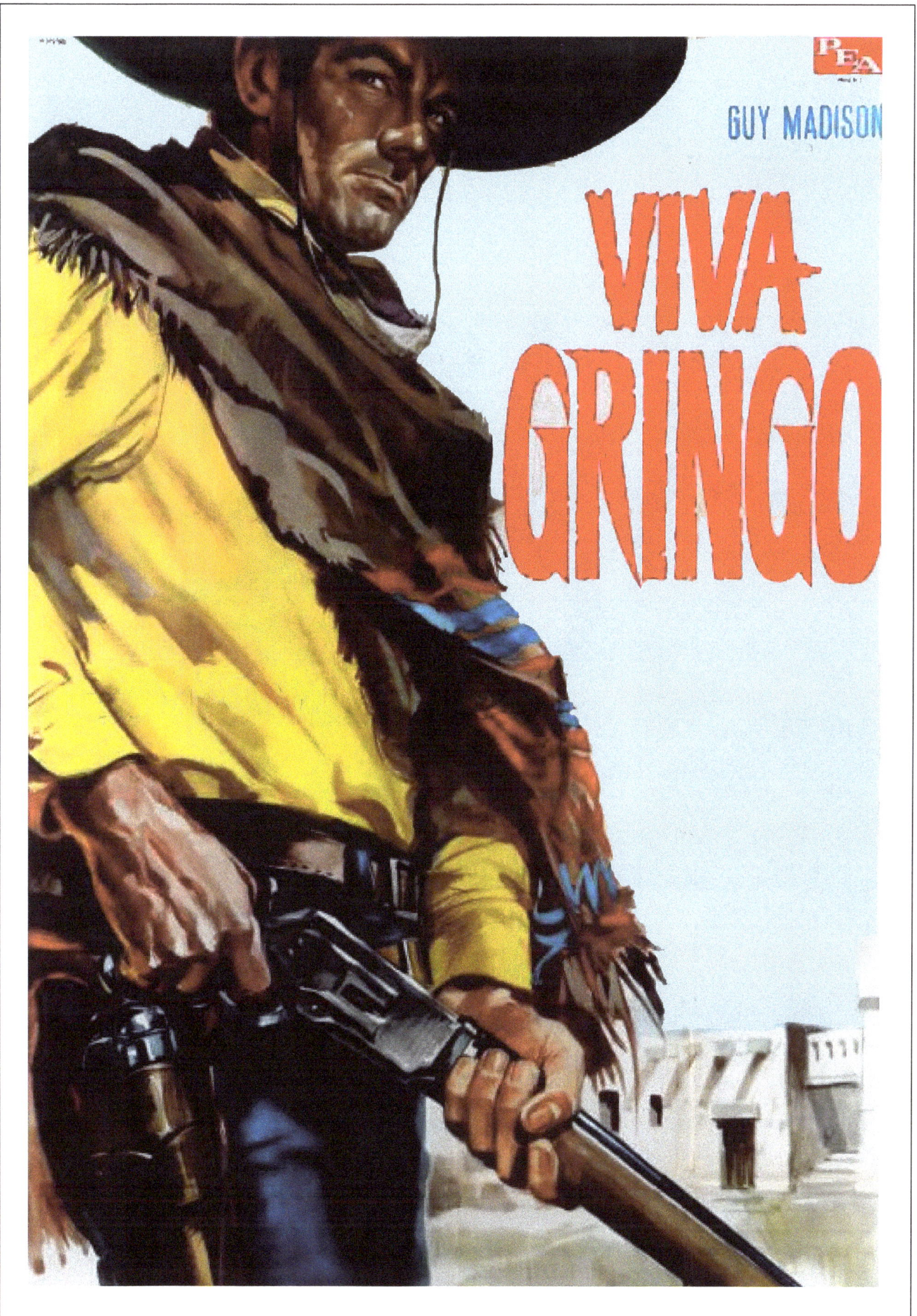

VIVA GRINGO

("Long Live The Gringo"). Artist: Renato Casaro. Original Title: **Das Vermächtnis Des Inka** (1965, Germany/Italy/Spain/Bulgaria).

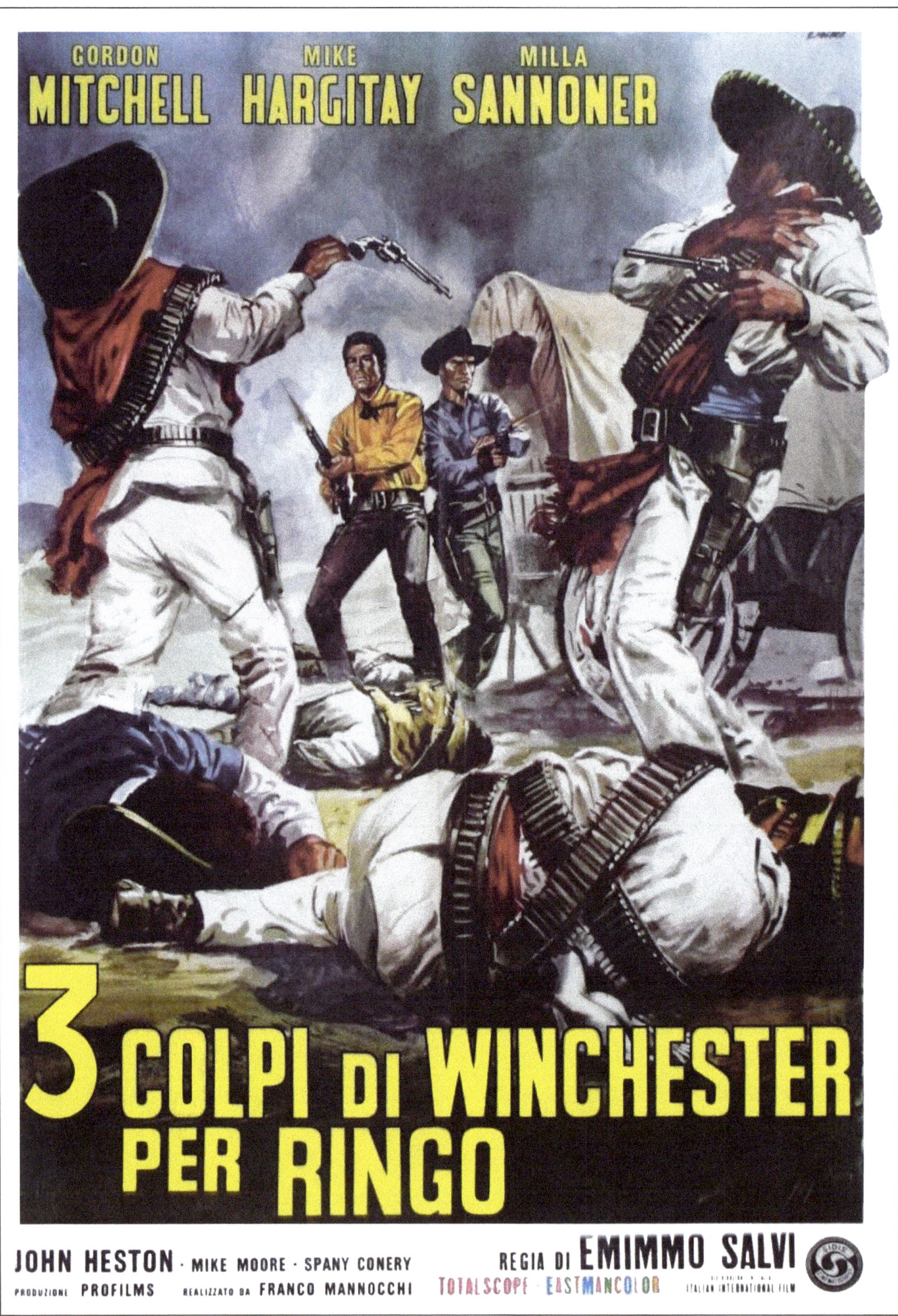

3 COLPI DI WINCHESTER PER RINGO

("3 Winchester Shots For Ringo"). Artist: Renato Casarod. Original Title: **3 Colpi Di Winchester Per Ringo** (1966, Italy).

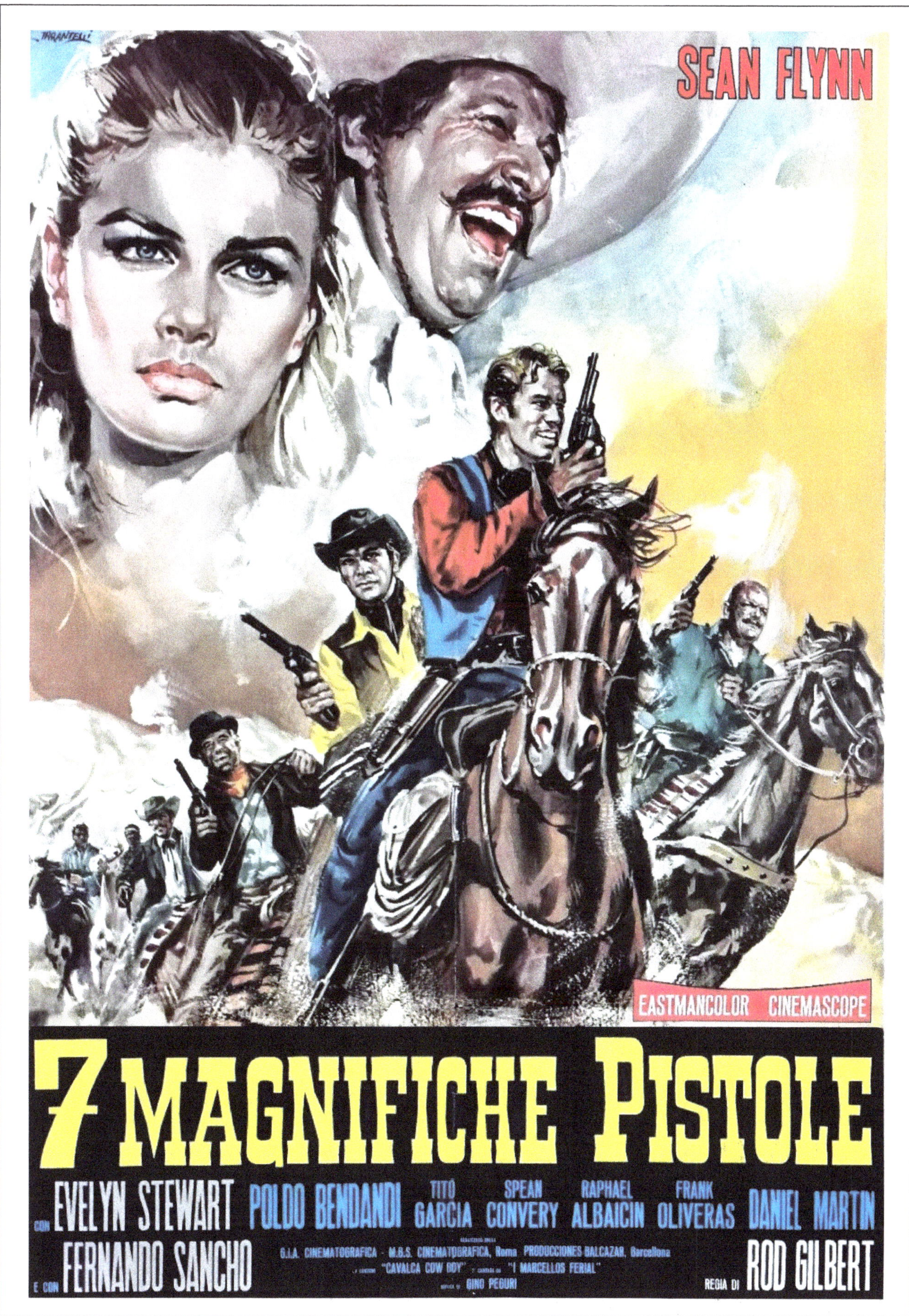

7 MAGNIFICHE PISTOLE

("7 Magnificent Guns"). Artist: Ezio Tarantelli. Original Title: **7 Magnifiche Pistole** (1966, Italy).

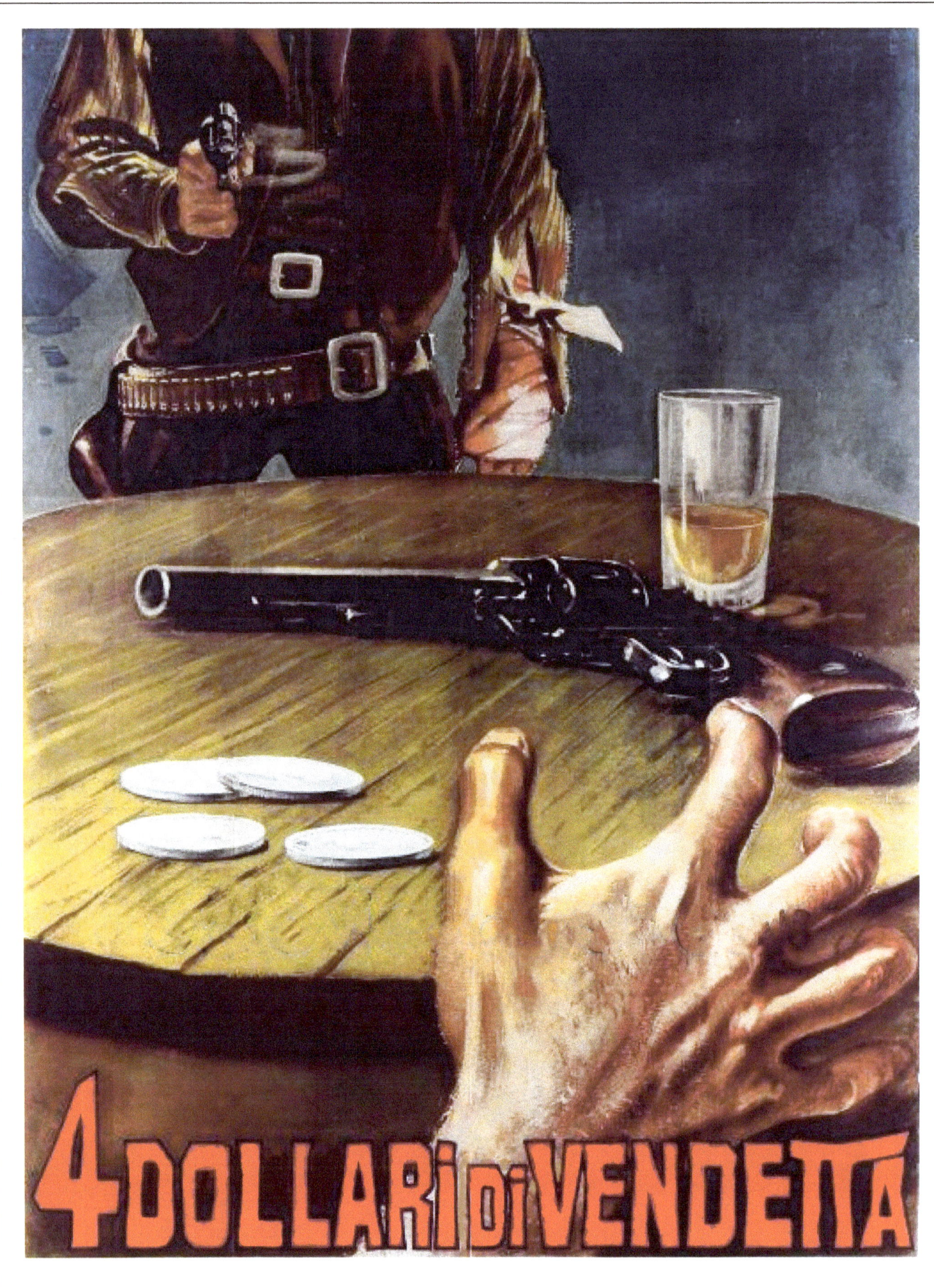

4 DOLLARI DI VENDETTA

("4 Dollars Of Vengeance"). Artist: unsigned. Original Title: **Cuatro Dólares De Venganza** (1966, Spain/Italy).

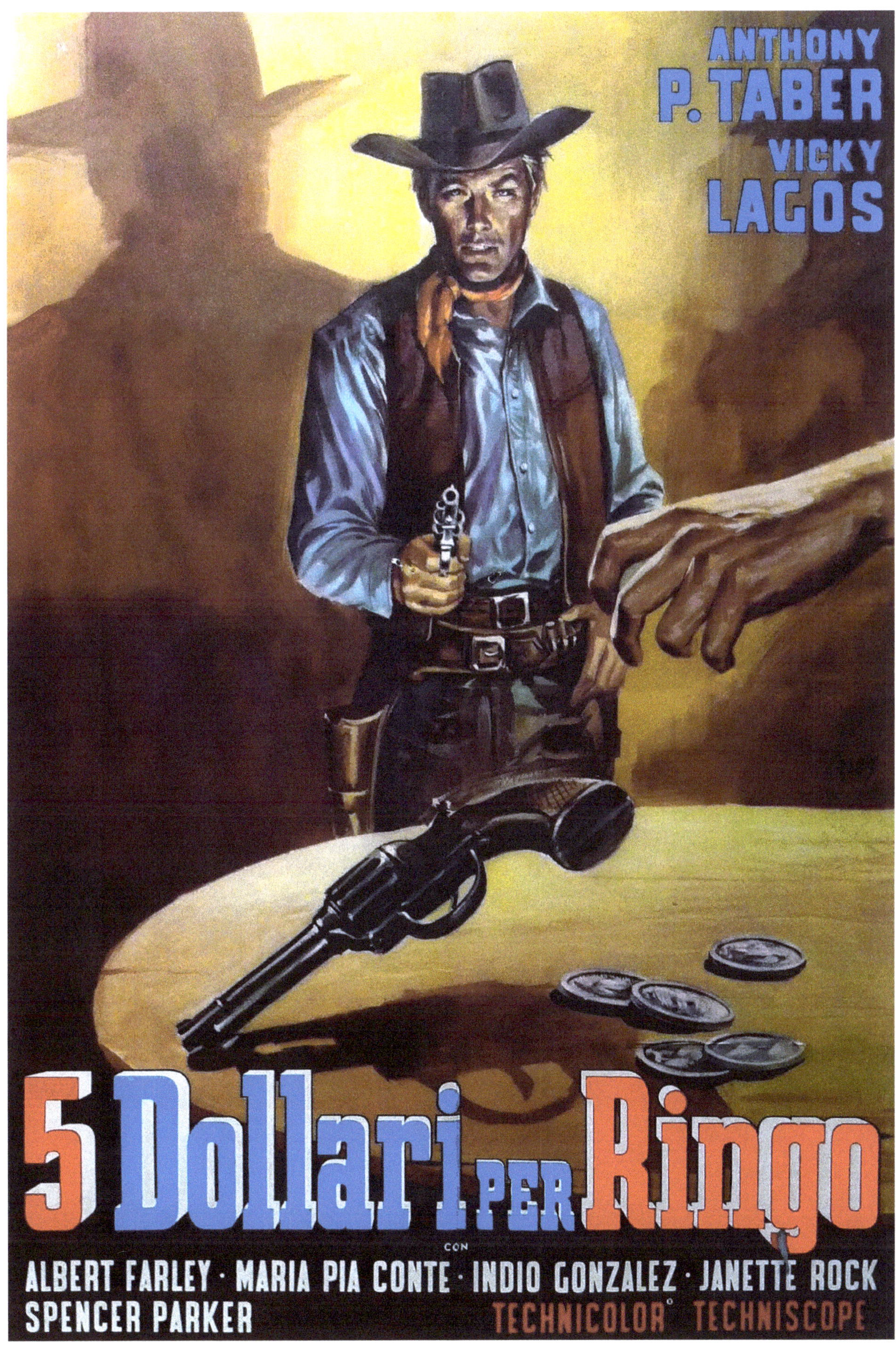

5 DOLLARI PER RINGO

("5 Dollars For Ringo"). Artist: Moz. Original Title: **Cinco Pistolas De Texas** (1966, Spain/Italy).

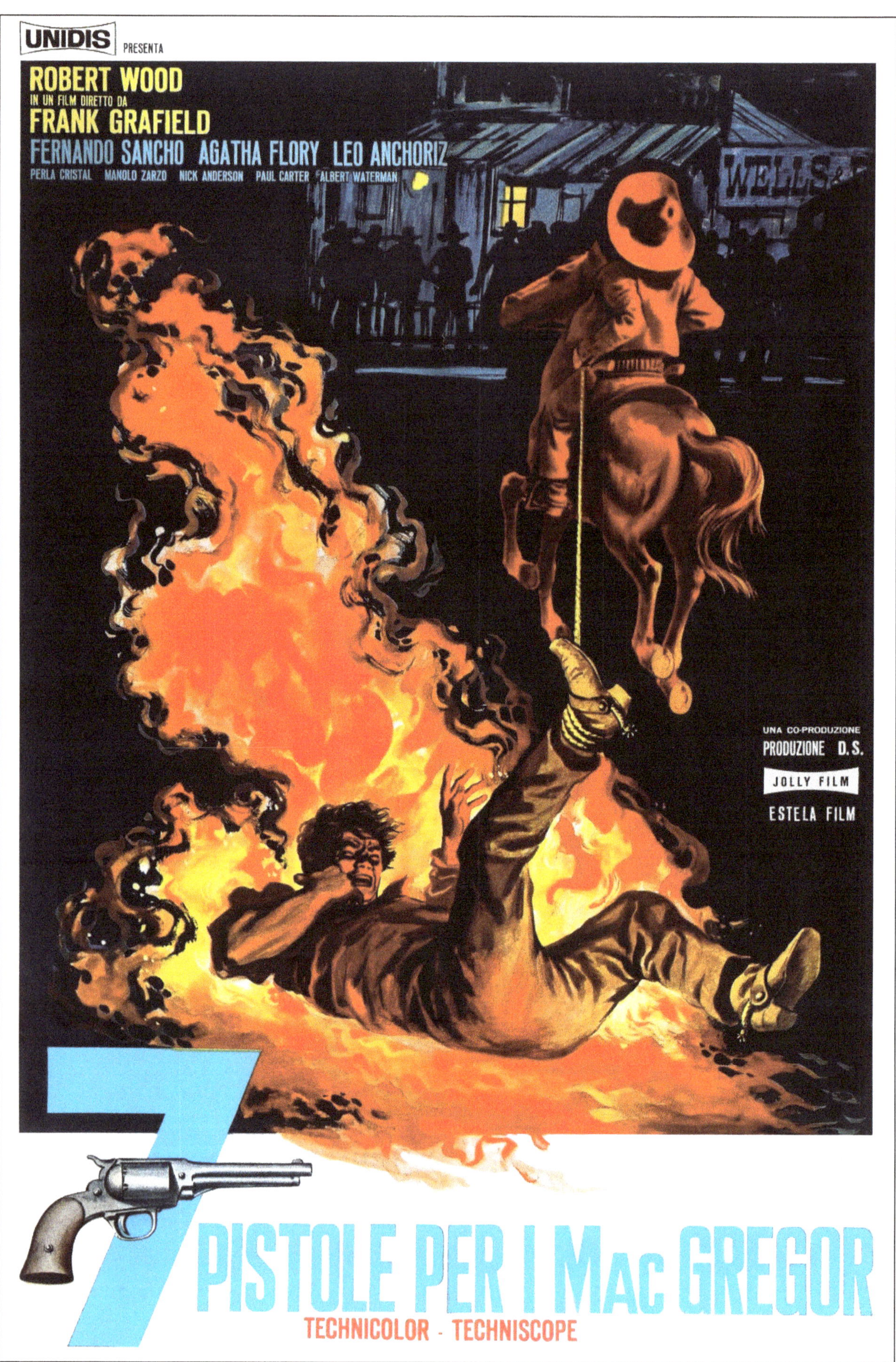

7 PISTOLE PER I MACGREGOR

("Seven Guns For The MacGregors"). Artist: unsigned. Original Title: **Sette Pistole Per I MacGregor** (1966, Italy/Spain).

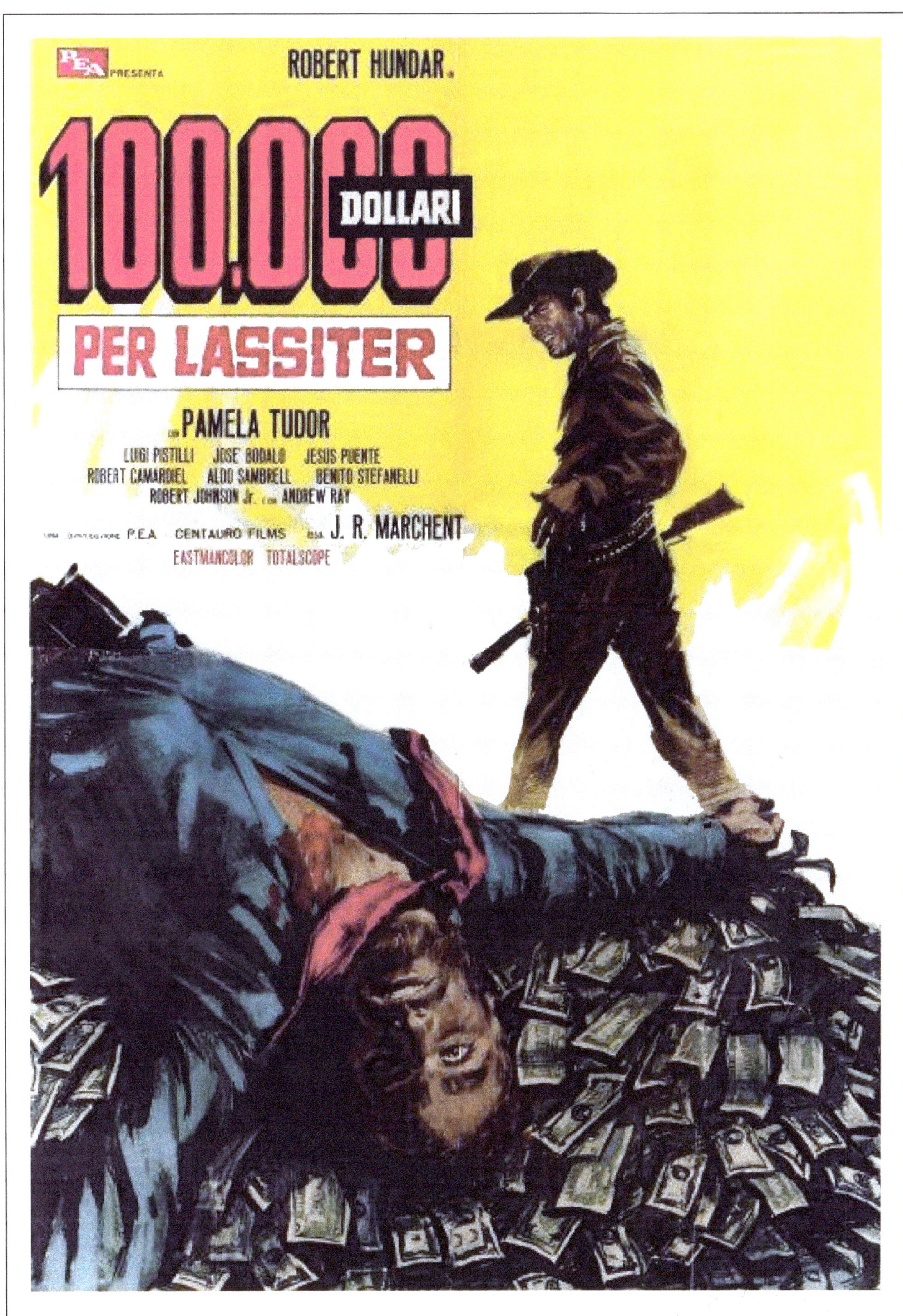

100.000 DOLLARI PER LASSITER

("$100,000 For Lassirt"). Artist: unsigned. Original Title: **La Muerte Cumple Condena** (1966, Spain/Italy).

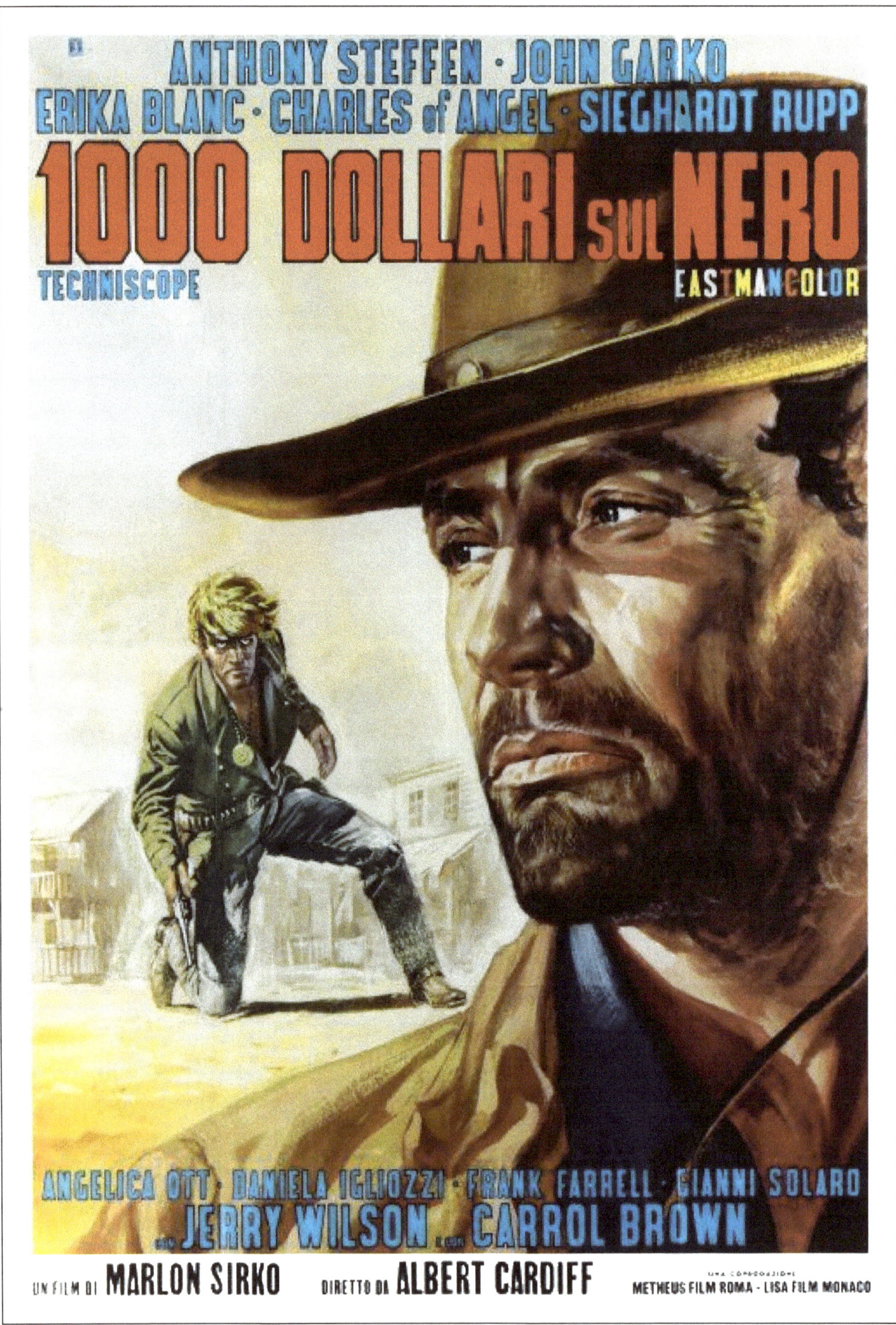

1000 DOLLARI SUL NERO

("$1,000 On Black"). Artist: unsigned. Original Title: **Mille Dollari Sul Nero** (1966, Italy/Germany).

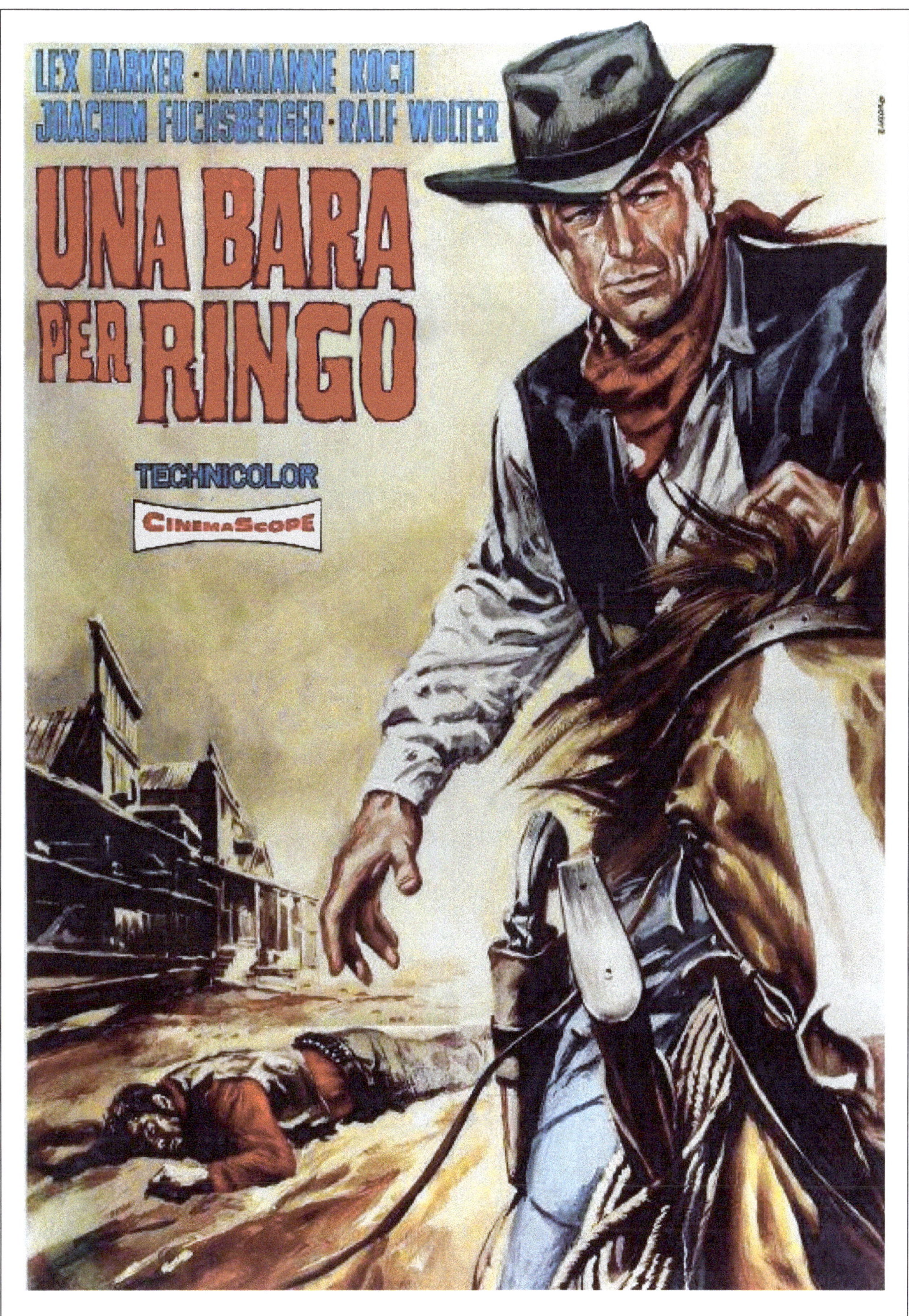

UNA BARA PER RINGO

("A Coffin For Ringo"). Artist: Renato Casaro. Original Title: **Wer Kennt Jonny R.?** (1966, Germany/Spain).

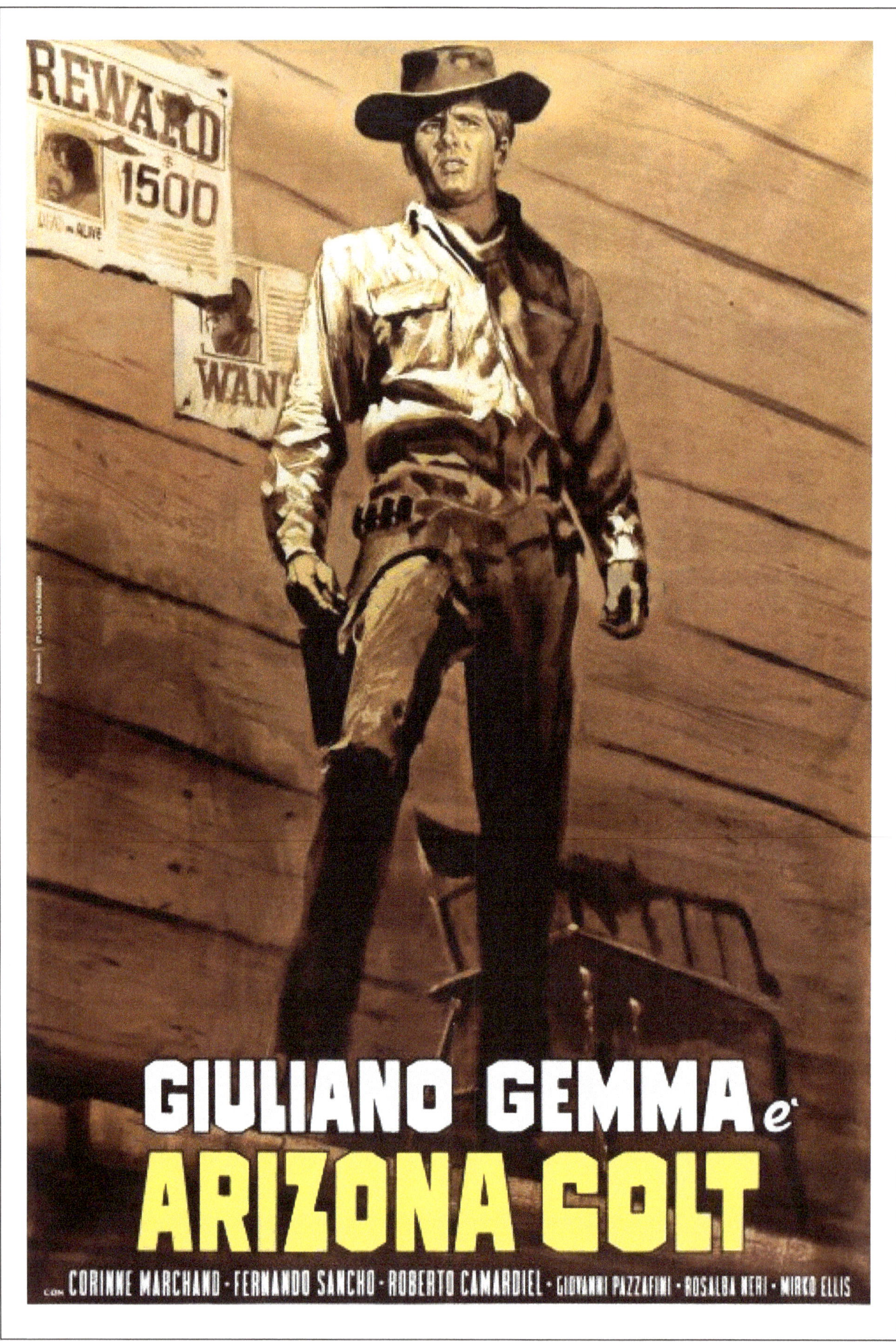

ARIZONA COLT

("Arizona Colt"). Artist: Mario Piovano. Original Title: **Arizona Colt** (1966, Italy).

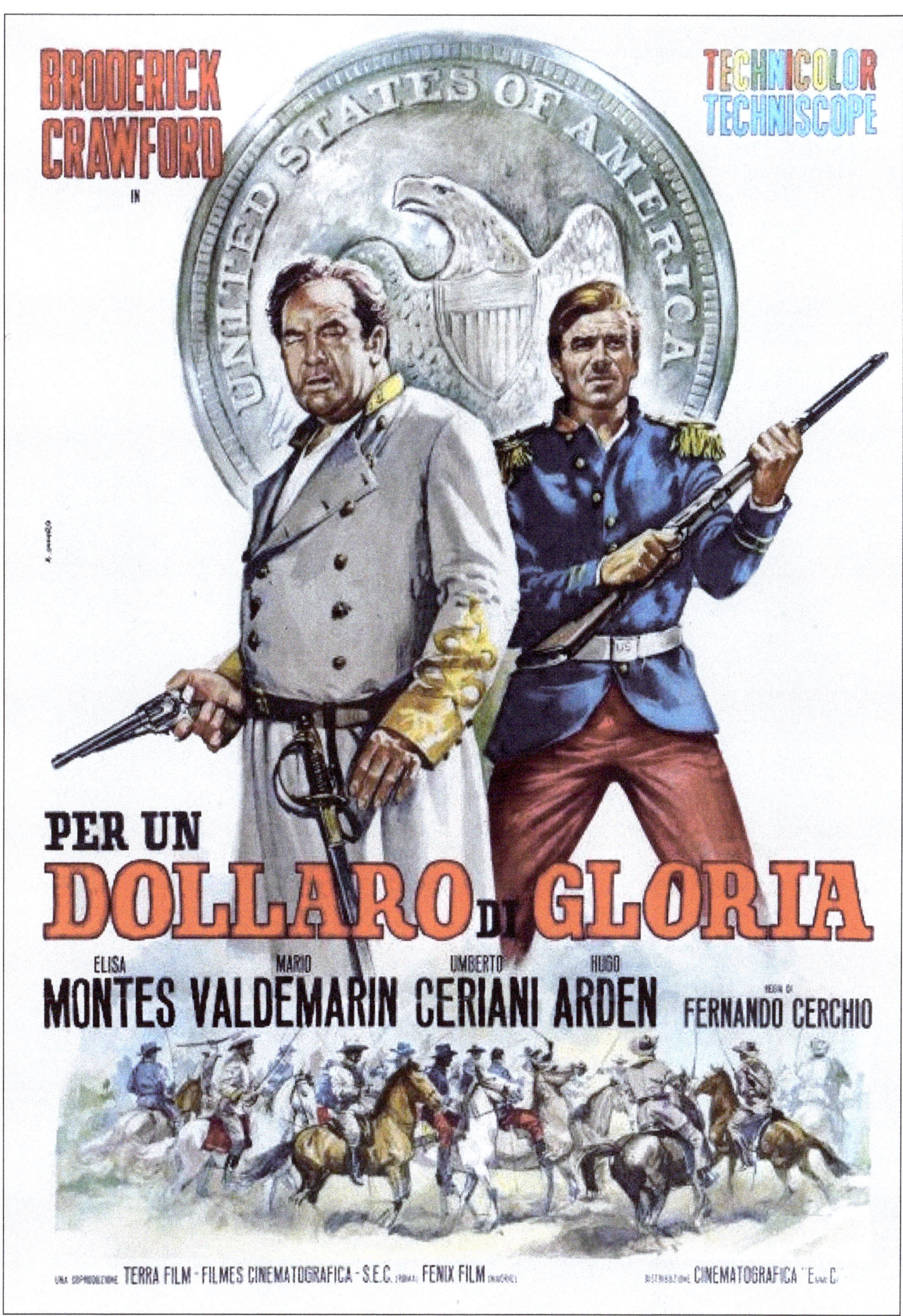

PER UN DOLLARO DI GLORIA

("For A Dollar Of Glory"). Artist: Renato Casaro. Original Title: **Per Un Dollaro Di Gloria** (1966, Italy/Spain).

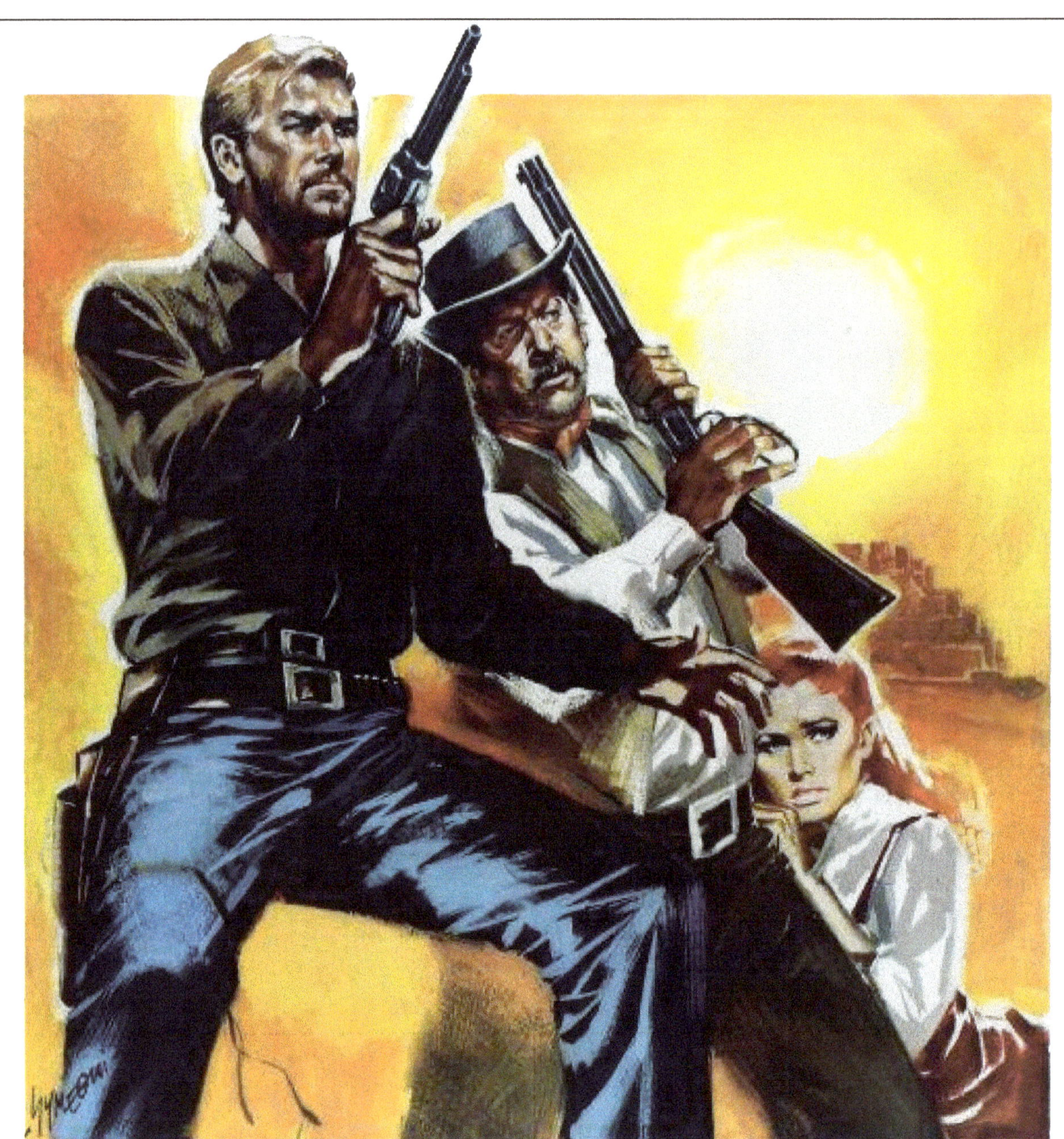

DJANGO SPARA PER PRIMO

("Django Shoots First"). Artist: Sandro Symeoni. Original Title: **Django Spara Per Primo** (1966, Italy).

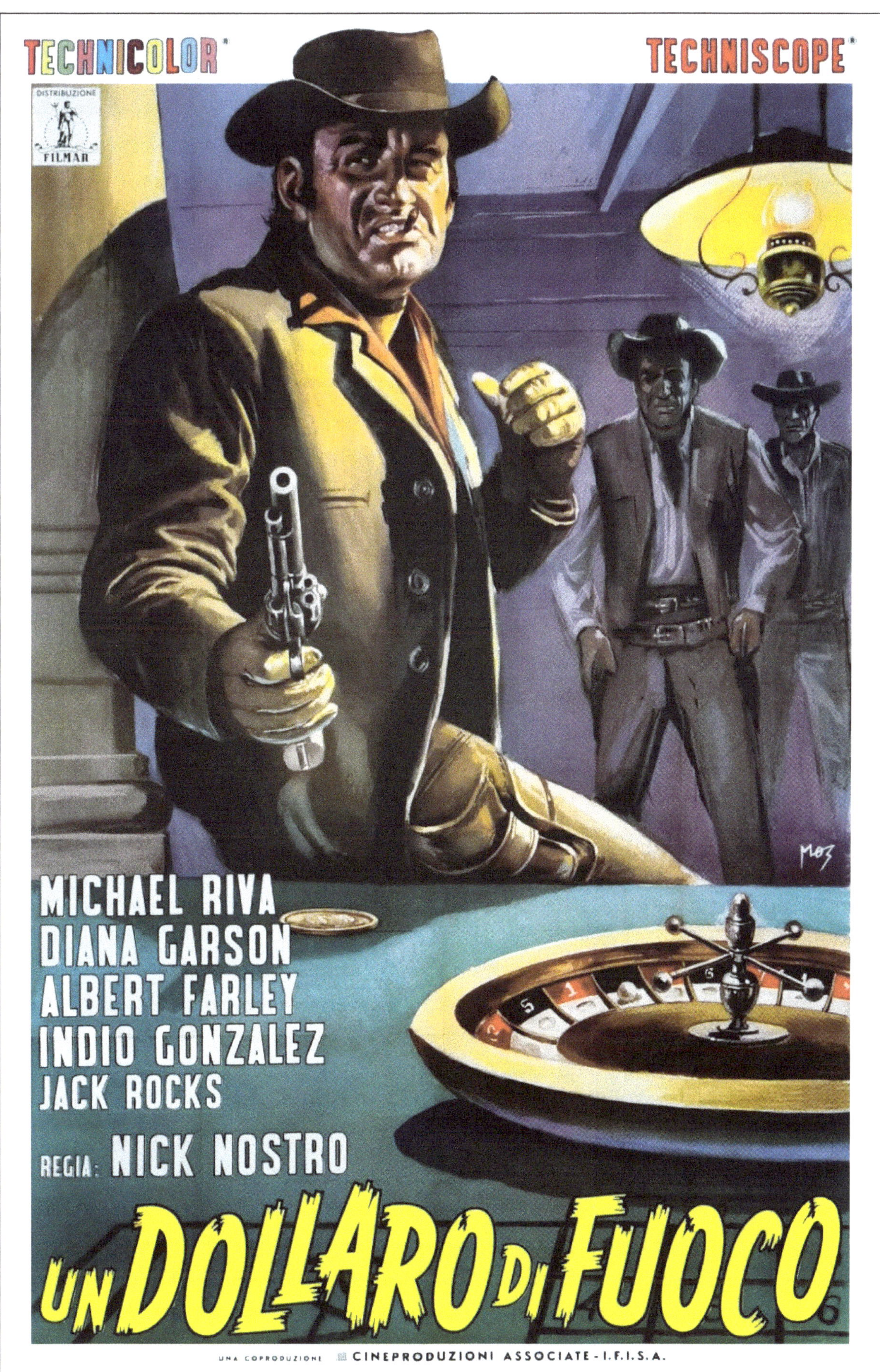

UN DOLLARO DI FUOCO

("One Dollar Of Fire"). Artist: Moz. Original Title: **Un Dólar De Fuego** (1966, Spain/Italy).

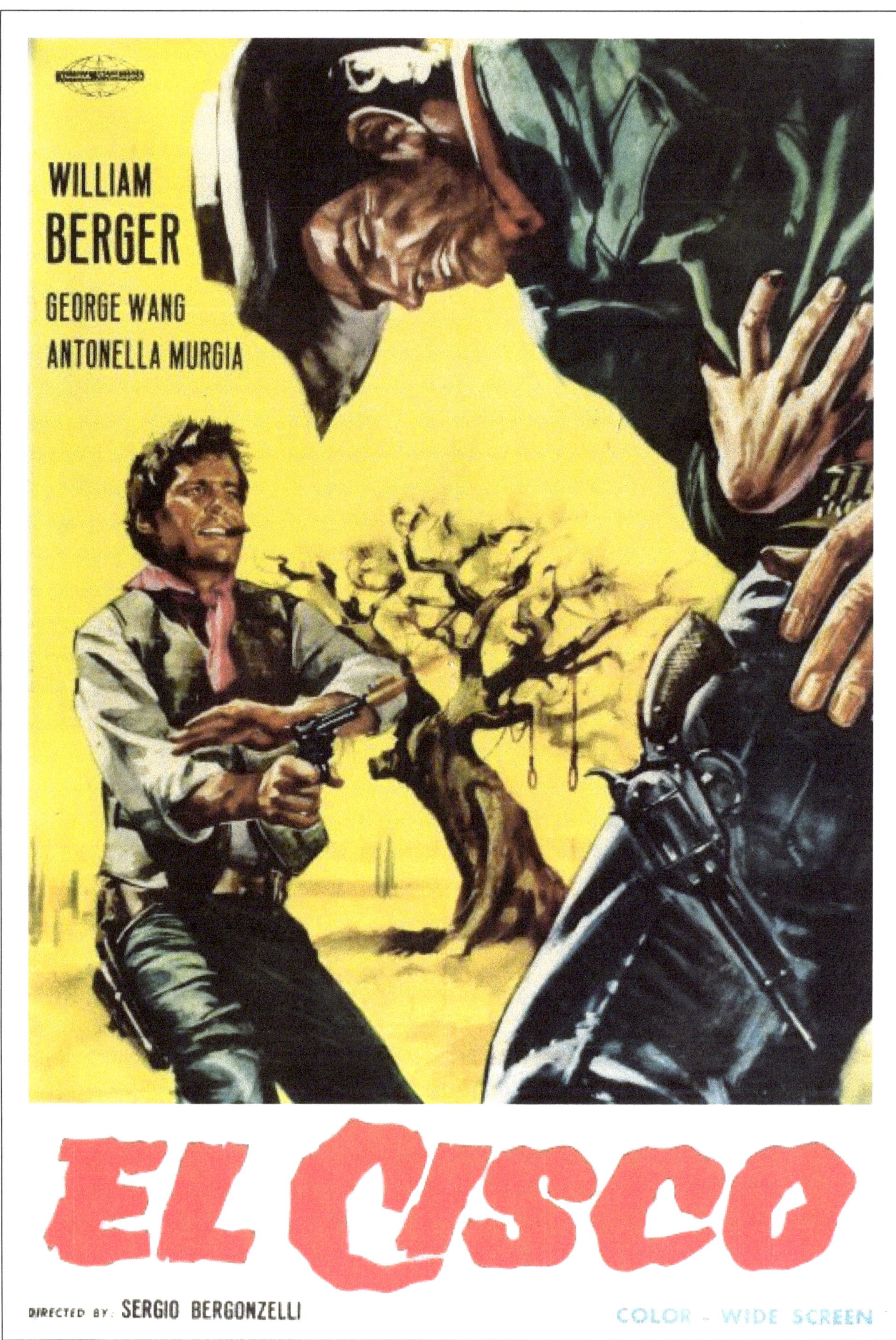

EL CISCO

("El Cisco"). Artist: unsigned. Original Title: **El Cisco** (1966, Italy).

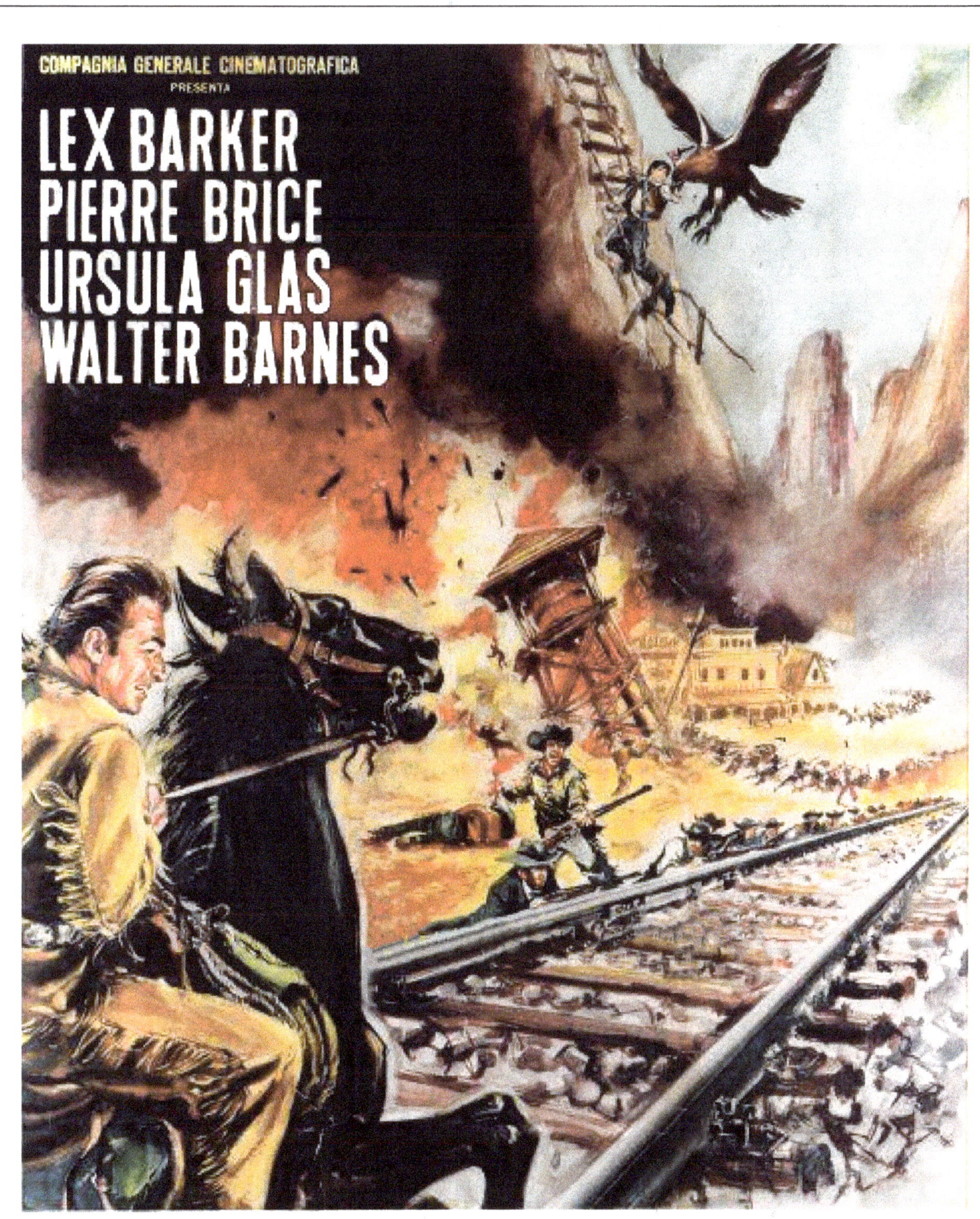

IL GIORNO PIÙ LUNGO DI KANSAS

("The Longest Day In Kansas City"). Artist: Morini. Original Title: **Winnetou Und Das Halbblut Apanatschi** (1966, Germany).

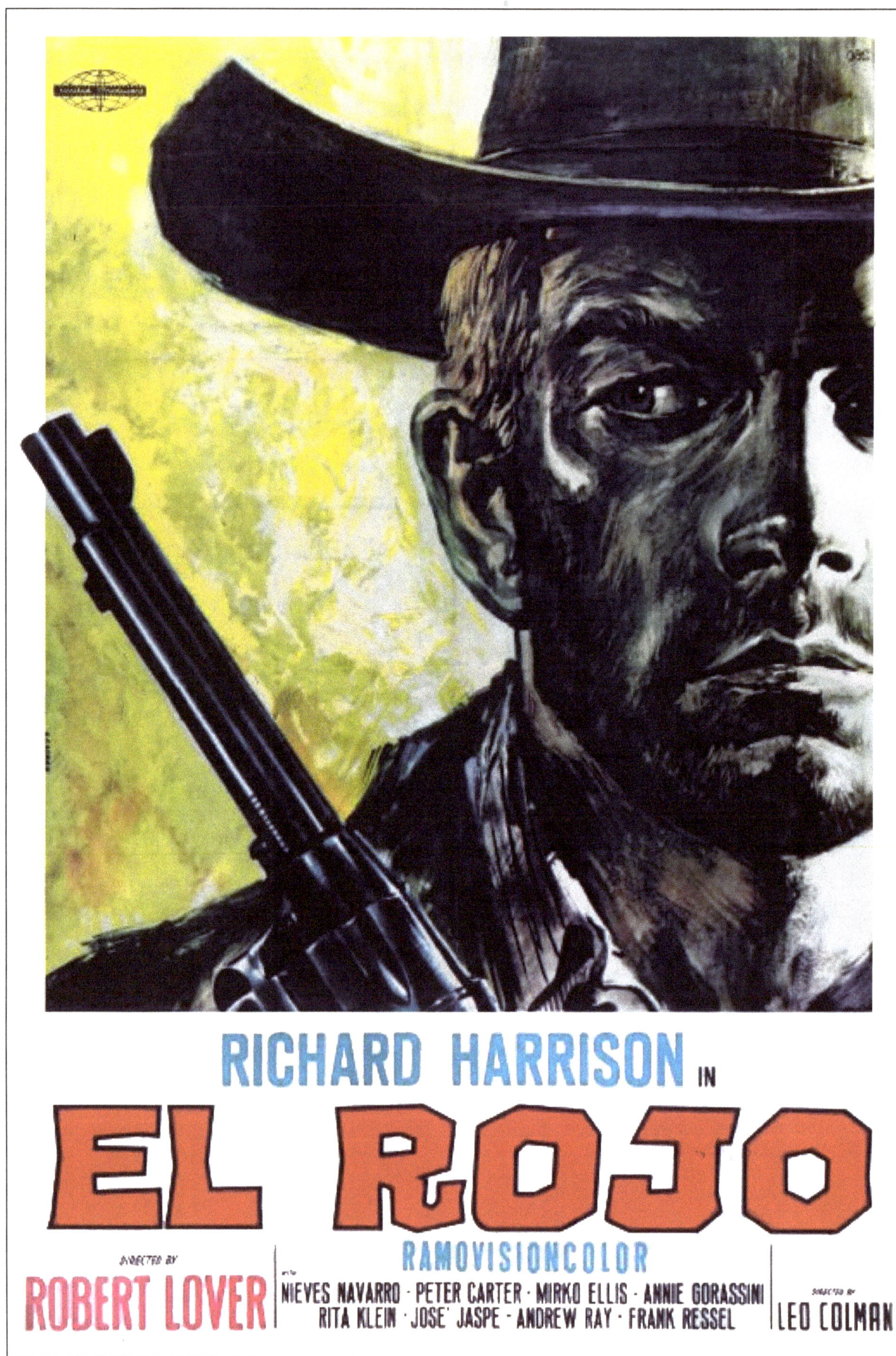

EL ROJO

("El Rojo"). Artist: Renato Casaro. Original Title: **El Rojo** (1966, Italy/Spain).

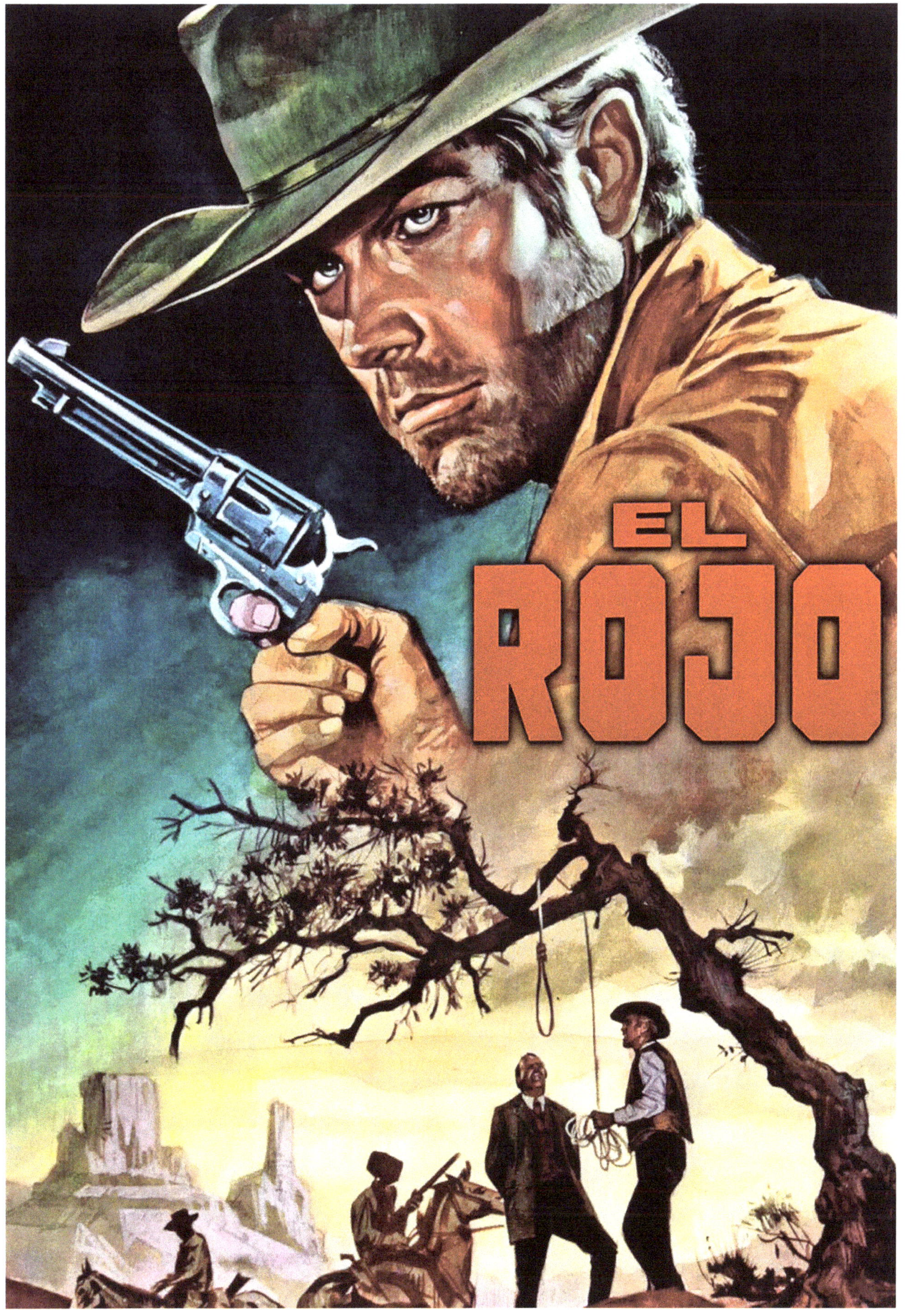

EL ROJO

("El Rojo"). Artist: unsigned. Original Title: **El Rojo** (1966, Italy/Spain).

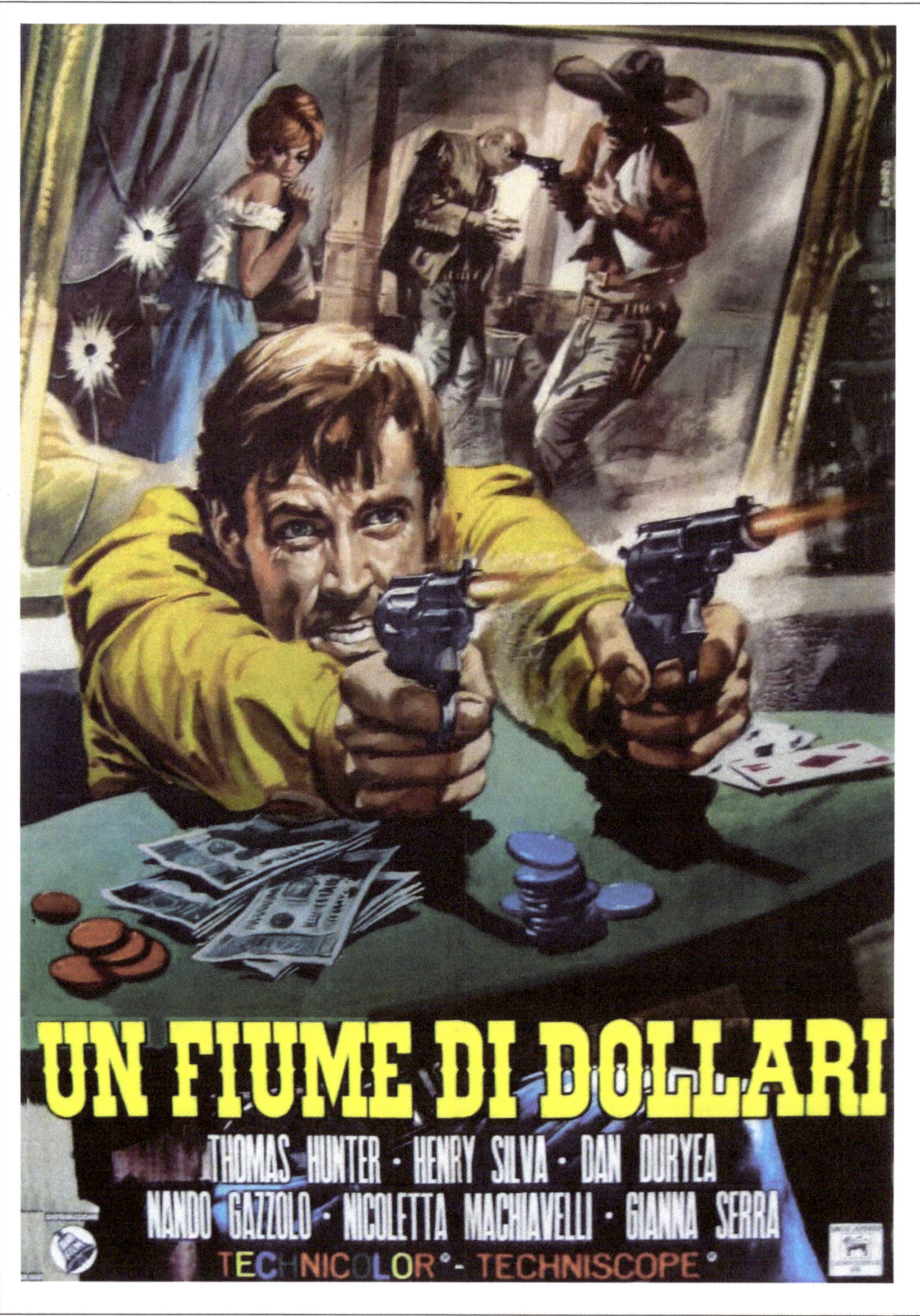

UN FIUME DI DOLLARI

("A River Of Dollars"). Artist: Renato Casaro. Original Title: **Un Fiume Di Dollari** (1966, Italy).

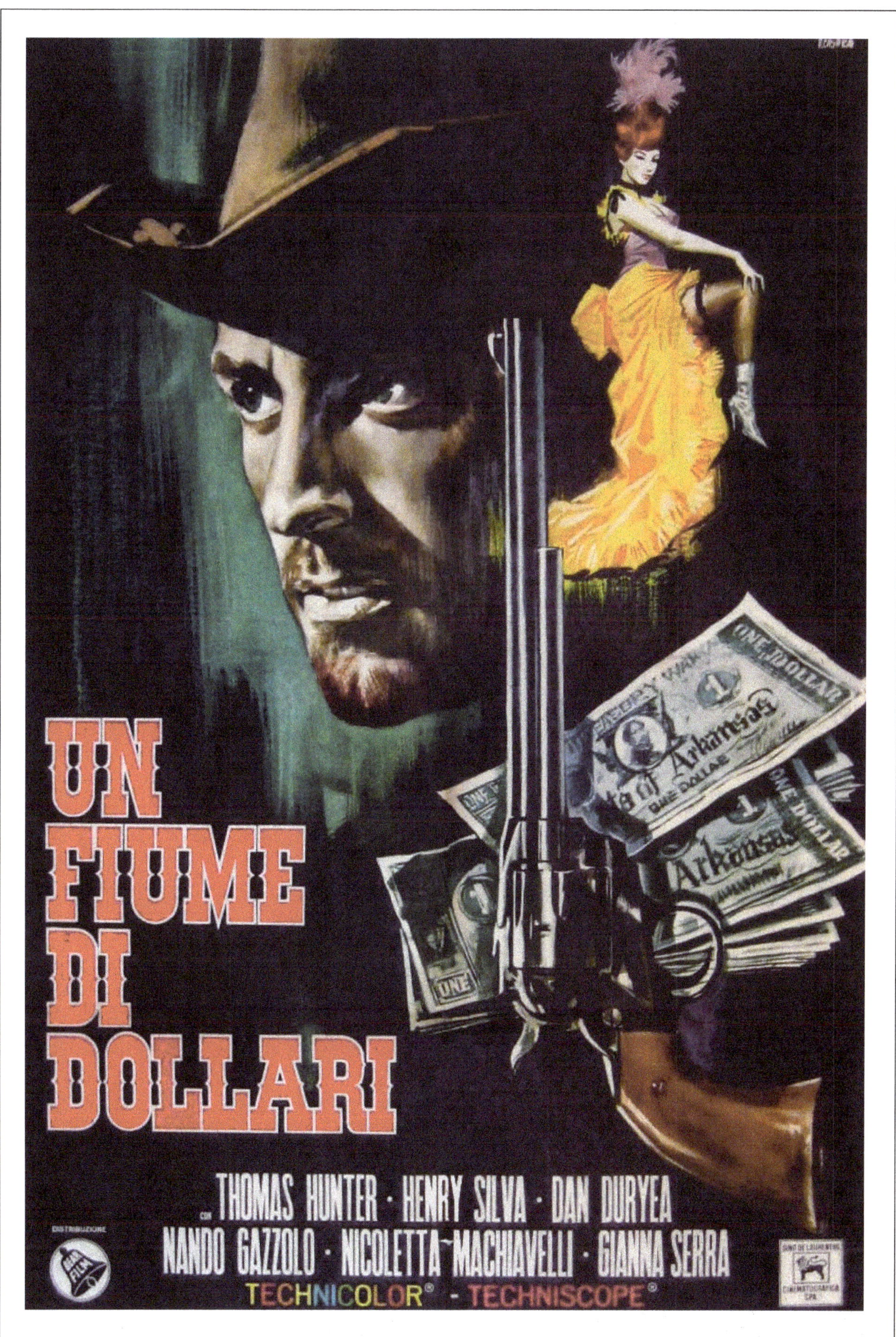

UN FIUME DI DOLLARI

("A River Of Dollars"). Artist: Renato Casaro. Original Title: **Un Fiume Di Dollari** (1966, Italy).

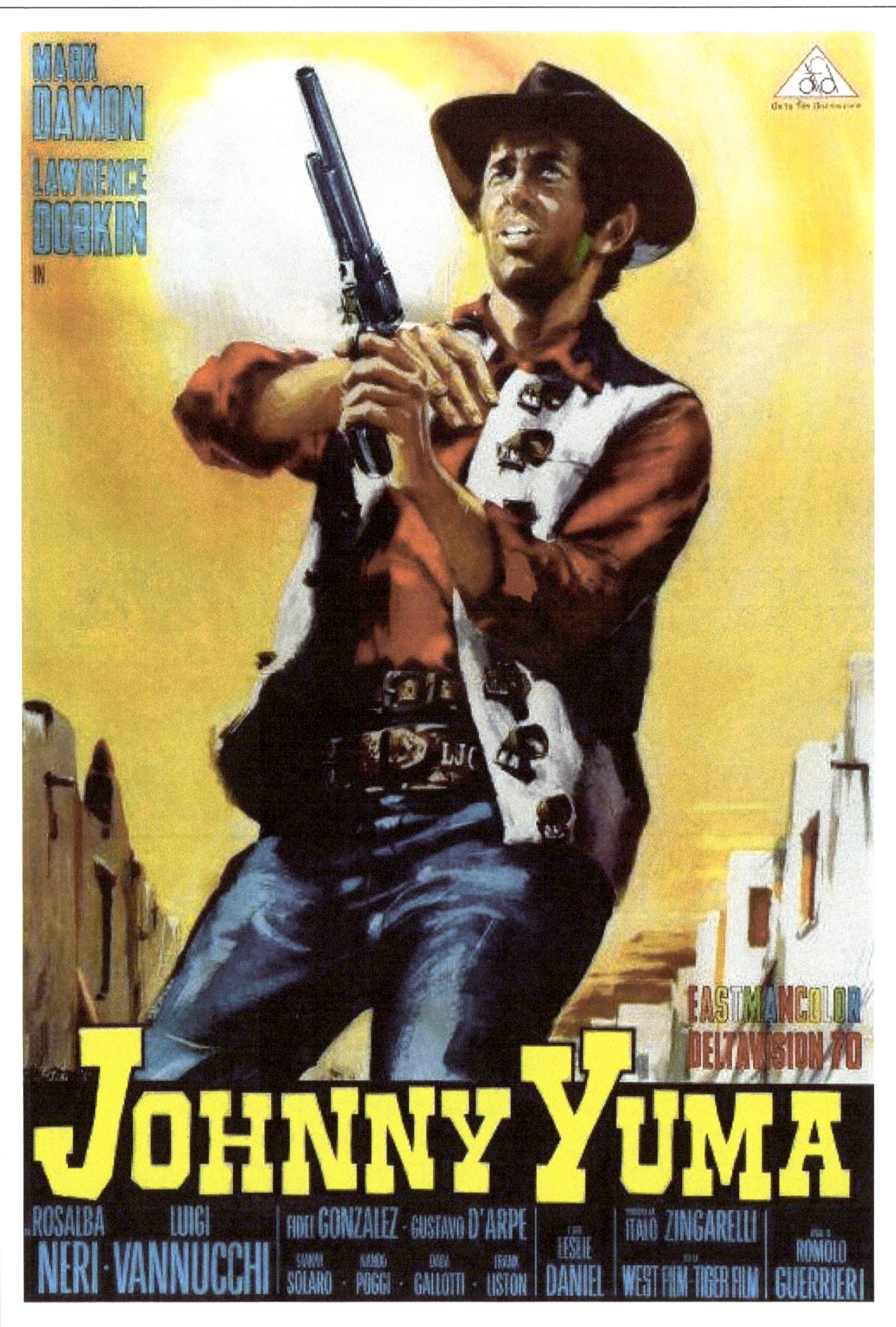

JOHNNY YUMA

("Johnny Yuma"). Artist: G. Di Stefano. Original Title: **Johnny Yuma** (1966, Italy).

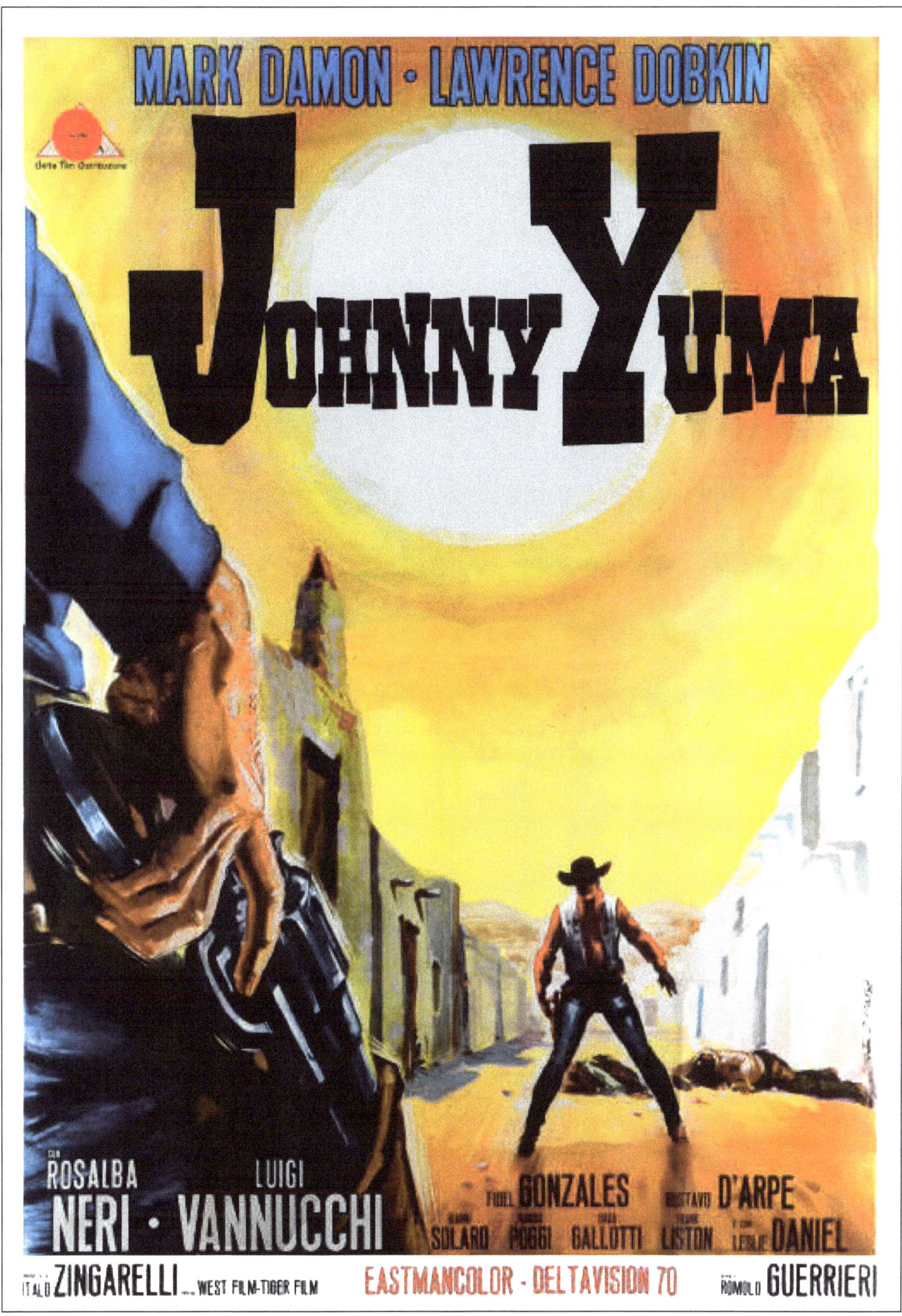

JOHNNY YUMA

("Johnny Yuma"). Artist: G. Di Stefano. Original Title: **Johnny Yuma** (1966, Italy).

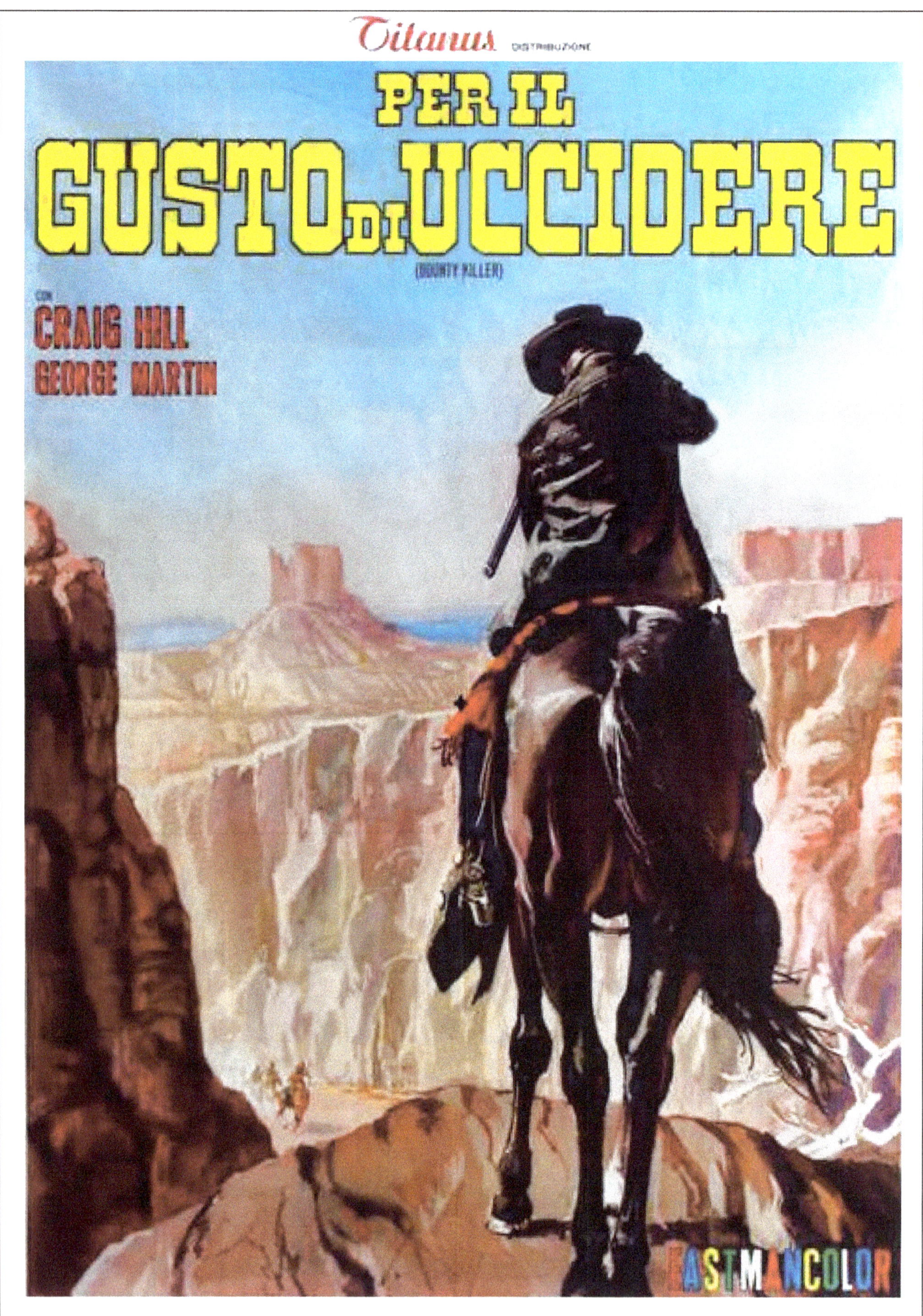

PER IL GUSTO DI UCCIDERE

("For The Taste Of Killing"). Artist: unsigned. Original Title: **Per Il Gusto Di Uccidere** (1966, Italy/Spain).

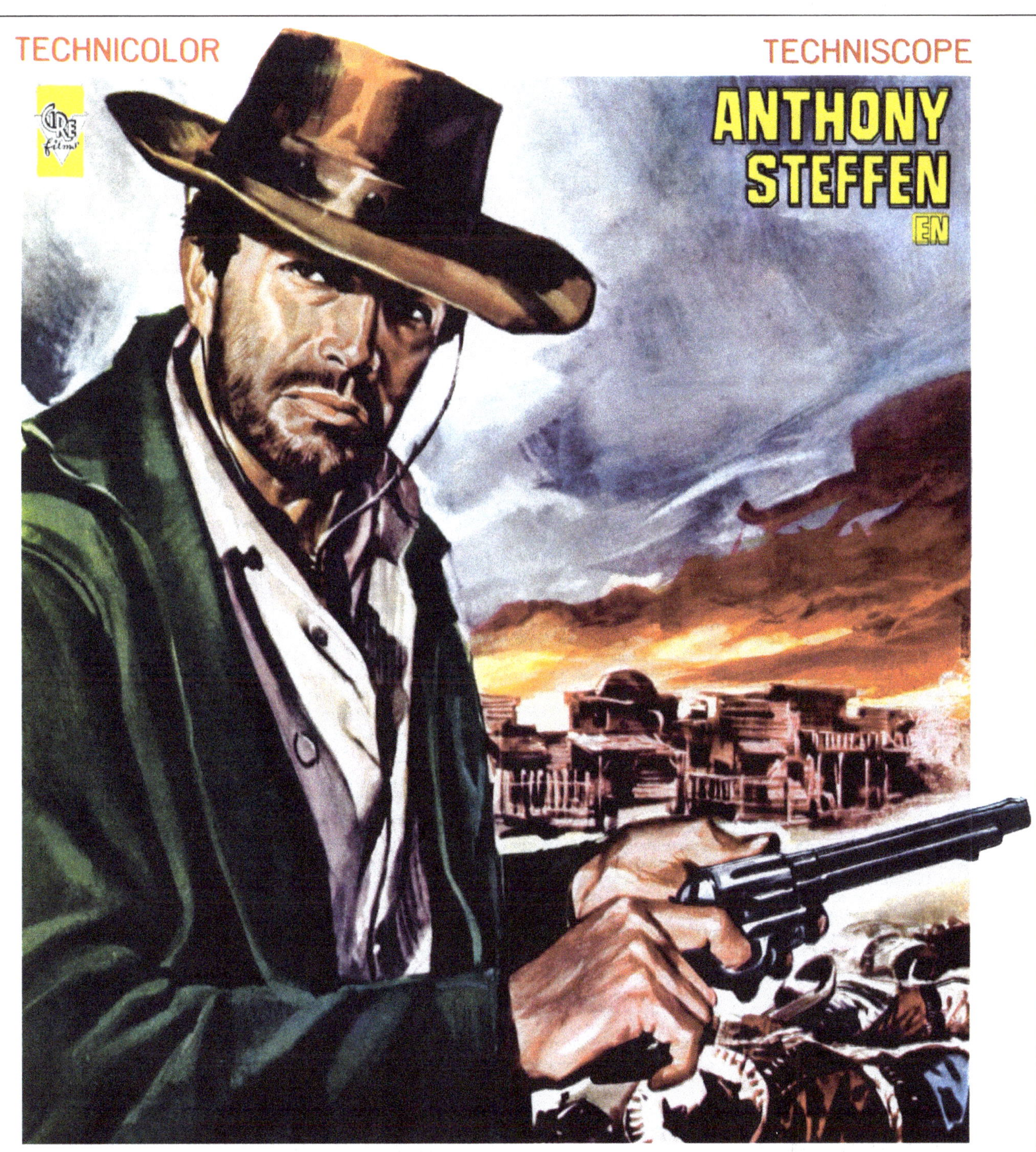

POCHI DOLLARI PER DJANGO

("A Few Dollars For Django"). Artist: Renato Casaro. Original Title: **Pochi Dollari Per Django** (1966, Italy/Spain).

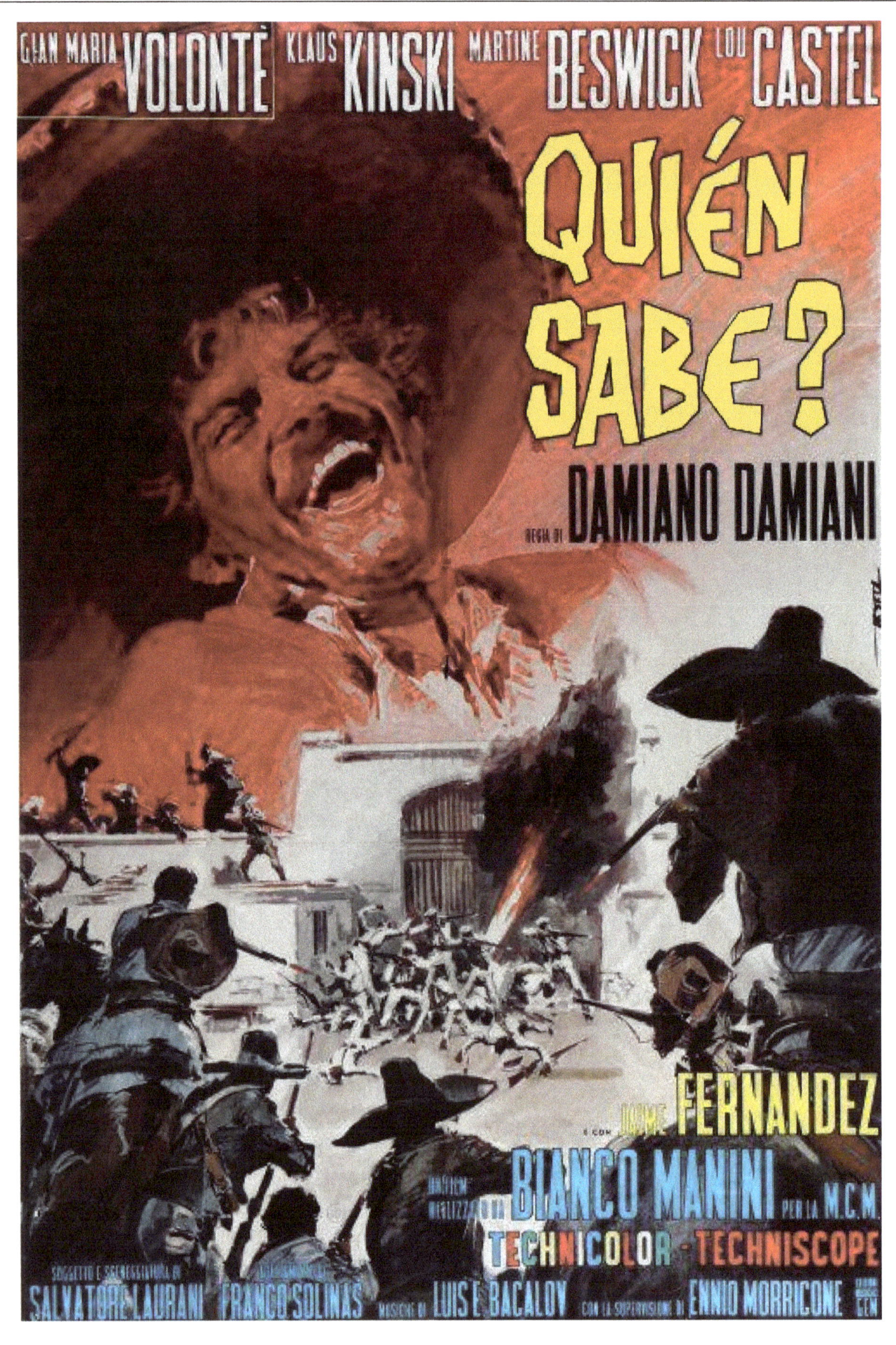

QUIÉN SABE?

("Who Knows?"). Artist: Enrico De Seta. Original Title: Quién Sabe? (1966, Italy).

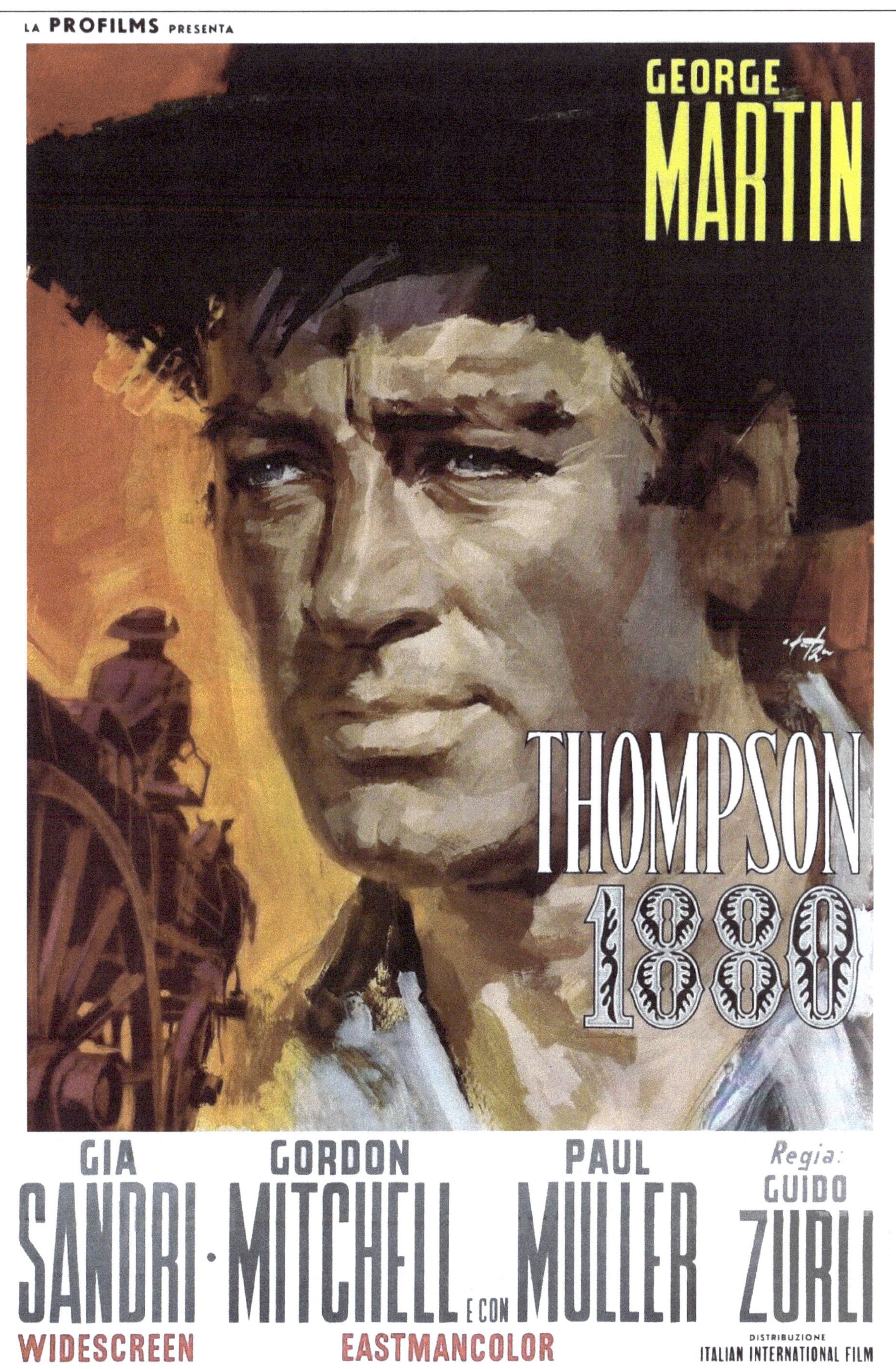

THOMPSON 1880

("Thompson 1880"). Artist: Arnaldo Putzu. Original Title: **Thompson 1880** (1966, Italy/Spain).

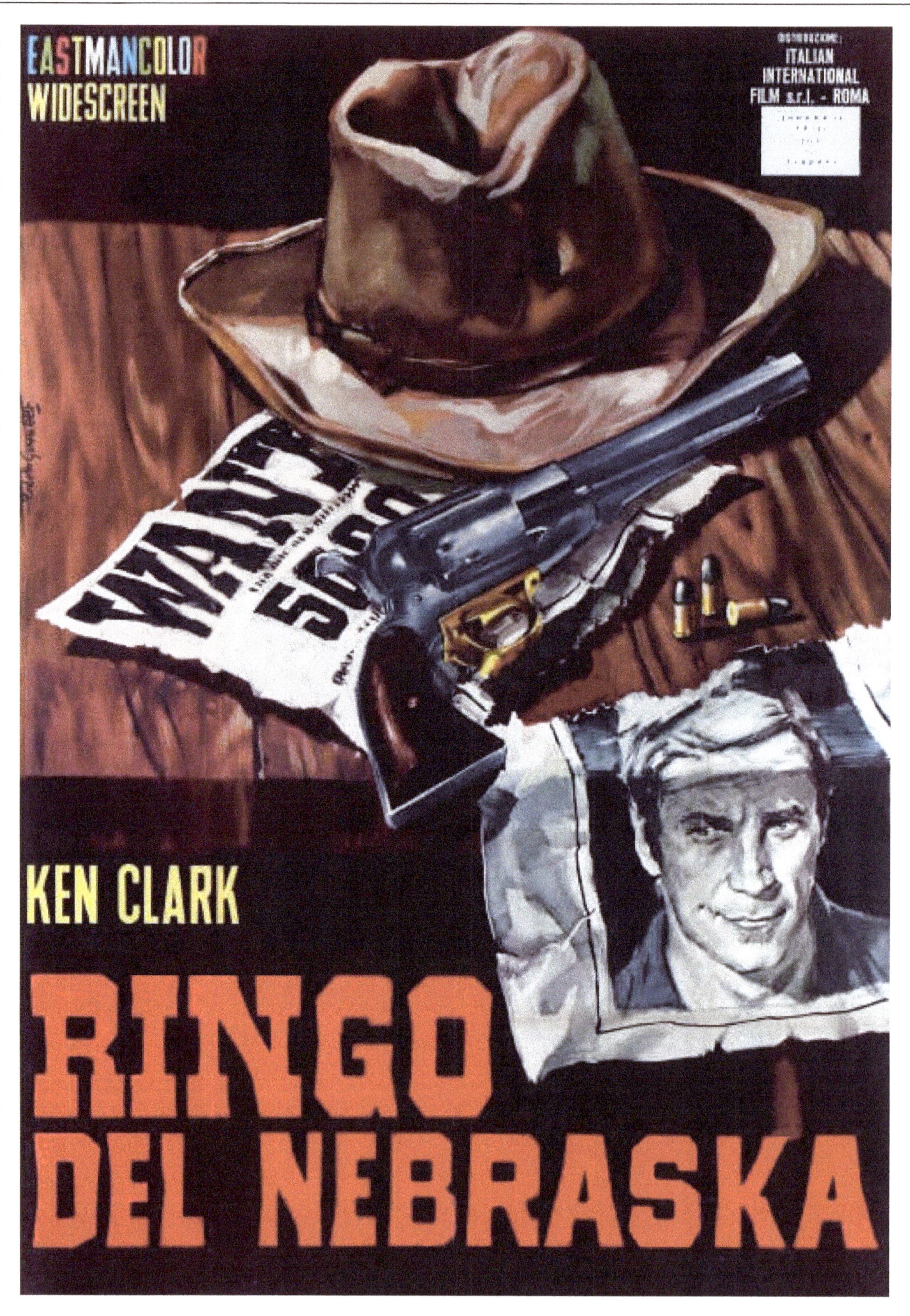

RINGO DEL NEBRASKA

("Ringo From Nebraska"). Artist: Rodlfo Gasparri. Original Title: **Ringo Del Nebraska** (1966, Italy/Spain).

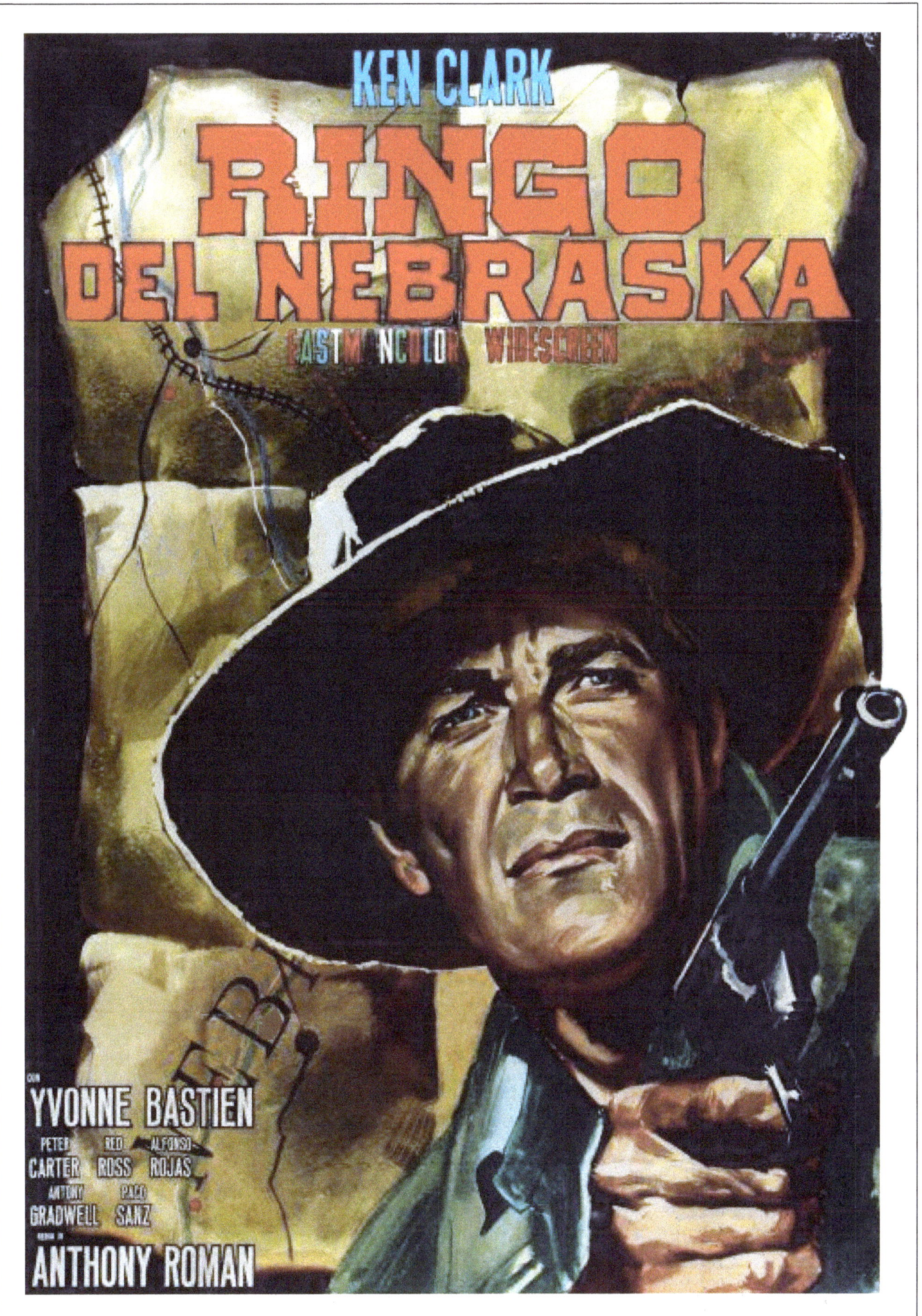

RINGO DEL NEBRASKA

("Ringo From Nebraska"). Artist: Rodlfo Gasparri. Original Title: **Ringo Del Nebraska** (1966, Italy/Spain).

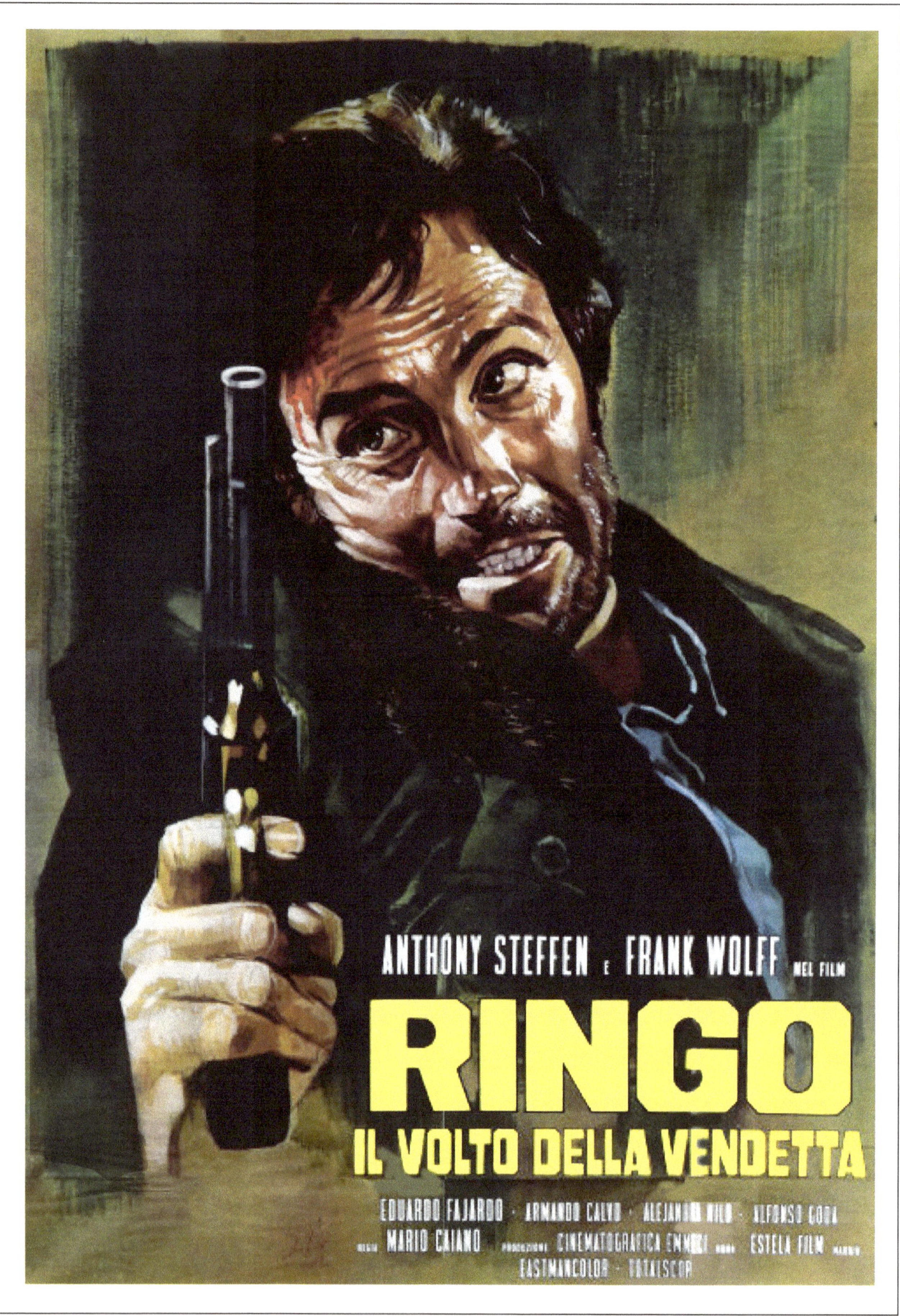

RINGO, IL VOLTO DELLA VENDETTA

("Ringo, The Face Of Vengeance"). Artist: Mario Piovano. Original Title: **Ringo, Il Volto Della Vendetta** (1966, Italy/Spain).

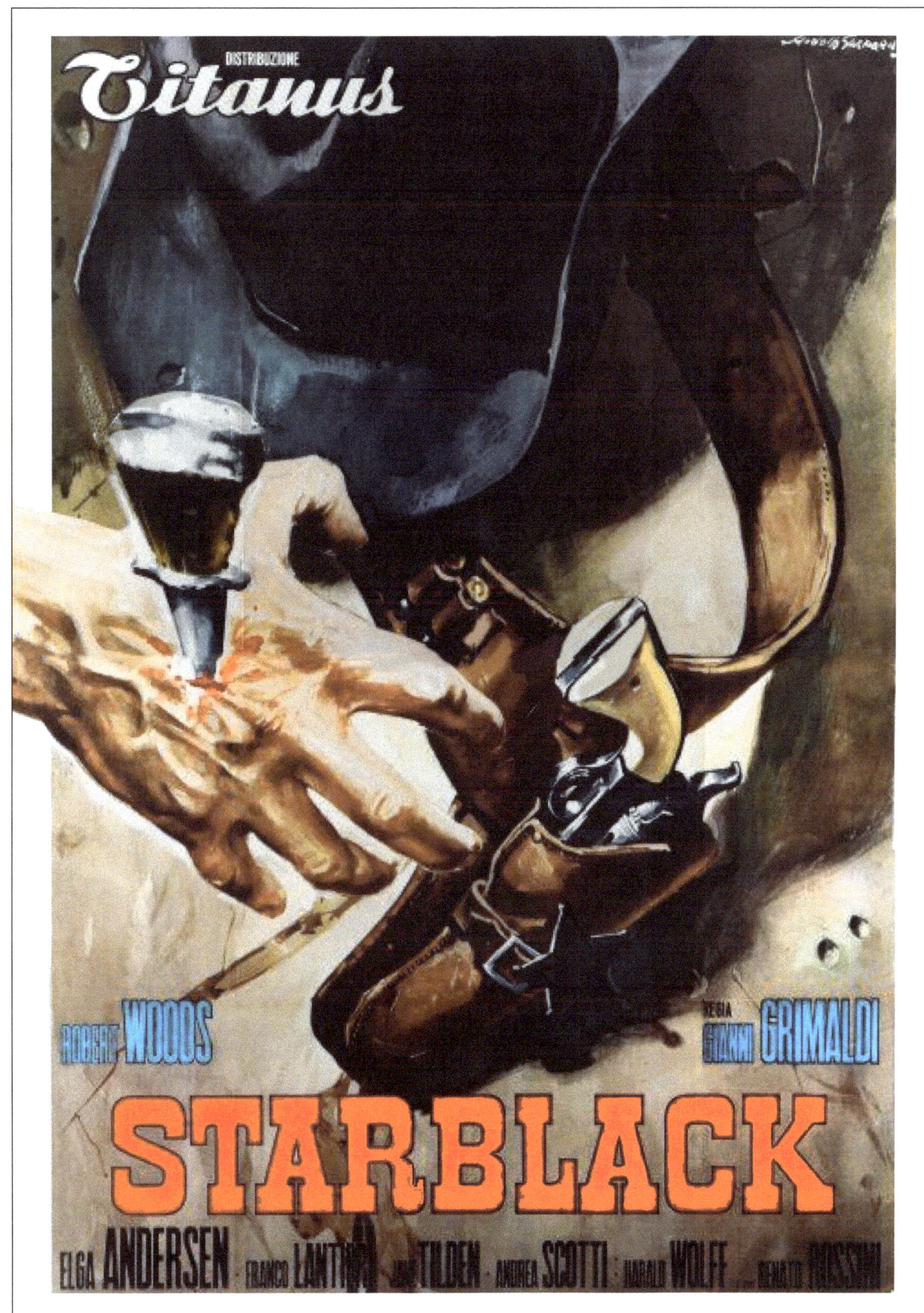

STARBLACK

("Starblack"). Artist: Rodolfo Gasparri. Original Title: **Starblack** (1966, Italy/Germany).

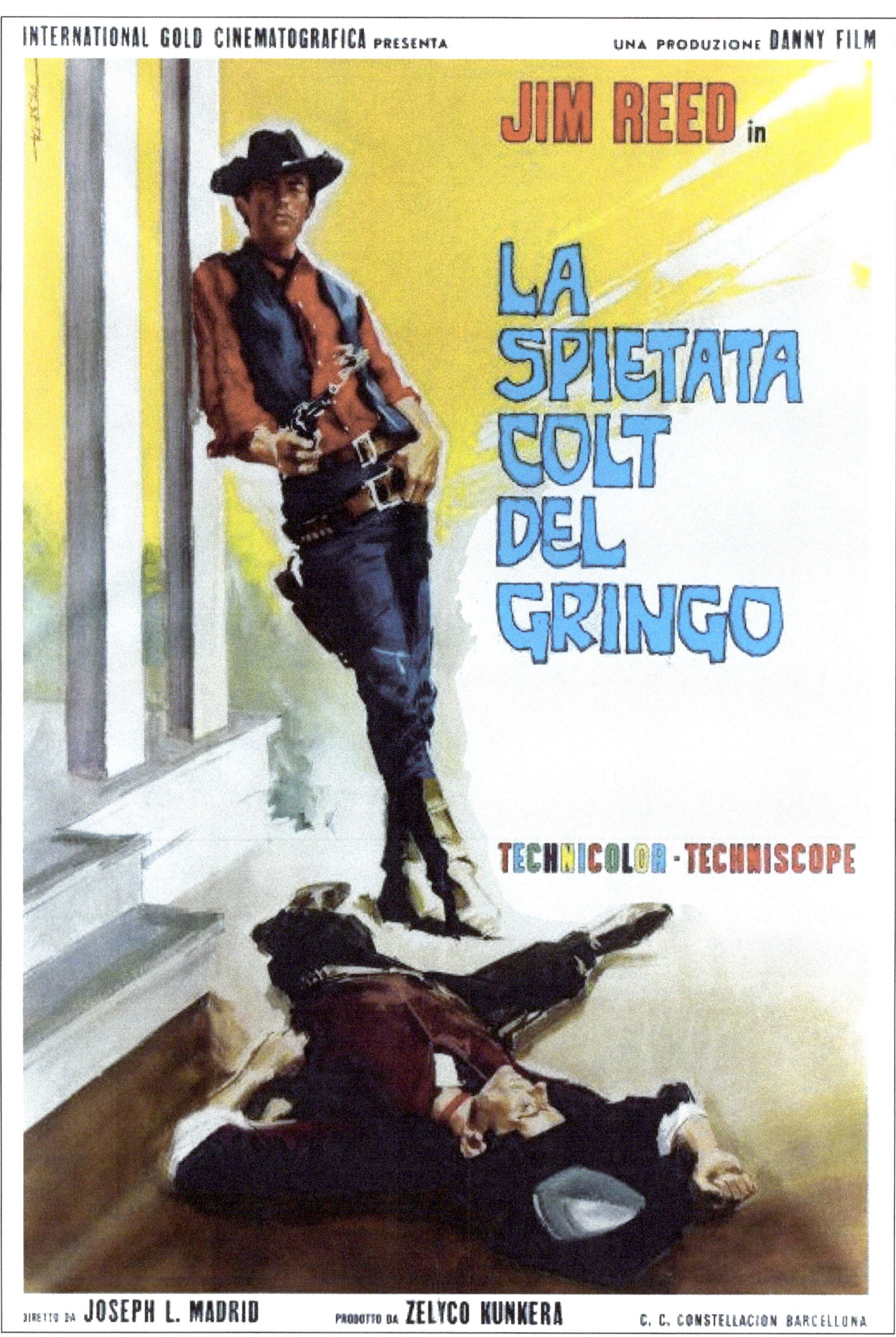

LA SPIETATA COLT DEL GRINGO

("Ruthless Colt Of The Gringo"). Artist: uEnrico De Seta. Original Title: **La Venganza De Clark Harrison** (1966, Spain/Italy).

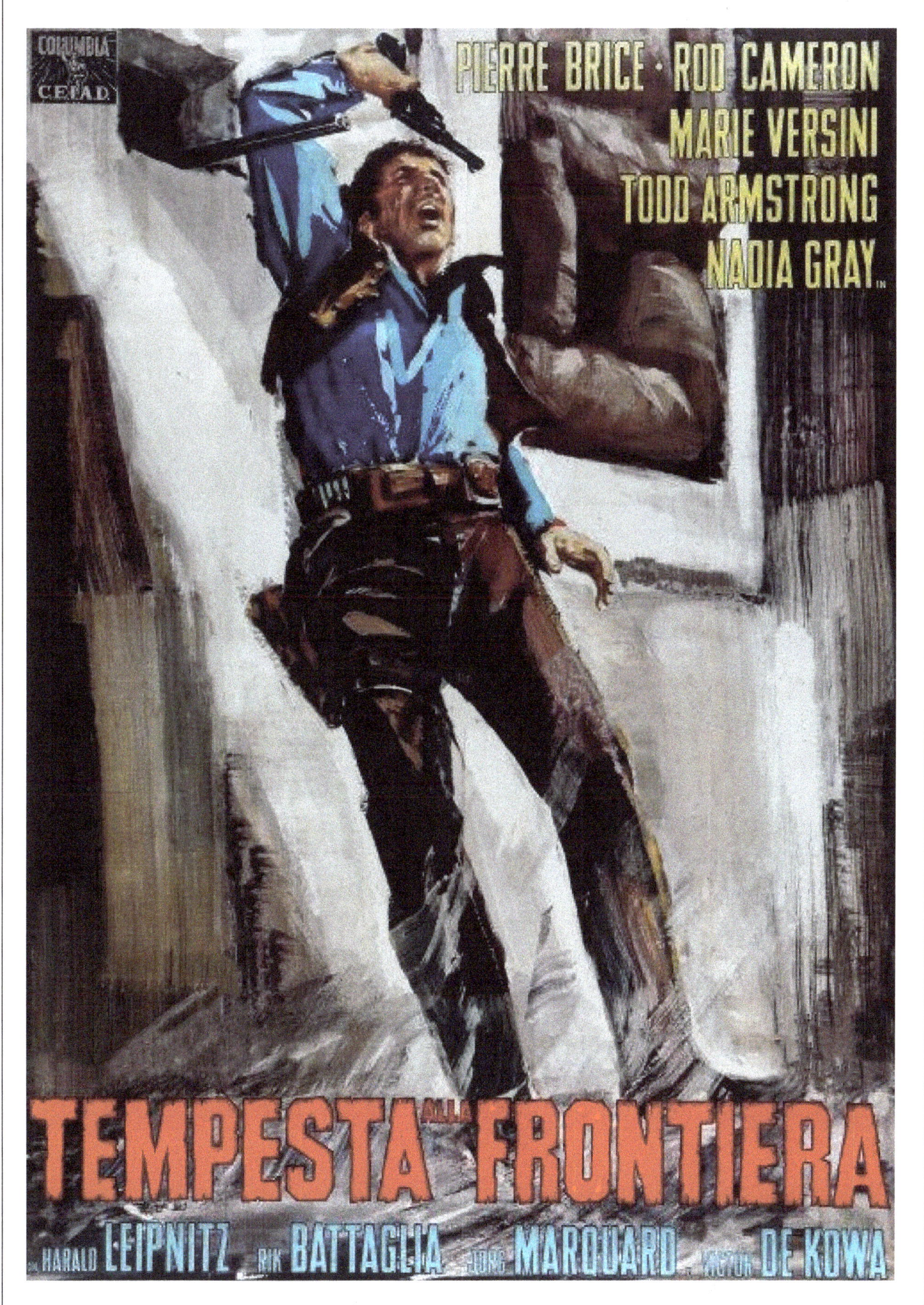

TEMPESTA ALLA FRONTIERA

("Storm At The Border"). Artist: unsigned. Original Title: **Winnetou Und Sein Freund Old Firehand** (1966, Germany/Yugoslavia).

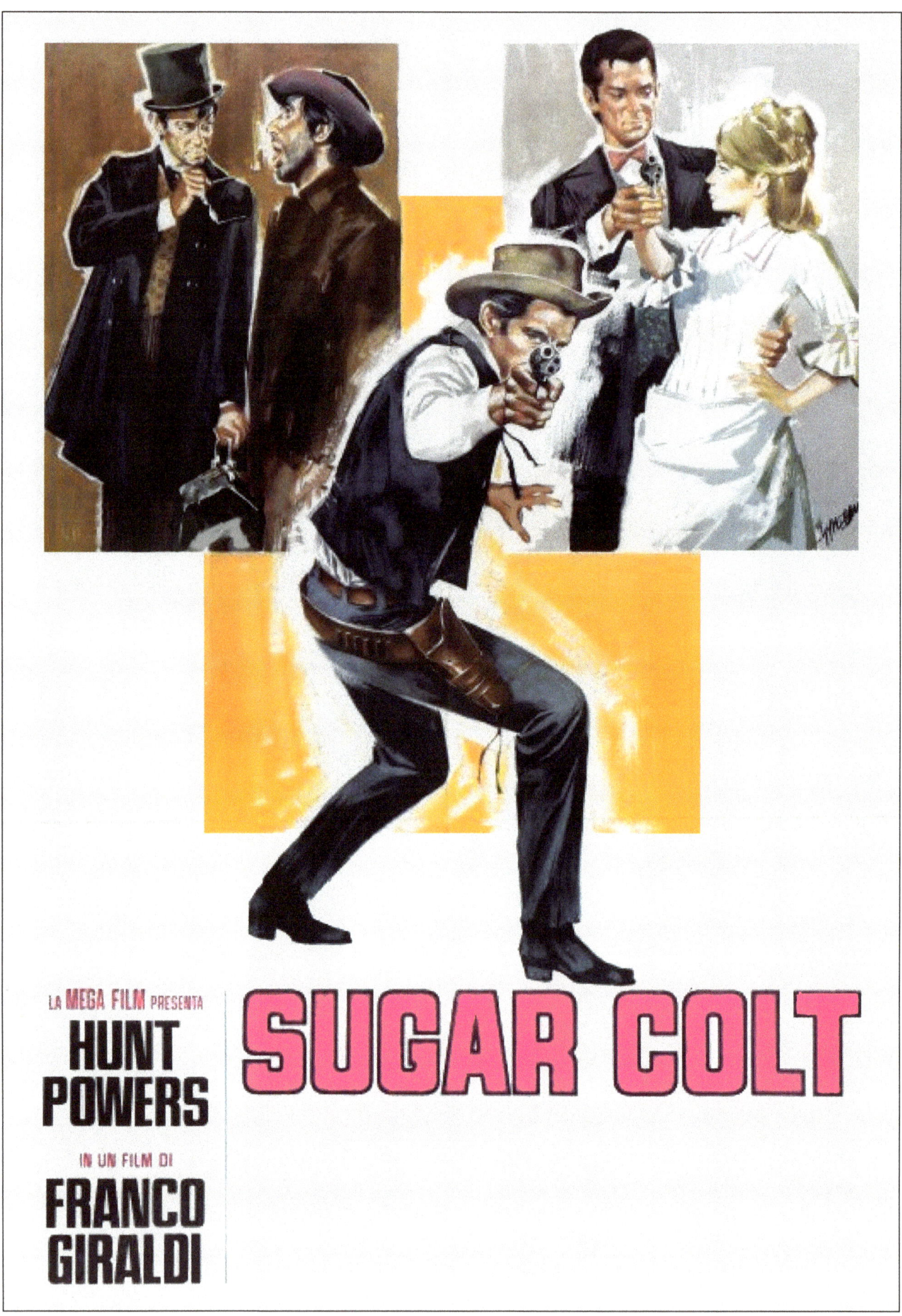

SUGAR COLT

("Sugar Colt"). Artist: Sandro Symeoni. Original Title: **Sugar Colt** (1966, Italy/Spain).

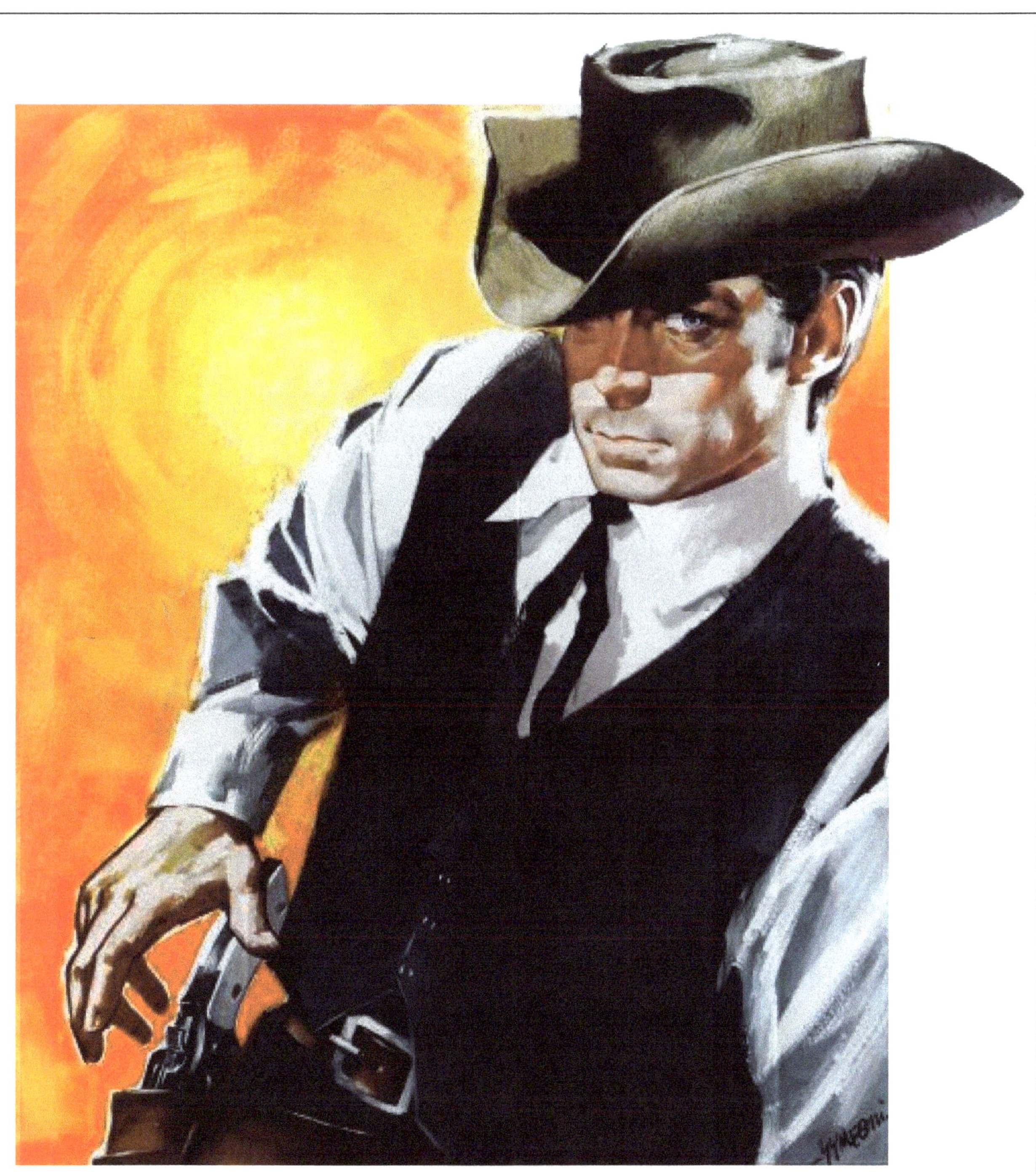

SUGAR COLT

("Sugar Colt"). Artist: Sandro Symeoni. Original Title: **Sugar Colt** (1966, Italy/Spain).

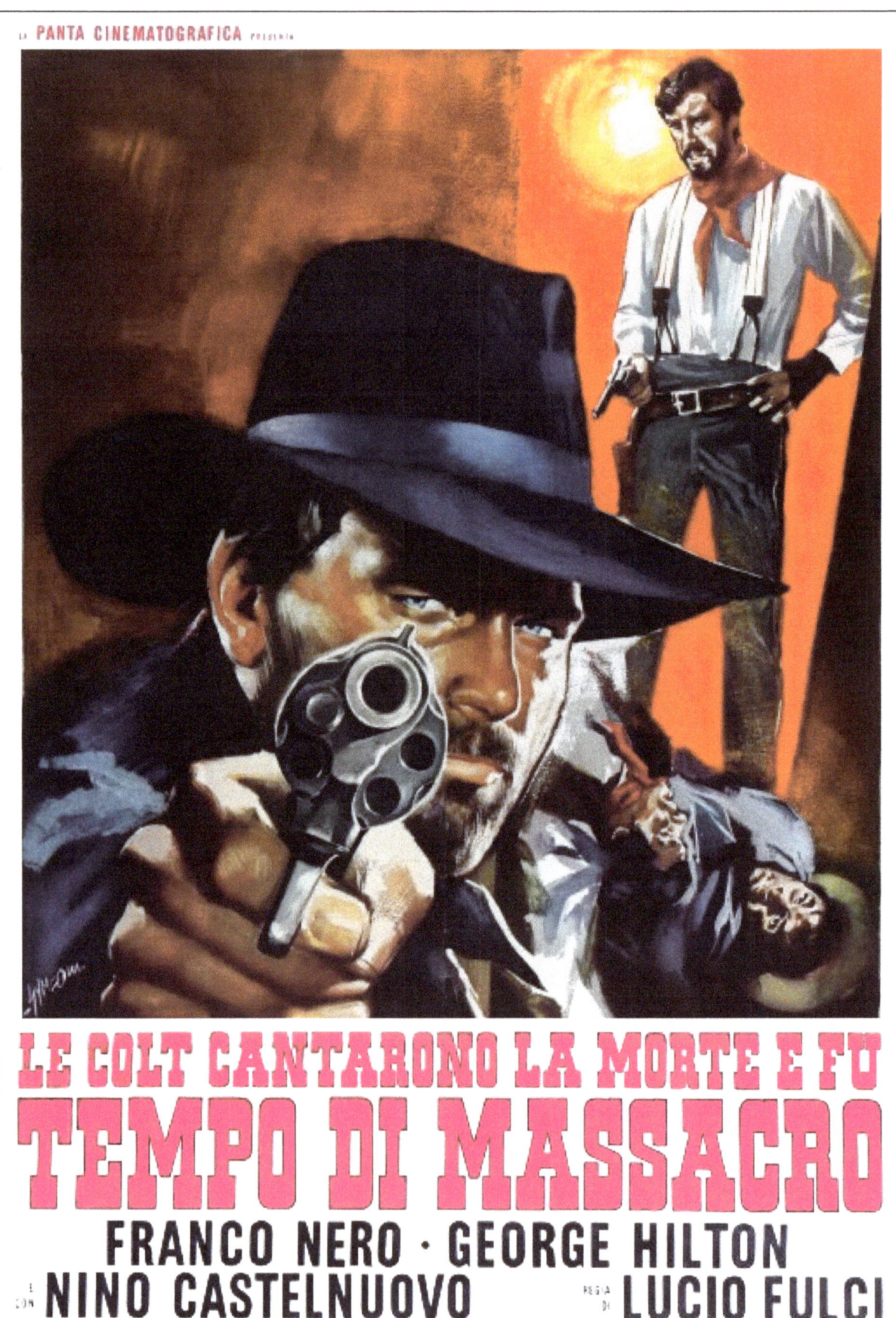

TEMPO DI MASSACRO

("Massacre Time"). Artist: Sandro Symeoni. Original Title: **Tempo Di Massacro** (1966, Italy).

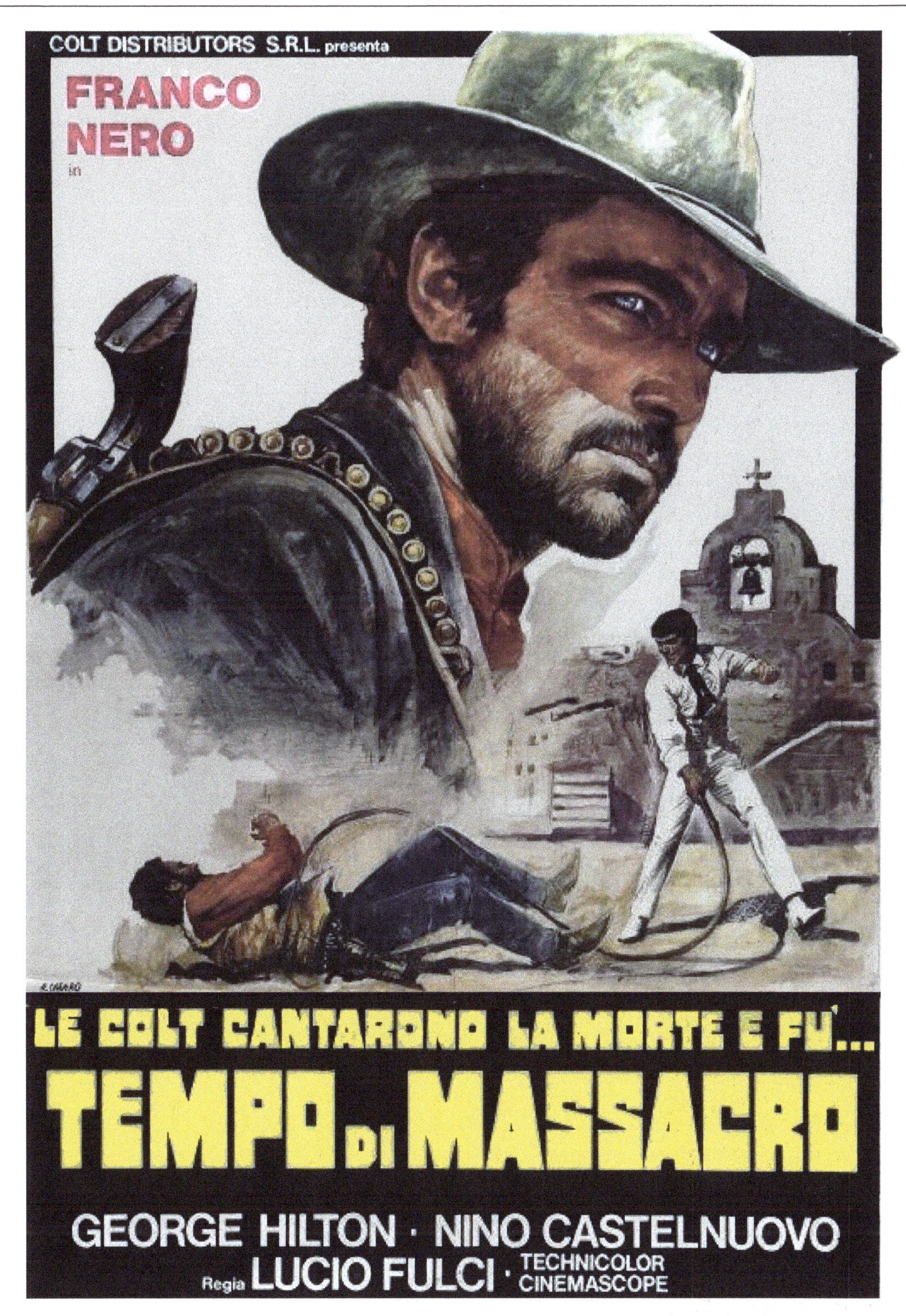

TEMPO DI MASSACRO

("Massacre Time"). Artist: Renato Casaroi. Original Title: **Tempo Di Massacro** (1966, Italy).

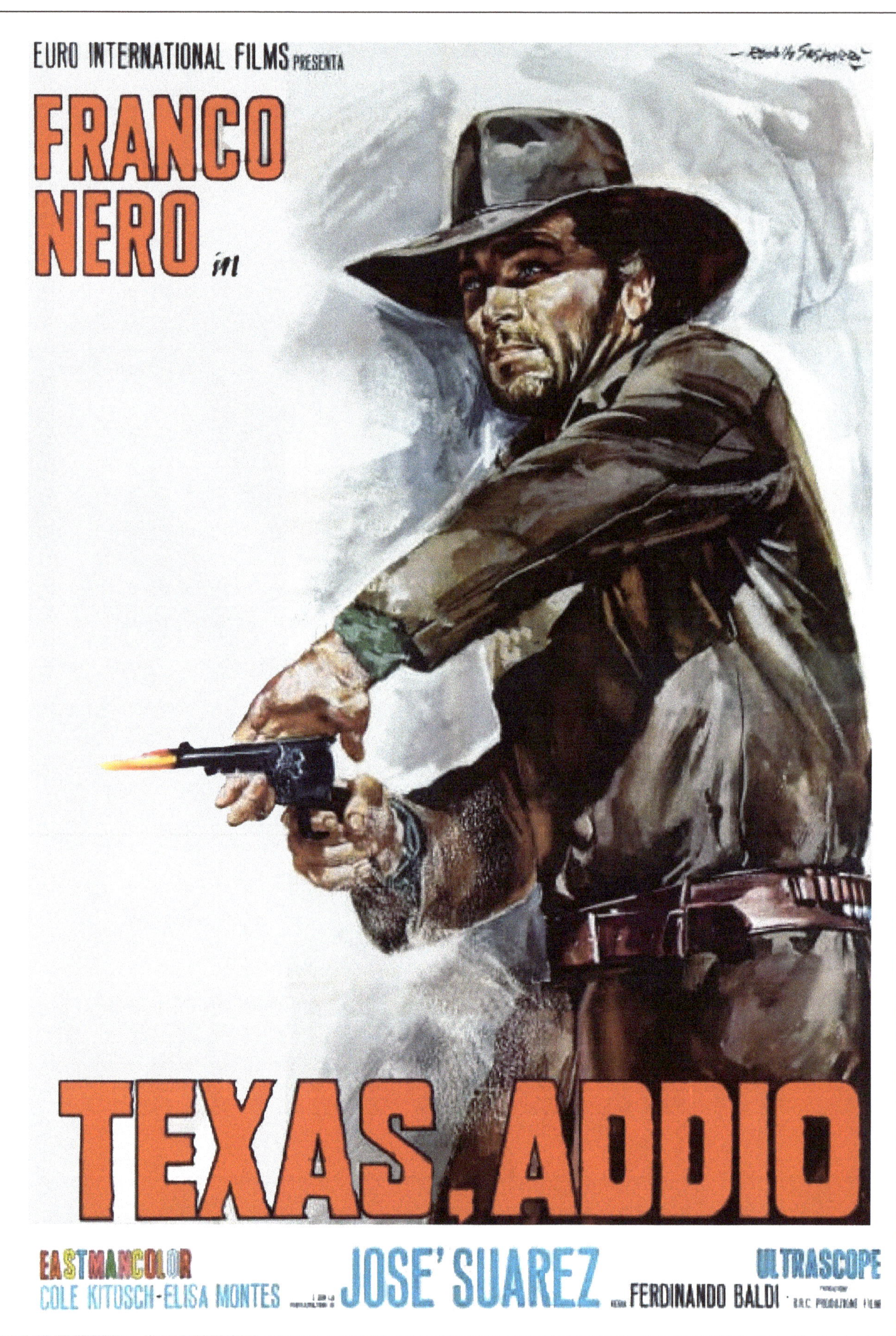

TEXAS, ADDIO

("Farewell, Texas"). Artist: Rodolfo Gasparri. Original Title: **Texas, Addio** (1966, Italy/Spain).

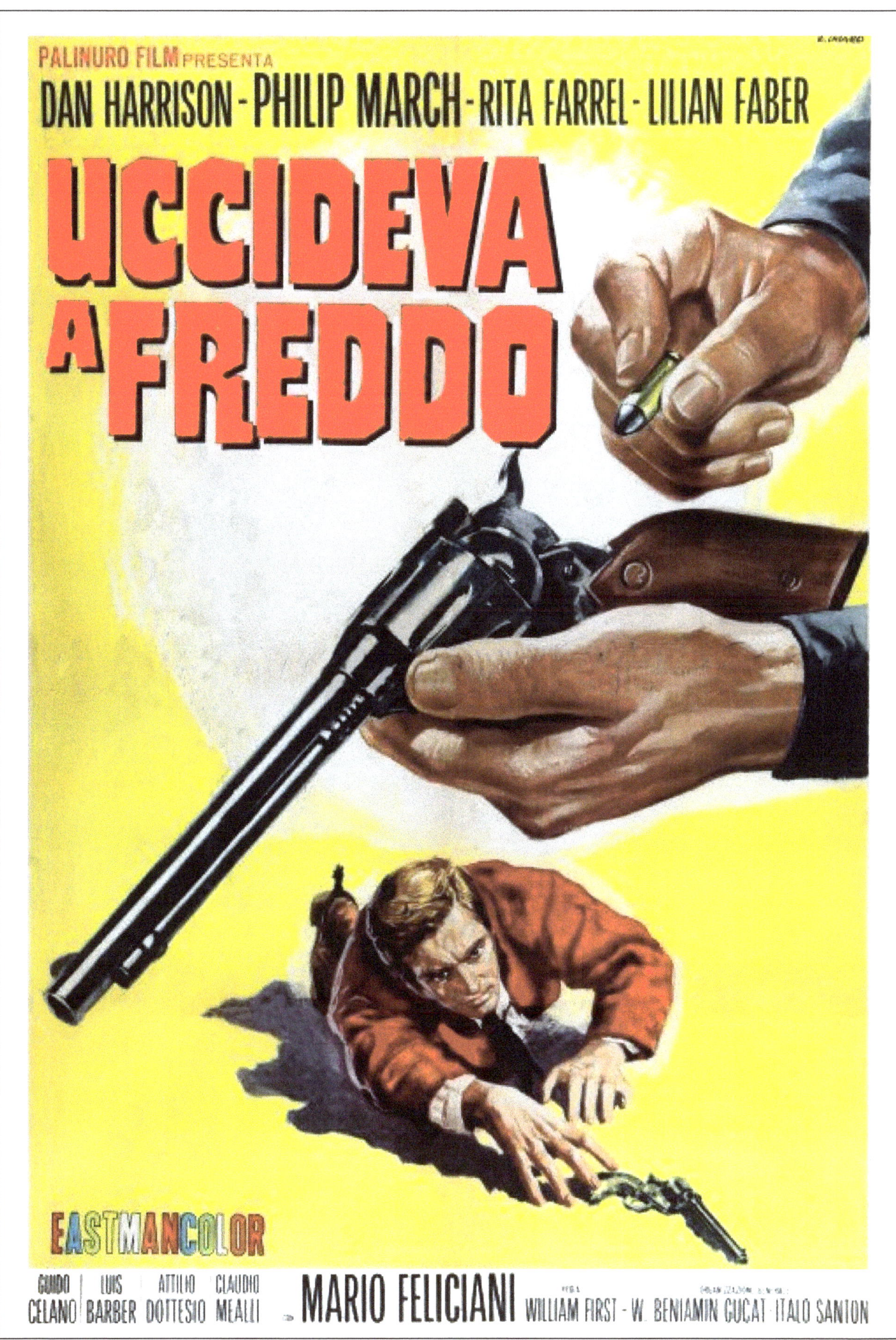

UCCIDEVA A FREDDO

("He Killed In Cold Blood"). Artist: Renato Casaro. Original Title: **Uccideva A Freddo** (1966, Italy).

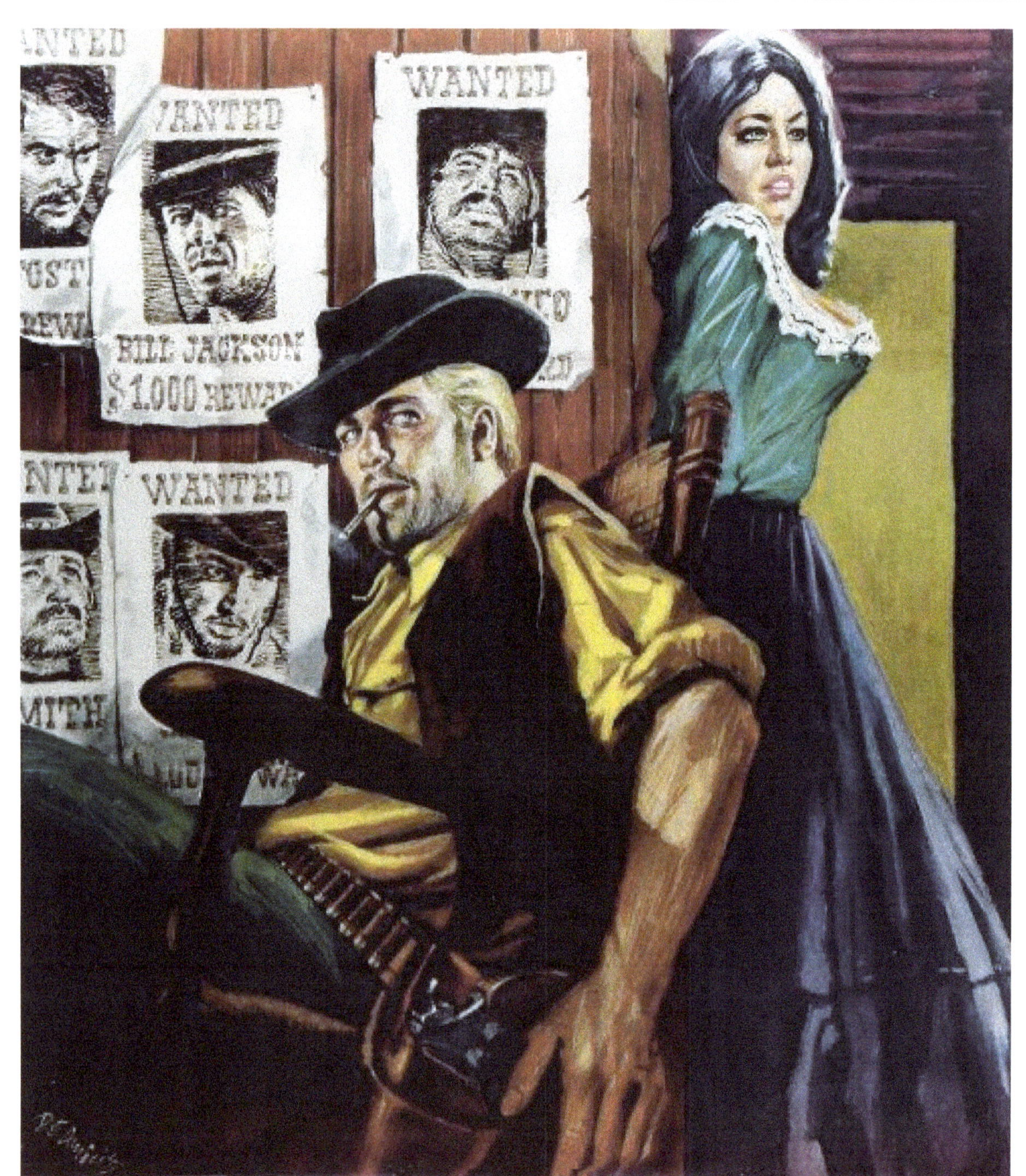

VAYAS CON DIOS, GRINGO

("Go With God, Gringo"). Artist: De Amicis. Original Title: **Vayas Con Dios, Gringo** (1966, Italy).

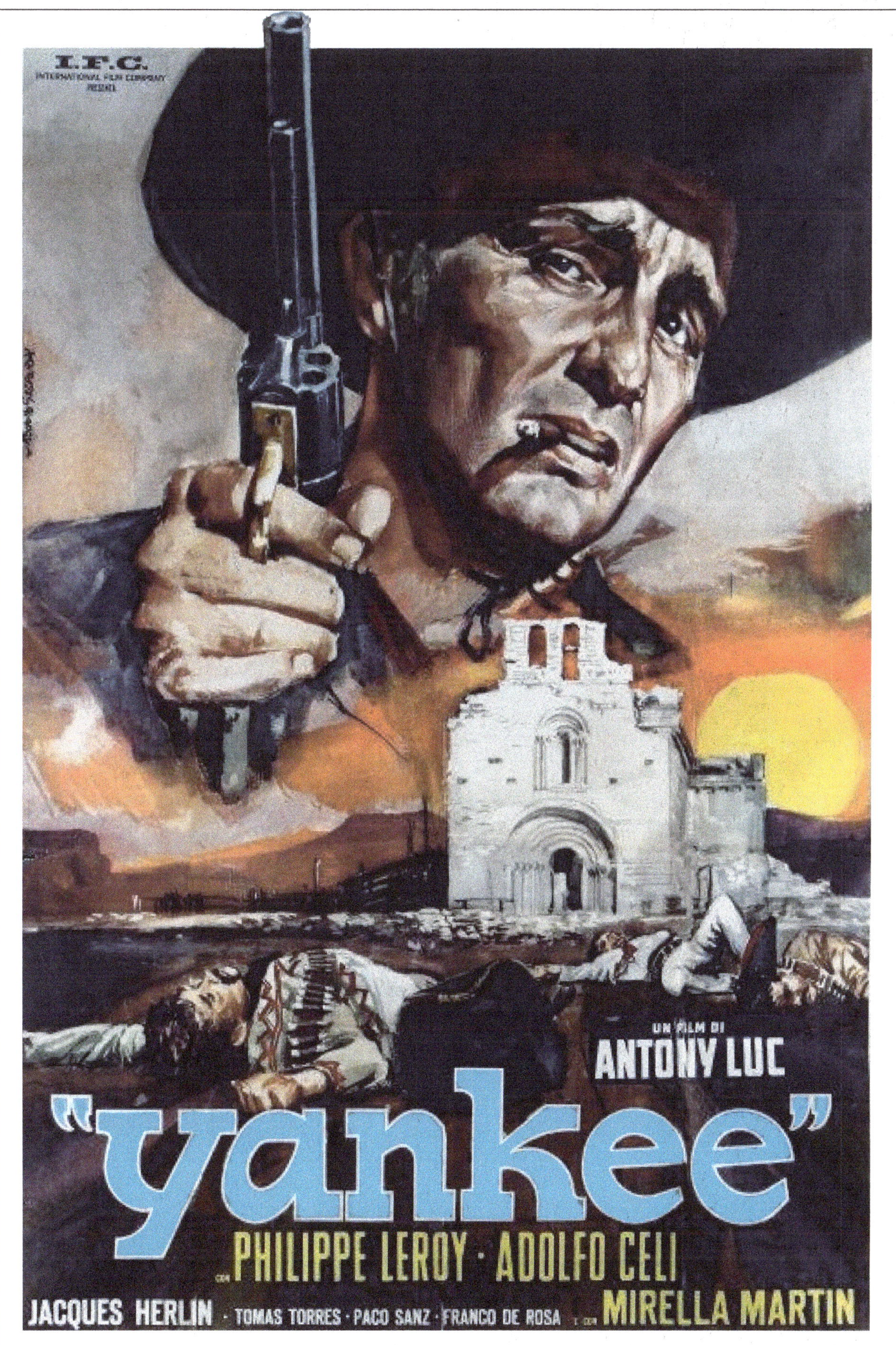

YANKEE

("Yankee"). Artist: Rodolfo Gasparri. Original Title: **Yankee** (1966, Italy/Spain).

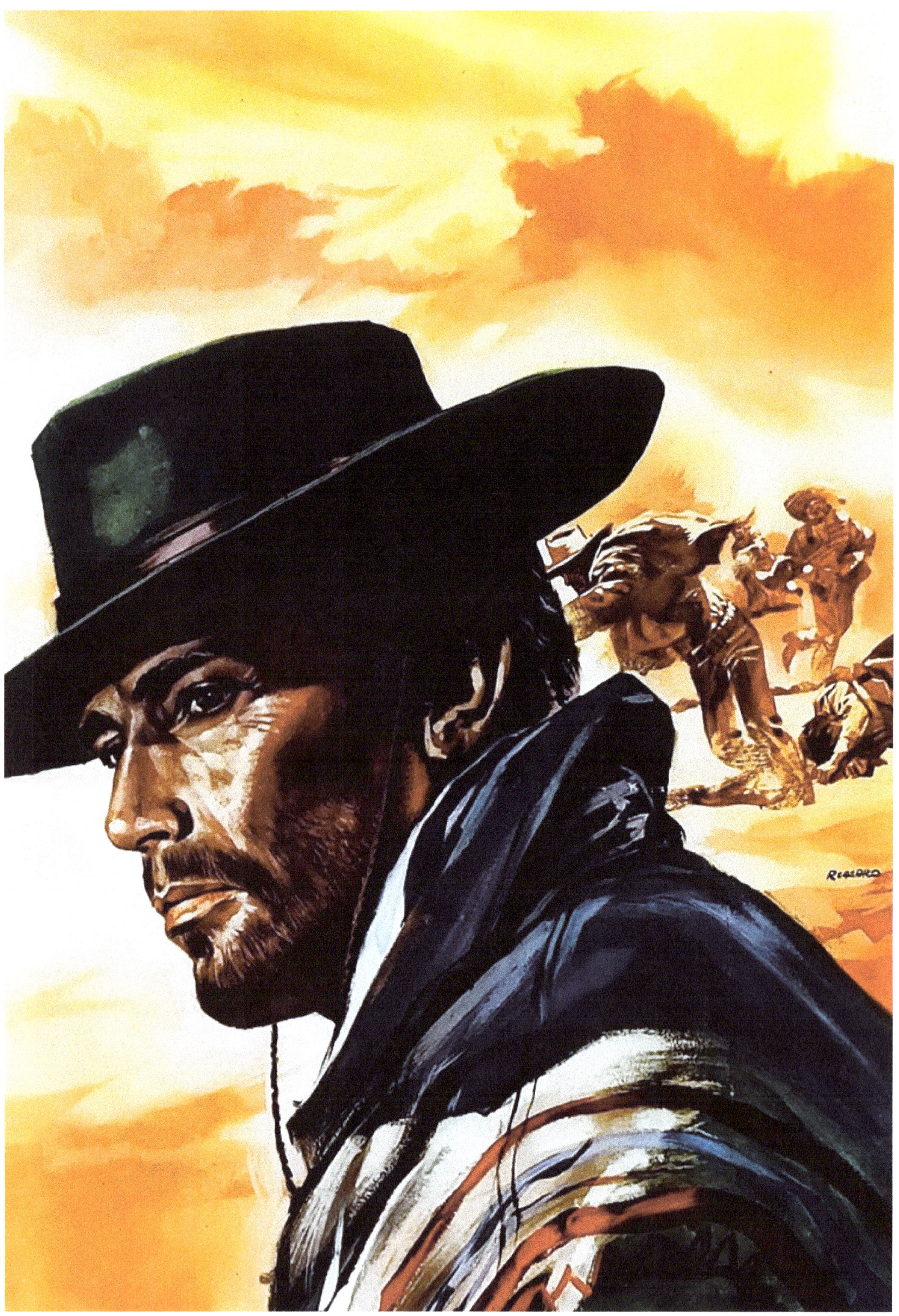

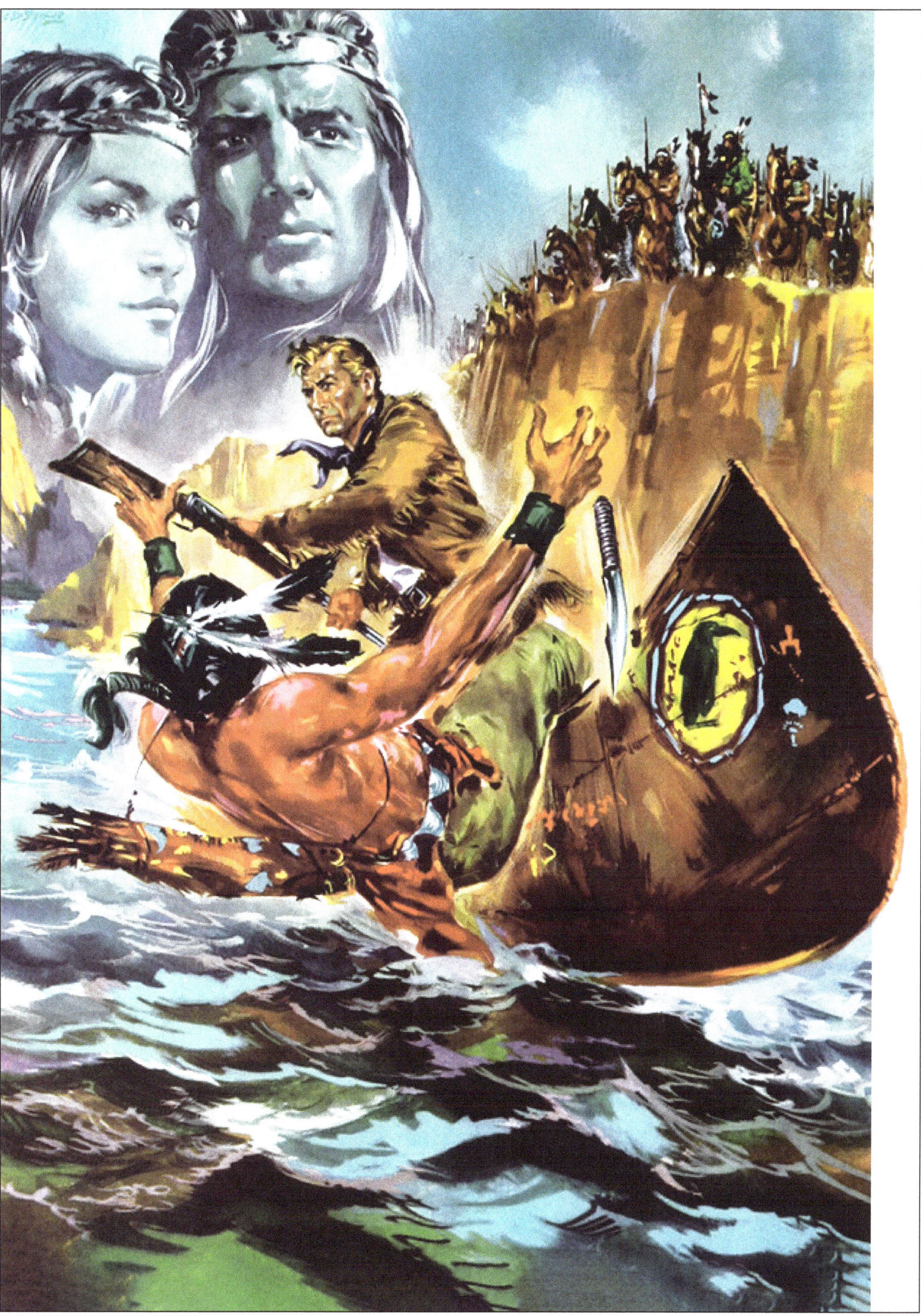

LIST OF ARTWORKS

Front cover: **Le Pistole Non Discutono** (1964; art by Rodolfo Gasparri).
Back cover: **Per Un Pugno Di Dollari** (1964; art by Renato Casaro).
Page 1: **Navajo Joe** (1966; art by Renato Casaro).
Page 2: **Duello nel Texas** (1963; art by Mauro Colizzi).
Page 106: **Pochi Dollari Per Django** (1966; art by Renato Casaro).
Page 107: **La Valle Dei Lunghi Coltelli** (1963; art by G. Di Stefano).

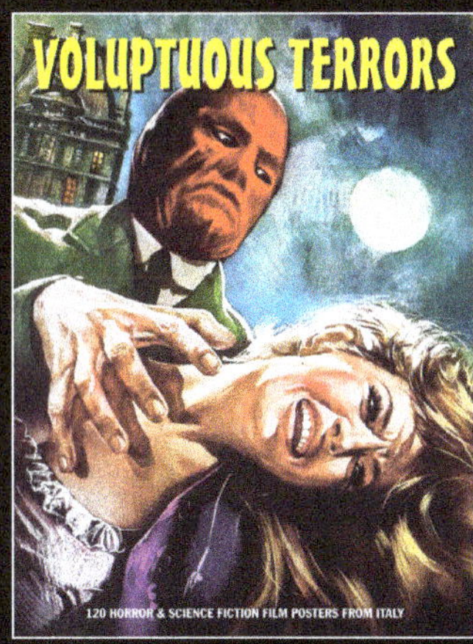
VOLUPTUOUS TERRORS
120 HORROR & SCIENCE FICTION FILM POSTERS FROM ITALY

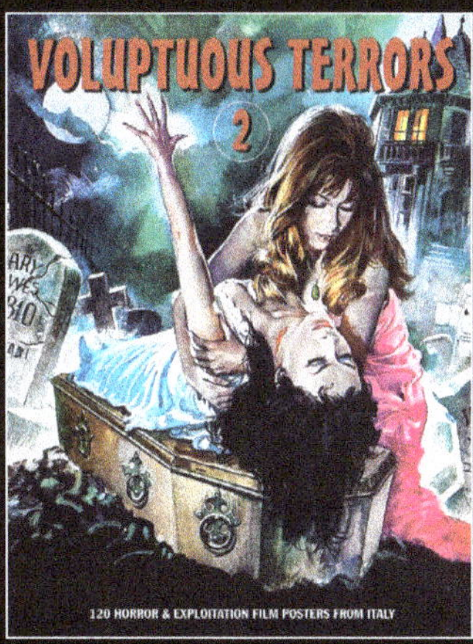
VOLUPTUOUS TERRORS
2
120 HORROR & EXPLOITATION FILM POSTERS FROM ITALY

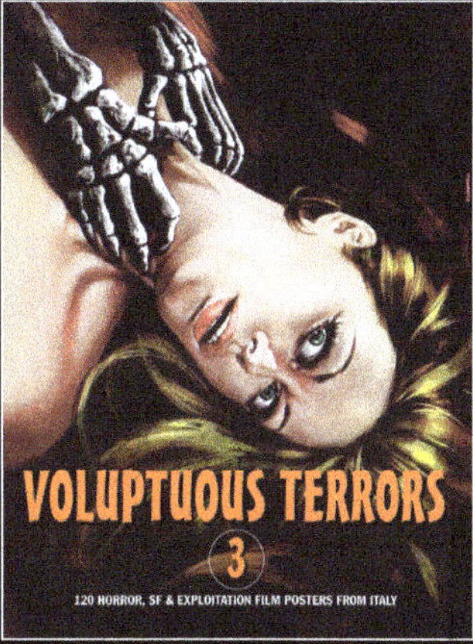
VOLUPTUOUS TERRORS
3
120 HORROR, SF & EXPLOITATION FILM POSTERS FROM ITALY

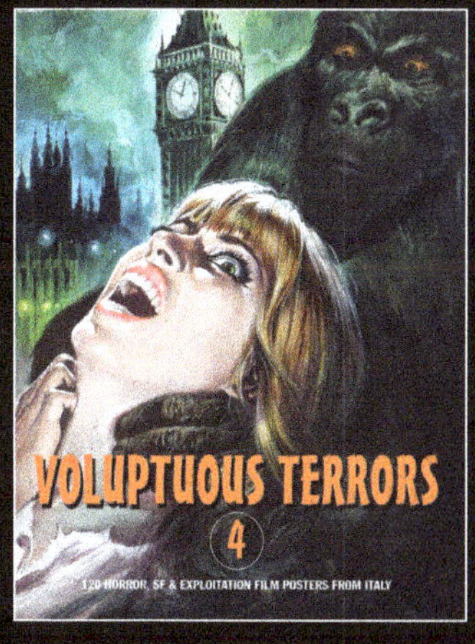
VOLUPTUOUS TERRORS
4
120 HORROR, SF & EXPLOITATION FILM POSTERS FROM ITALY

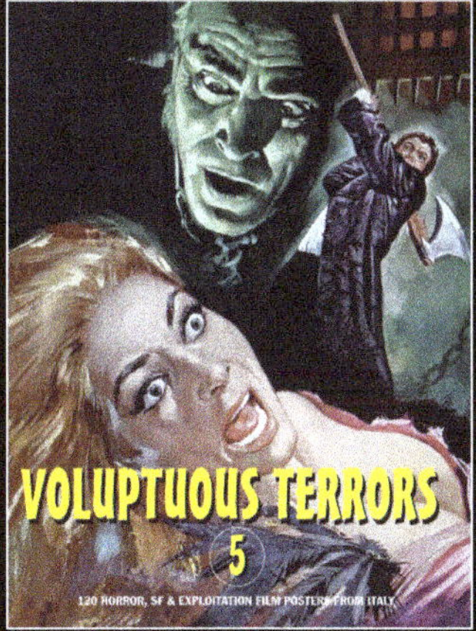
VOLUPTUOUS TERRORS
5
120 HORROR, SF & EXPLOITATION FILM POSTERS FROM ITALY

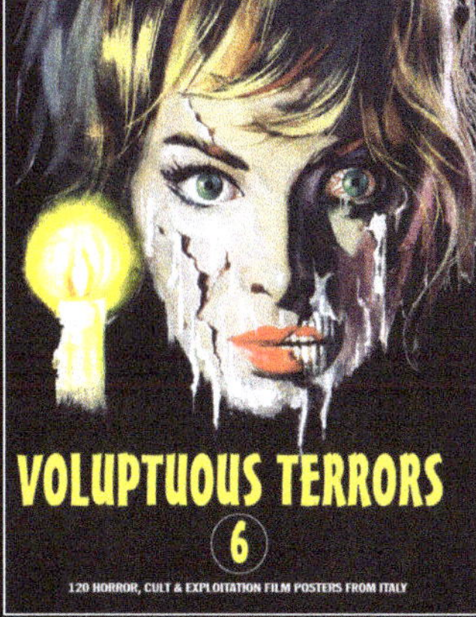
VOLUPTUOUS TERRORS
6
120 HORROR, CULT & EXPLOITATION FILM POSTERS FROM ITALY

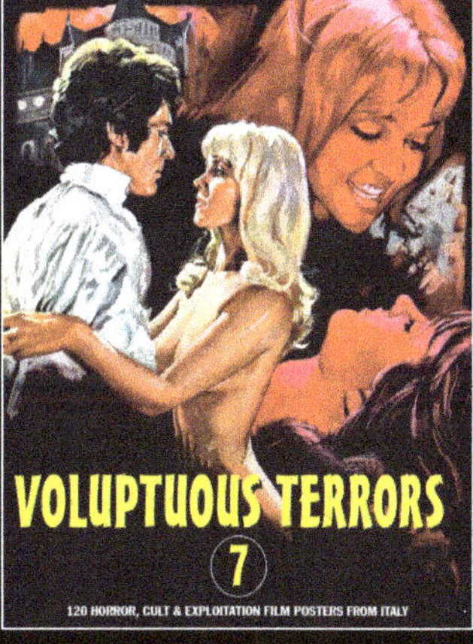
VOLUPTUOUS TERRORS
7
120 HORROR, CULT & EXPLOITATION FILM POSTERS FROM ITALY

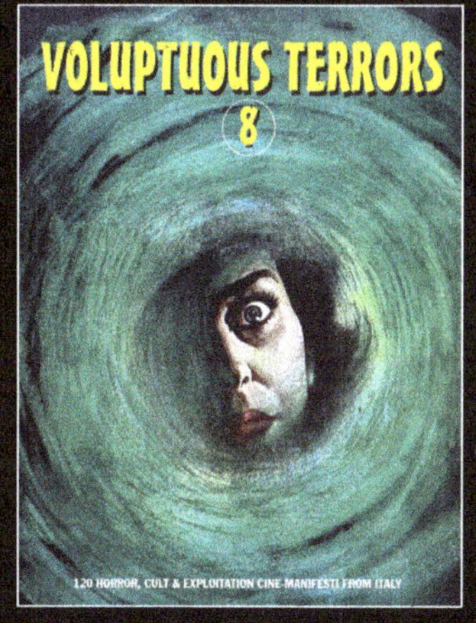
VOLUPTUOUS TERRORS
8
120 HORROR, CULT & EXPLOITATION CINE-MANIFESTI FROM ITALY

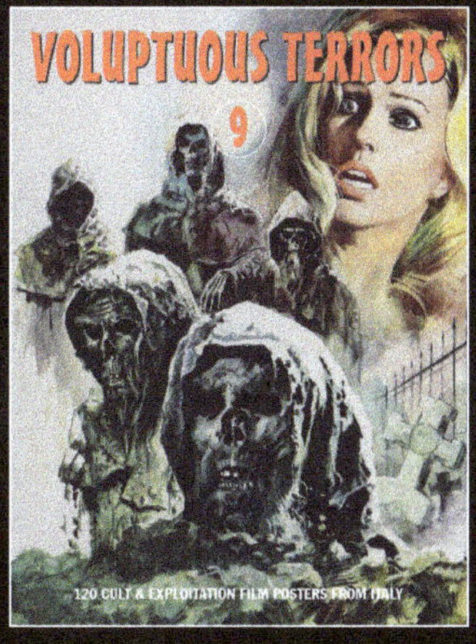
VOLUPTUOUS TERRORS
9
120 CULT & EXPLOITATION FILM POSTERS FROM ITALY

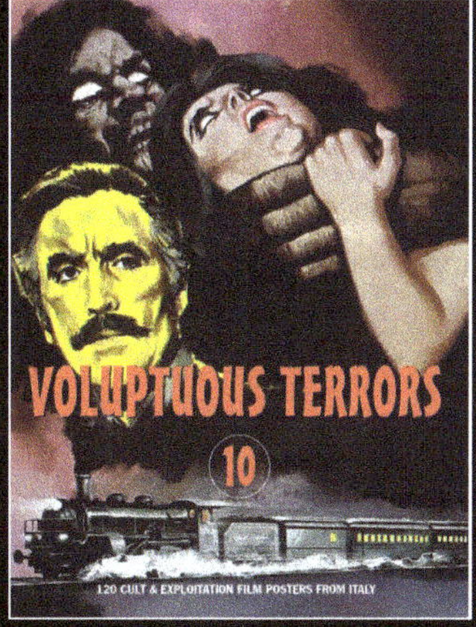
VOLUPTUOUS TERRORS
10
120 CULT & EXPLOITATION FILM POSTERS FROM ITALY

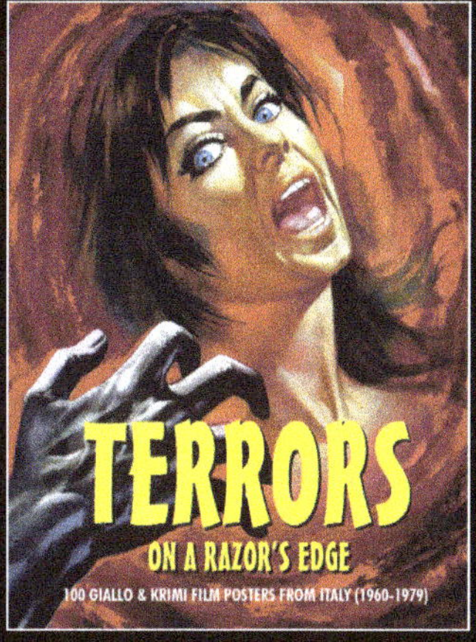
TERRORS
ON A RAZOR'S EDGE
100 GIALLO & KRIMI FILM POSTERS FROM ITALY (1960-1979)

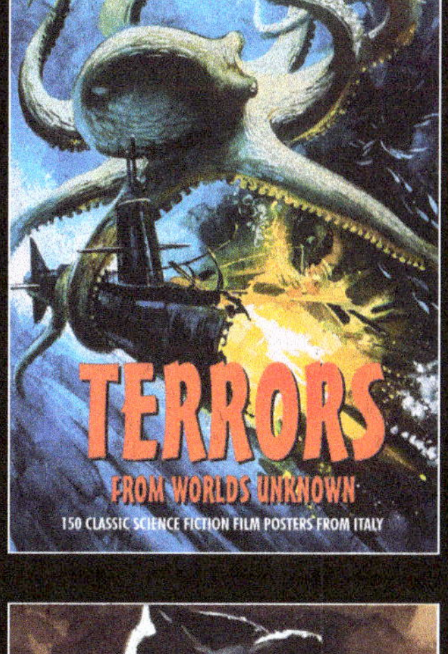
TERRORS
FROM WORLDS UNKNOWN
150 CLASSIC SCIENCE FICTION FILM POSTERS FROM ITALY

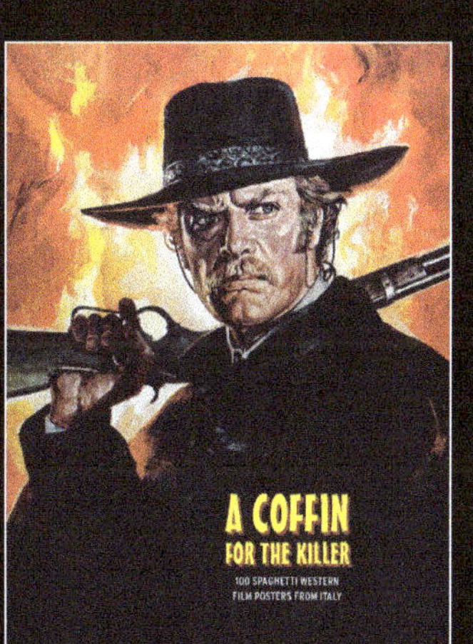
A COFFIN
FOR THE KILLER
100 SPAGHETTI WESTERN FILM POSTERS FROM ITALY

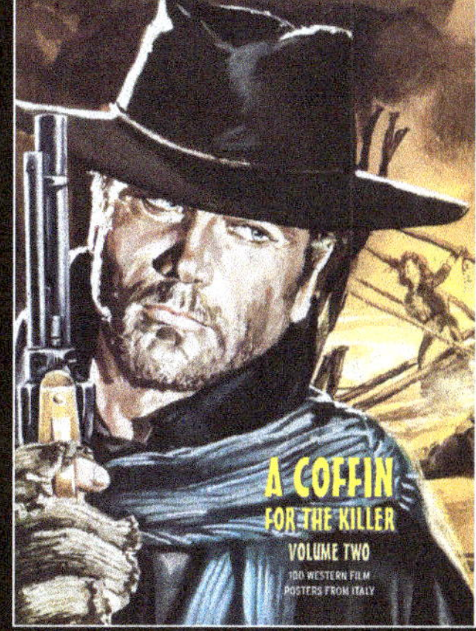
A COFFIN
FOR THE KILLER
VOLUME TWO
100 WESTERN FILM POSTERS FROM ITALY

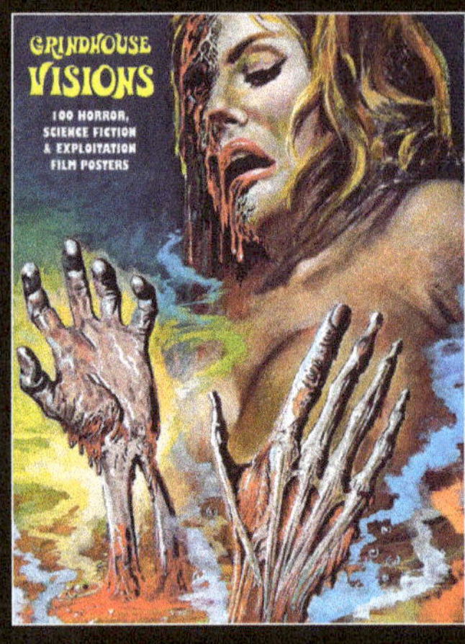
GRINDHOUSE
VISIONS
100 HORROR, SCIENCE FICTION & EXPLOITATION FILM POSTERS

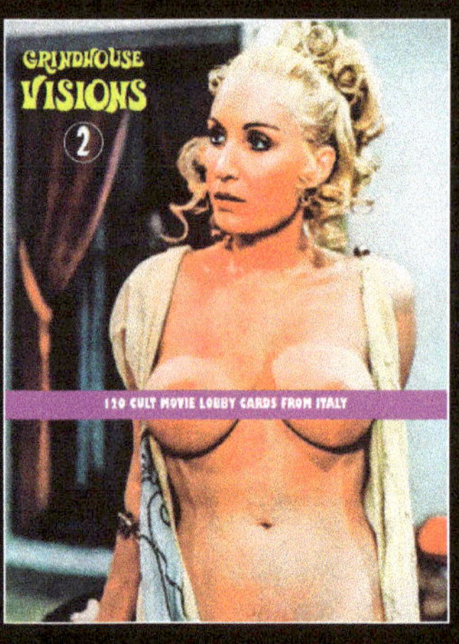
GRINDHOUSE
VISIONS
2
120 CULT MOVIE LOBBY CARDS FROM ITALY

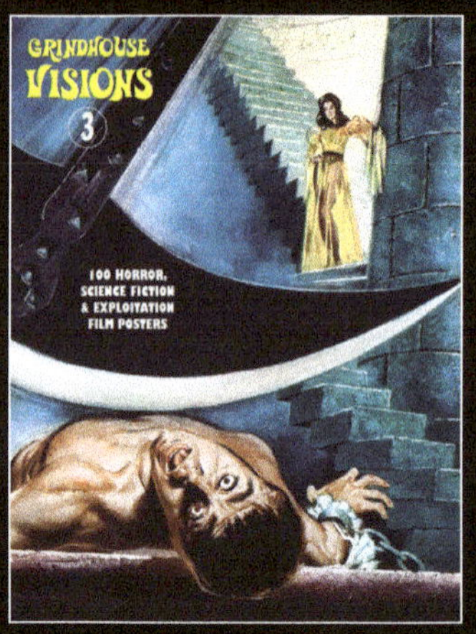
GRINDHOUSE
VISIONS
3
100 HORROR, SCIENCE FICTION & EXPLOITATION FILM POSTERS

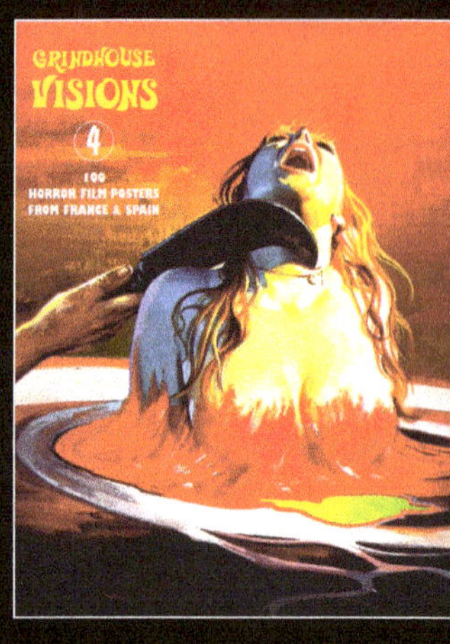
GRINDHOUSE
VISIONS
4
100 HORROR FILM POSTERS FROM FRANCE & SPAIN

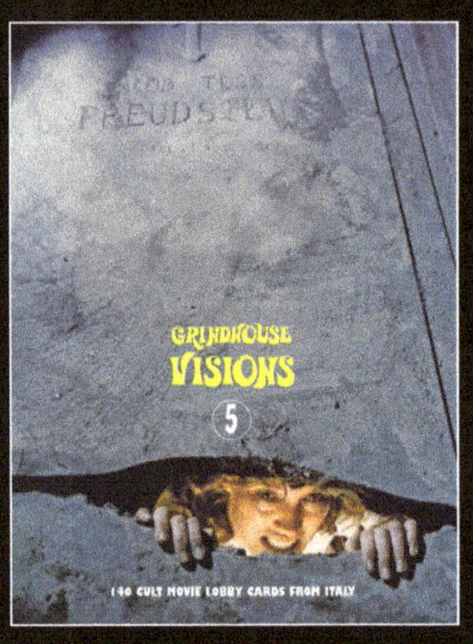
GRINDHOUSE
VISIONS
5
140 CULT MOVIE LOBBY CARDS FROM ITALY

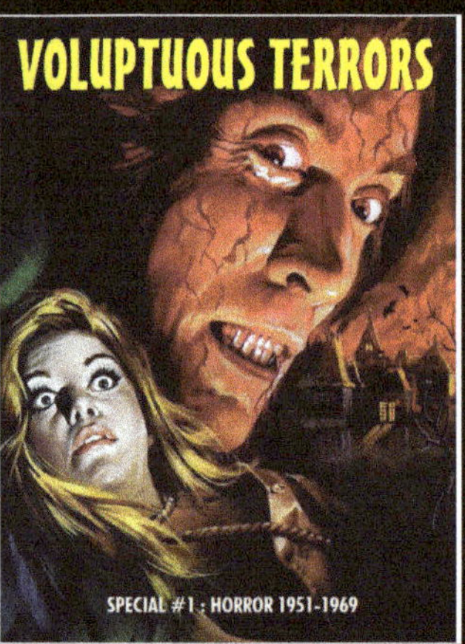
VOLUPTUOUS TERRORS
SPECIAL #1 : HORROR 1951-1969

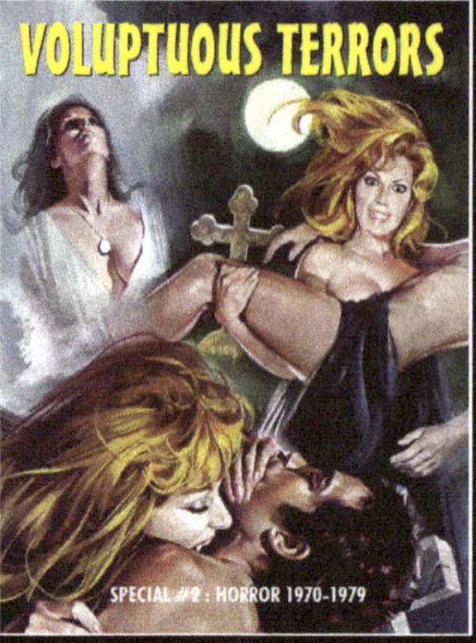
VOLUPTUOUS TERRORS
SPECIAL #2 : HORROR 1970-1979

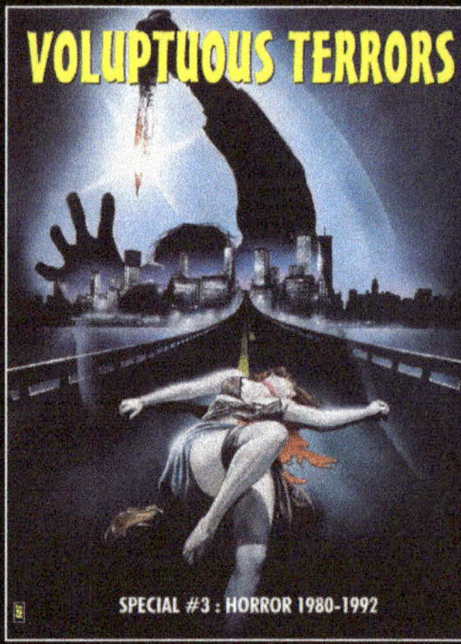
VOLUPTUOUS TERRORS
SPECIAL #3 : HORROR 1980-1992

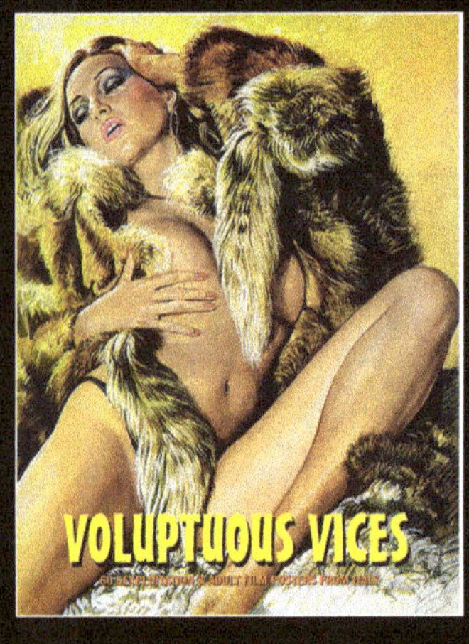
VOLUPTUOUS VICES

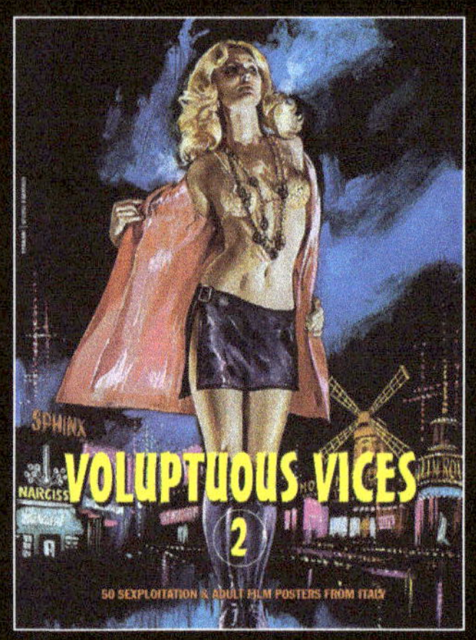
VOLUPTUOUS VICES
2
50 SEXPLOITATION & ADULT FILM POSTERS FROM ITALY

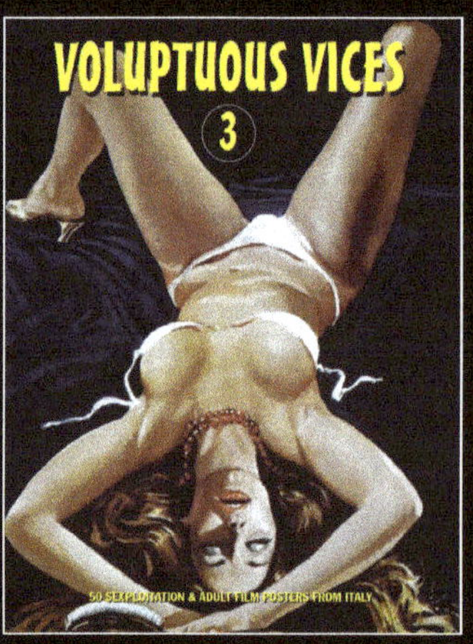
VOLUPTUOUS VICES
3
50 SEXPLOITATION & ADULT FILM POSTERS FROM ITALY

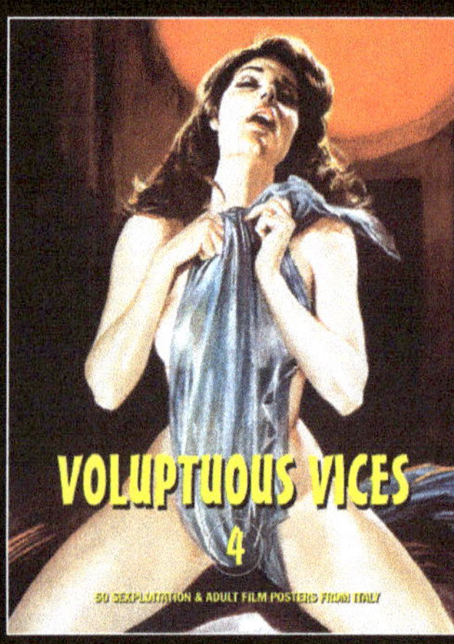
VOLUPTUOUS VICES
4
50 SEXPLOITATION & ADULT FILM POSTERS FROM ITALY

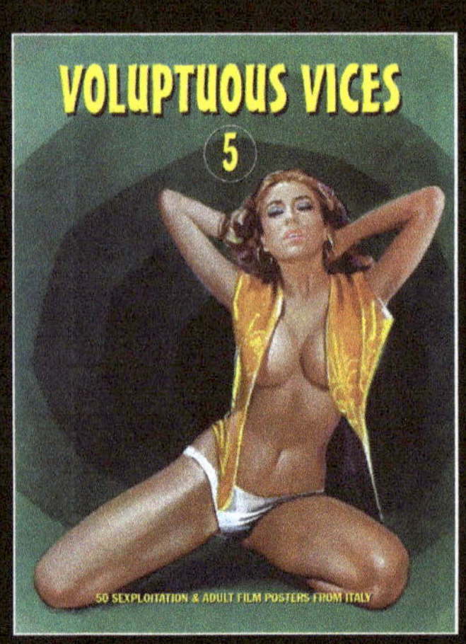
VOLUPTUOUS VICES
5
50 SEXPLOITATION & ADULT FILM POSTERS FROM ITALY

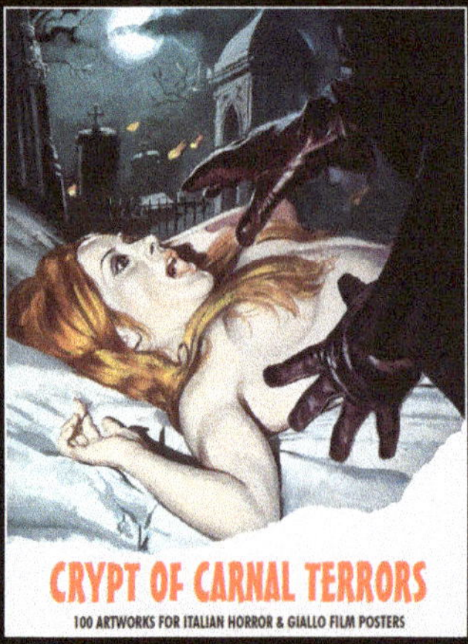
CRYPT OF CARNAL TERRORS
100 ARTWORKS FOR ITALIAN HORROR & GIALLO FILM POSTERS

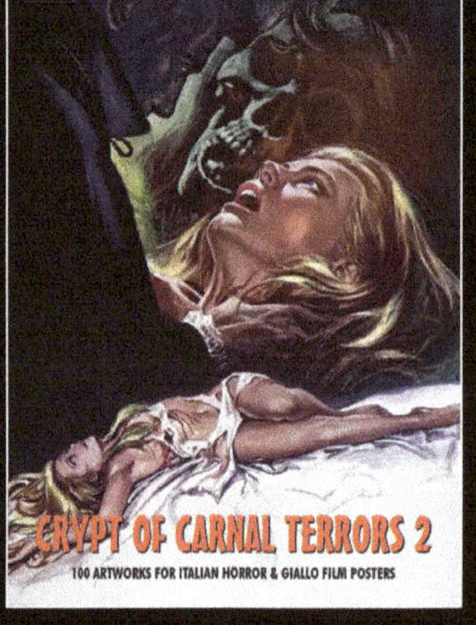
CRYPT OF CARNAL TERRORS 2
100 ARTWORKS FOR ITALIAN HORROR & GIALLO FILM POSTERS

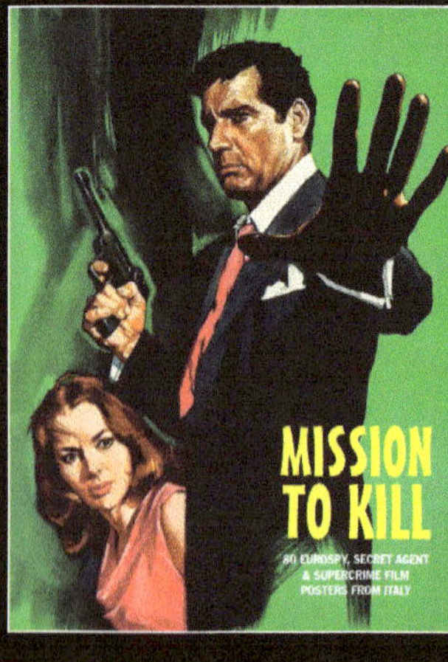
MISSION TO KILL
80 EUROSPY, SECRET AGENT & SUPERCRIME FILM POSTERS FROM ITALY

www.ingramcontent.com/pod-product-compliance
Lightning Source LLC
LaVergne TN
LVHW070935160826
845679LV00021B/1812
9781917285551